AF581260

“Clearing a Jam, Great Falls of the Ausable.” (406). *92.41.6A.*

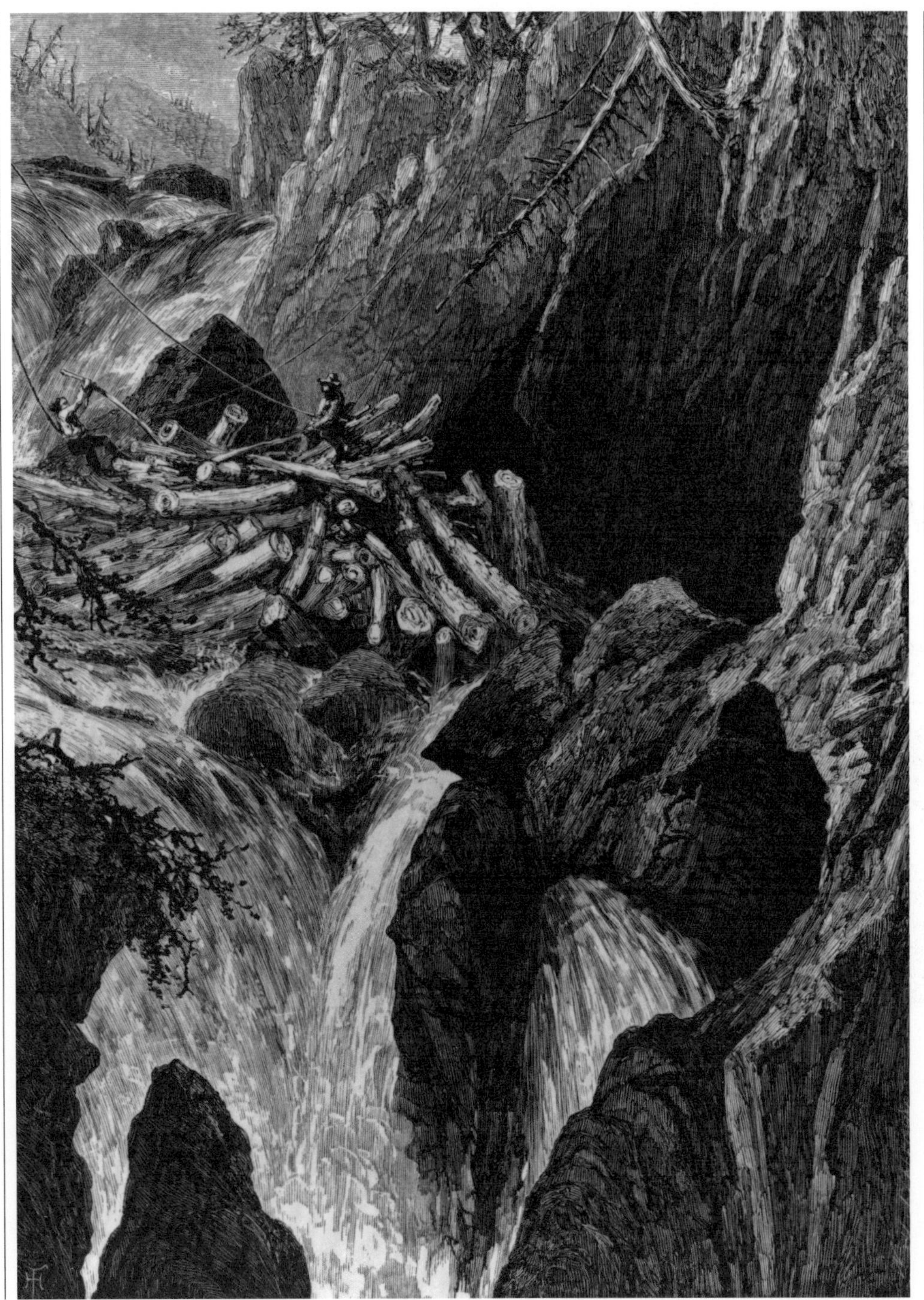

The Adirondacks on Paper

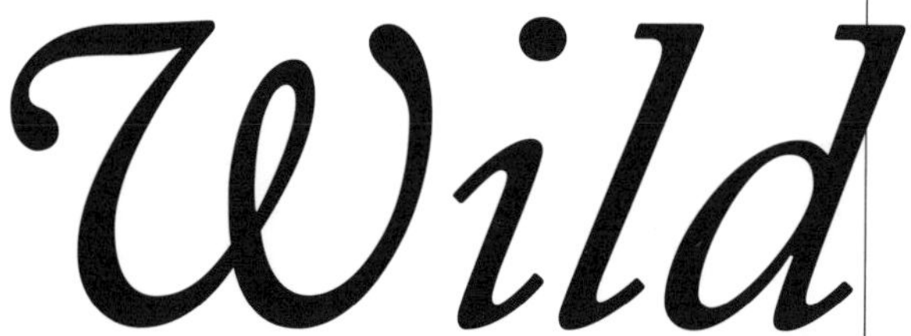

Prints in the Collection of the Adirondack Museum

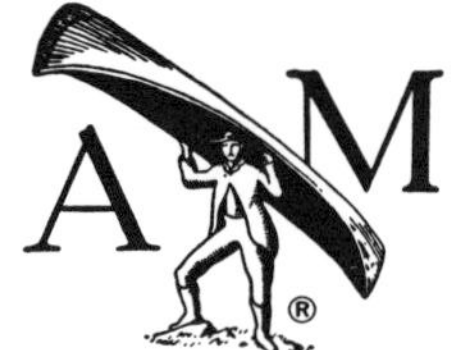

Impressions

by Georgia B. Barnhill

with an introduction by David Tatham

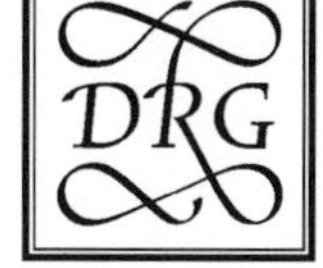

The Adirondack Museum & David R. Godine · *Publisher* · *Boston*

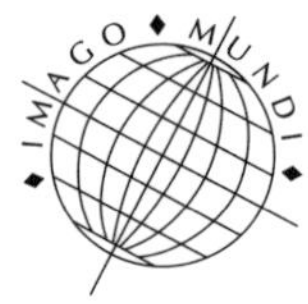

Exhibit and Project Director: Caroline Mastin Welsh
Catalogue Editor: Alice Wolf Gilborn
Checklist Editor: Jane Mackintosh Storms

Designed by Wynne Patterson
Photography by Erik Borg
Printed by Mercantile Printing Company, Inc.

Wild Impressions: The Adirondacks on Paper
is printed on Mohawk Vellum.

First edition 1995
Pinted in the United States of America
Library of Congress Catalog Card Number:
95-060362

Cover: *American Speckled Brook Trout.* A. F. Tait, artist. Chromolithograph, 16 x 22. Printed by Charles Parsons (1821-1910). 1864. Checklist no. 234.

Frontispiece: "Clearing a Jam, Great Falls of the Ausable." Harry Fenn (1845-1911), artist. Wood engraving, 9 1/8 x 6 1/4, 1873. William J. Linton (1812-97), engraver. Checklist no. 406.

ISBN 1-56792-041-1 HC

WILD IMPRESSIONS WAS set in Adobe Caslon, an adaptation of the great eighteenth century English old style face that probably has suffered more degradation and useless "improvement" than any face in the classic library. Sturdy in its appearance, slightly quirky in its italic, clearly based on Dutch models, Caslon has been a favorite of printers like Whittingham, publishers like Pickering and writers like George Bernard Shaw and T. E. Lawrence for three centuries.

D. B. Updike in his monumental *Printing Types* proclaims, "In the class of types which appear to be beyond criticism from the point of view of beauty and utility, the original Caslon type stands first." This lovely recutting, designed by Carol Twombly and made available digitally through Adobe Originals, is a worthy successor to its charming forebear.

Contents

This volume is dedicated to
Patricia Carroll FitzGerald Mandel
scholar,
friend of art, and
friend of the Adirondacks

Foreword

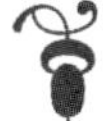

The Adirondack Museum is located at the center of the Adirondack Park, a vast mosaic of state owned and private land that comprises the largest public park in the contiguous United States. Since 1894, close to half of the Adirondack Park's six million acres have been protected as "forever wild" by the New York State constitution. The changing face of the Adirondacks as a wilderness place is one of the central themes of the Adirondack Museum.

Since the museum opened to the public in 1957, its exhibitions and publications have documented the complex interaction between people and the land as well as shifting cultural attitudes towards nature. The changing relationship between people and nature has influenced recreation, work, and the creative imagination in the Adirondacks. The American experience of the wilderness has been in part defined in this region where the reality of everyday life and work was transformed through the myth making imagination of its artists and other observers.

The exhibition and publication project "Wild Impressions" culminates five years of research and conservation of the Adirondack Museum's important collection of historic prints. Museum staff and consultants, under the able leadership of curator Caroline Welsh, have worked with great energy and commitment to bring this project to completion. These prints provide a rich vein of visual information that documents the land and its people. The images are also a reflection of culture, and of the beliefs and values of the artists who depicted the region visually and helped shape it as well. The collection provides an opportunity to study the changing aesthetic responses to the Adirondacks through the prints that popularized the region to an increasingly fascinated public throughout the nineteenth century. The study of these images expands our understanding of the Adirondacks and the American experience of wilderness.

Jacqueline F. Day
Director

Acknowledgments

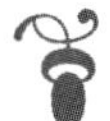

Any exhibition is a collaborative effort; this one is no exception. My greatest debt is to Caroline Mastin Welsh, curator, who invited me to undertake this project in the summer of 1990 at the time of the symposium that accompanied the exhibition *Fair Wilderness.* Combining trips to the Museum with weekend visits to family and friends at Lake George seemed to be an ideal plan for several summers. I did not realize at the outset how much fun I would have with the Welsh family at Tupper Lake. The Welsh's hospitality has always been superb and I thank Peter, Caroline, and Jamie for making me a part of their family.

Caroline was more than the perfect hostess. Her planning of the exhibition was detailed and thoughtful, encompassing photography, conservation, framing, and hanging. We shared the task of selecting the prints and arranging them in the galleries. Tracy Meehan, registrar, and Jane Mackintosh, curatorial associate, helped at all stages of the cataloguing process and in the creation of the checklist. I appreciate their real interest in this project and their ability to keep the paper flowing smoothly. Jerold Pepper, librarian, answered many questions and was very hospitable to me. I am particularly grateful to Alice Wolf Gilborn for her editorial skill. Her careful work immeasurably improved the essay. This project began during the directorship of Craig Gilborn and was completed under that of Jacqueline F. Day. I am indebted to both directors for giving me the opportunity to undertake this project. I have enjoyed the subject, the process, and the people. Not often is so much work such a pleasure.

David Tatham, professor of fine arts at Syracuse University, has been a very helpful advisor to this entire project. He believes in the ability of prints to inform us about the past, and I am particularly pleased that he chose to contribute an essay to this catalogue. Finally, I should like to express my appreciation to my own institution, the American Antiquarian Society, where much of the research for this project was done in its collections of nineteenth-century books and periodicals.

Georgia B. Barnhill

Preface

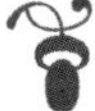

An infinite variety of prints were sold by the millions to a voracious American public in the nineteenth century. Prints, primarily lithographs, adorned offices and parlors. Distributed widely, they catered directly to popular taste and provide an extraordinary record for the social historian of nineteenth-century America. Prints document Victorian taste, values and attitudes with images of heroic exploits, technological innovations, politics and politicians, rural pleasures, women and the family, sports and recrea-tion, the gentlemanly pastimes of hunting and fishing, and the natural grandeur of the American and Adirondack landscapes. Lithographic reproductions of original paintings disseminated fine art to a broad middle class in an affordable manner and thus exemplified a pervasive nineteenth-century faith that art could enrich the life of everyone. Chromolithographs of the works of prominent nineteenth century painters speeded the acceptance of this popular medium.

Along with the growing demand for printed art came an explosion of educational materials. "Self-help" broadsides outlining ways to "better ones-self" through formal courses and other means paralleled the proliferation of state universities, agricultural and public schools. Advances in the technology of printing vastly increased the production of illustrated newspapers, magazines and books. The printed image quickly became one of the most powerful communication devices in modern times. William M. Ivins, Jr., in *Prints and Visual Communication,* describes prints as "exactly repeatable pictorial statements" and, as such, they make "the accepted report of an event...of greater importance than the event, for what we think about and act upon is the symbolic report and not the concrete event itself." As prints "reported the events" of the Adirondacks, they contributed directly to the development of the region as a tourist mecca.

Prints introduced thousands of people to the Adirondacks. Fortunately for the wilderness, not everyone experienced it first hand. Many of those who did not come had their ideas about the north woods formed by reading guidebooks by authors such as Joel T. Headley, William H. H. Murray and Seneca Ray Stoddard. Illustrated with metal and wood engravings, these books conveyed what the land looked like, what took place there and the nature of its human and animal residents.

Images or illustrations published in the popular press had a variety of intentions and effects. Some lured tourists to the region; others ridiculed conditions in the Adirondacks; still others informed the public about conservation issues or documented the vacation habits of American presidents. The Annual Meeting of the American Canoe Association at Lake George in 1891 was reported in great detail with illustrations and text. The anonymous wood engraving "Rush to the Wilderness," published in *Harper's New Monthly Magazine* in 1869, ridiculed hapless tourists. Julian Rix's wood engraving "Destruction of Forests in the Adirondacks" (Harper and Brothers, 1884) poignantly documented a conservation issue that persists today. President Cleveland's visits were chronicled pictorially in various magazines between 1885 and 1888.

Artists illustrated the major geologic and topographic surveys of New York State made to document and catalog the largely unexplored wilderness. Charles Cromwell Ingham accompanied New York State Geologist Ebenezer Emmons as he surveyed the High Peaks; *The Great Adirondack Pass,* which Ingham painted "on the spot," was reproduced as a lithograph by John Bufford and included in Emmons' 1838 report to the State legislature. Verplanck Colvin, who comprehensively mapped the region in the 1870s and '80s, illustrated his multi-volume *Topographical Survey of the Adirondack Wilderness* with lithographs produced by the Albany firm of Weed and Parsons, made from Colvin's drawings. The museum collection is rich with examples of prints from both of these works.

Artists who came to the Adirondacks to paint the scenery also reproduced it in prints. John Henry Hill made etchings of Lake George; Frederic Rondel made a lithograph of the Raquette River; Stephen Parrish's etchings of sites along the upper Hudson are exceptionally fine and also rare. Significant engravings in the collection are prints reproduced from the works of Asher B. Durand, John William Casilear, James M. Hart, Winslow Homer and Homer Dodge Martin, among others. The museum owns the original paintings from which several of the prints were made. Wood engravings after paintings appeared in fine art publications such as *The Aldine* in the 1870s and William Cullen Bryant's *Picturesque America* of 1874. Harry Fenn produced illustrations for Bryant's popular volume which not only capture the texture of the Adirondack landscape but also include dramatic views of loggers, river drivers, teamsters, boatmen, fishermen and hikers. This publication placed the Adirondack mountains on the itinerary of nineteenth-century tourists. Scenes of hunting, fishing, camping and winter activities reveal the accoutrements of the gentleman "sport" at play in the latter nineteenth-century, as well as a slice of outdoor life in the Adirondacks, which goes beyond their original intent. The museum's excellent and comprehensive collection of

Currier & Ives prints, particularly those after A.F. Tait, does this best of all.

In the last twenty-five years there has been an extraordinary scholarly and popular interest in American historical prints. Annual conferences, sponsored by museums, libraries and historical societies, have resulted in a substantial body of literature about prints. Inclusive rather than exclusive, the Adirondack Museum's eclectic images of the Adirondacks, assembled over the last thirty-five years, comprise common as well as rare and precious ones. The collection's focus on one region and the index it provides to study that region's artistic and social history is invaluable. The museum is fortunate that the late William K. Verner, former curator, and Edward Comstock, Jr., former assistant curator, guided the beginning years of the collection with such discernment and knowledge. This curator is indebted to her mentors, the late Anthony N. B. Garvan and Peter C. Welsh, who applied George Peter Murdock's *Outline of Material Culture* to the analysis of prints and thereby provided her with a point of view for studying prints.

In 1991, the Adirondack Museum undertook the study and analysis of its own collection of prints. In that year, Georgia B. Barnhill, Andrew W. Mellon Curator of Graphic Arts at the American Antiquarian Society, joined the curatorial staff as guest curator to catalogue and provide a context for the collection of seven hundred prints. Ms. Barnhill performed an item by item survey which yielded substantial information as to publication data, conservation requirements and value. In addition, she photographed each print, in many cases for the first time. This contribution to the records is an immeasurable one. We are indebted to her for compiling this extremely useful checklist of the collection. Ms. Barnhill has spent her career studying, writing and lecturing on book illustrations and American historical prints. Her wide knowledge, insightful observations and thorough scholarship make this book a major contribution to the literature. Her flexibility, timeliness and meticulous attention to detail made this four-year project an organizational delight.

In 1993, David Tatham, professor of fine arts at Syracuse University, joined the Print Collection project team as an advisor. His cogent analysis of the contribution our exhibition and publication efforts could make to scholars and the public spurred us forward. His thoughtful critiques improved the content of this publication and that of the North American Print Conference Symposium and Proceedings. We are indeed grateful to this productive scholar and friend.

Others at the museum have contributed their time and expertise to the project. As Project Director, I was greatly assisted by Registrar Tracy N. Meehan, Curatorial Associate Jane Mackintosh and Curatorial Clerk Karen Joyce. Museum Editor Alice W. Gilborn edited the manuscripts for this volume and adroitly managed the production of the catalogue. Jane Mackintosh edited the checklist. David R. Godine graciously co-published and created this handsome book, designed by Wynne Patterson. Others have assisted with the formulation of programs, related events and publicity.

The project also owes a debt of gratitude to Deedee Wigmore, Mara Jayne Miller and the Adirondack Museum's Art Committee for their efforts to raise money to defray the costs of publication. Former Museum Director Craig Gilborn presided over the early stages of this project and Director Jacqueline F. Day assisted and encouraged the successful fruition of it. *Wild Impressions: The Adirondacks on Paper* continues the Adirondack Museum's tradition of contributing to regional scholarship and publishes for the first time a singular collection of regional images.

Caroline M. Welsh

Adirondack Prints

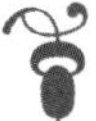

A number of years ago, as I browsed through a bin of nineteenth-century lithographs in an east coast shop that had long specialized in American historical graphic arts, a young woman entered and told the clerk that she would like to see some Adirondack prints. He knitted his brow, thought for a few moments as he quietly repeated the word "Adirondack," and then asked, just a bit sheepishly, "Did you have a particular place in mind?" Mention of Long Lake and Paul Smith's brought no response from the clerk, who seemed to be sorting through the shop's stock in his mind, but when his patron asked, "What about Trenton Falls?," his countenance brightened as he said, "Oh, yes!," and turned to a drawer marked "New Jersey."

His mistake was common enough among people who did not know that Trenton Falls, located at the southwestern margin of the Adirondacks, had once been one of New York State's scenic wonders. His vagueness about Adirondack localities probably had less to do with geographic uncertainty, however, than it did with the way in which thinking about American historical prints had developed in the United States. Early in the twentieth century, when prints from older generations first began to attract a following, collectors, dealers, and curators found it necessary to impose some kind of order on the vast and dauntingly diverse body of pictorial material that had poured forth from the nation's presses throughout the previous century. They did so by establishing clear-cut categories of interest. The chief categories included publishers (such as Currier & Ives), artists (Winslow Homer, Charles Parsons, and others), specialty subjects (including birds, sailing ships, race horses), historical events (the Civil War, political campaigns, disasters), views of localities (such as New Orleans and Niagara Falls), media (etching, chromolithography), and many others.

This approach created well-defined targets for a rapidly-growing population of collectors and the dealers who served them, and it became the basis of important private collections, but it left many interesting prints straddling two or more categories and others fitting no category at all. Though scenic views in the Adirondacks constituted a lively category for a few knowledgeable print dealers, and a sub-category of New York State for some others, it was the common experience of Adirondack collectors to find that most print dealers knew little about the region's geography, its place names, its history, or its art. Neither collectors nor dealers could turn to a reference work on the subject of pictorial images pertaining to the Adirondacks; none had ever been published.

Though the standard subject categories prevailed, there were, of course, alternate ways of thinking about and organizing historical prints, and in time one emerged that focused not on subject classifications but on geographic entities. It cut across categories to bring together prints by any maker in any medium on any subject that pertained to any aspect of a region. For a region that had inspired significant activity in the graphic arts over a long time, as the Adirondacks had, this all-inclusive approach offered a richness of variety unmatched by any single category of print. Collections began to be formed that did not correspond to the labeled drawers and bins in most print shops, though a print or two from many of those drawers often found a place in an Adirondack collection. Such a collection might well include bird's eye views of towns, scenic landscapes, pictorial maps, portraits of notable Adirondack figures, sporting subjects, depictions of buildings, geological charts, illustrated broadsides, billheads, and advertising matter, and more.

Most of these prints had been produced in New York, Buffalo, Boston, and other cities where commercial printmaking thrived. The Adirondacks could claim no important center of print production. Indeed, as a region it could claim no center at all. None of its several towns held a position of real primacy over the others. The region's boundaries were famously imprecise—everyone agreed that part of the region lay outside the blue line that conventionally identifies the Adirondack Park on maps, but few would venture to say just where the region began or ended. Unlike urban centers, the Adirondacks had few resident printmakers; most of the graphic artists who have treated the land and life of the region have been visitors, many returning year after year. Some have been amateurs, making prints essentially for their own delectation. Nearly all have responded to a mystique of place.

Wilderness has always been at the heart of this mystique. From the earliest years of exploration to the present, images of the Adirondacks, in painting and photography as well as in the graphic arts, have emphasized the dominating presence of wild nature. In these pictorial arts, the Adirondack wilderness has rarely seemed daunting—it appears as a positive aspect of the region. Water has been another vital part of the mystique. No where else in the populated United States could one find so extensive a forestland network of lakes, ponds, and rivers set among mountains, serving simultaneously as routes of passage, places for sport, and locations for permanent and temporary residences in the wild. A sense of isolation from the bustle and complexities of the "outside" world contributed to the mystique as well, for while the region has seemed relatively close to urban centers, access to it in the nineteenth century was not a simple matter. Once the journey had been made, the Adirondack sojourner was inclined to close the door for a while on the "real" life outside. Even present-day locals harbor a belief that the Adirondacks are about a million miles away from urban life.

The White Mountains of New Hampshire offer a useful contrast. There the rapid development of a tourist culture began in the middle of the nineteenth century with the arrival of railroads, some of which soon ran directly through the heart of the region. Trains stopped at major resort hotels. The hotels, built on a grand scale, flourished by offering the comforts and amenities of modern urban life. Hotel keepers kept wild nature at a safe distance, and arranged for their patrons to visit summits and scenic outlooks transported in mountain wagons on graded roads.

In contrast, most Adirondack visitors roughed it, or seemed to. Hardly any of them arrived at their final destinations by train; rail lines never spread throughout the region. Most spent their time at water level rather than aspiring to mountain heights. They lodged at boarding houses or rustic hotels or even woodland lean-tos and shanties. Some built their own camps, nearly always in a style that seemed at home in the woods. Even those lodges erected by the wealthy on a manorial scale presented themselves essentially as overgrown log cabins.

Adirondack visitors tended to disdain, for the duration of their stay in the region, most things that smacked of urban life. They subscribed to the mystique of place. If truth be told, the Adirondacks had fine resort hotels, and the White Mountains offered ample opportunities to embrace wilderness. Without question, some Adirondackers climbed mountains and some White Mountain vacationers spent days on end at pondside. But the simpler reputations of the two places have endured, and are reflected in many of the prints associated with each region.

The broader range of prints in a regional collection enlarge on this rather limited understanding of the Adirondacks as a scenic watery wilderness, a sparsely-populated sportsman's paradise. They include well-groomed towns with people who are not demonstrably different than those in towns anywhere else in America. They remind us that the Adirondack region had a substantial local population whose lives were at once distinct from and similar to the lives of the visitors who arrived each season. In this and other ways, the pictorial information gained from the full range of the region's prints enlarges our understanding of Adirondack history. There was much truth in the region's mystique, but there was a larger truth as well.

A regional collection of Adirondack prints, such as the splendid one discerningly put together over many years at the Adirondack Museum, accomplishes a number of things. It offers documentation of the appearances of places, structures, and other objects now lost or transformed. It encourages useful comparisons of the different sensibilities of some of the nation's major artists, as in the striking contrasts between what Winslow Homer and Homer Martin each reported about the Adirondacks in wood engravings around 1870. It shows how graphic artists often undertook subjects, such as views of hotels and towns, that painters left untouched, and how, for the most part, graphic artists treated subjects that were of direct interest to the general public, and did so in accessible ways. The collection reveals as well that fine artist printmakers working in a more individual pictorial language for a smaller, sophisticated audience, created Adirondack works of impressive aesthetic strength. A truly inclusive Adirondack print collection tells us a great deal about the region while it also illuminates much about American art, modes of pictorial communications, changing attitudes toward the natural world, and, not least, the history of print collecting itself.

Recently, I returned to the east coast print shop where years before I had overheard the clerk and his patron search for Adirondack prints. I found the shop's subject categories much expanded. The name "Adirondacks" now graced a bin and a folio drawer. The present clerk asked if she could be of help, and I replied by expressing an interest in seeing prints of Adirondack hotels. "Certainly," she said, "We have a handsome lithograph of Paul Smith's and a few others in the Adirondack bin." "How about Trenton Falls?" I asked. "That's outside the blue line," she noted with a smile, "but we have a few pieces in the Adirondack bin, including some interesting illustrated hotel menus with views you won't find elsewhere." I asked, "Do you spend much time the Adirondacks?" "I've never been there," she replied, "but I'd like to drive through it sometime, and see the places that I've come to know through prints." I concluded that Adirondack prints were at last coming into their own.

David Tatham

The Adirondacks Delineated

Exploration, Promotion, Celebration

The Adirondacks encompass a vast portion of New York State bounded on the east by Lake George and Lake Champlain, on the west by Lake Ontario, on the north by the Saint Lawrence River, and on the south by the Mohawk River. The land enclosed by these geological features includes majestic mountains, almost innumerable lakes and ponds, meandering streams and rivers, swamps and bogs. At the end of the nineteenth century, as a result of legislative action, a portion of this region was established as a state forest preserve. Today, Adirondacks has lost its geological meaning and usually refers to just the area within the Adirondack Park. Only in the past one hundred and seventy-five years has this territory been thoroughly described and its natural resources, particularly its forest and mineral deposits, exploited. In the second half of the past century, writers and artists celebrated the region as a retreat from the pressures of urban life and a place for relaxation and enjoyment. This aspect of the area was secured by the creation of the Adirondack Park a century ago. These antecedents of the current economy of the Adirondacks, both the economic exploitation of natural resources and tourism, are well documented by printed images. In addition these prints reproduce the efforts of artists to delineate the landscape to bring the incomparable aesthetic qualities of the land to a public scattered far beyond its geographic boundaries.

Exploration

Prints to Describe the Topography

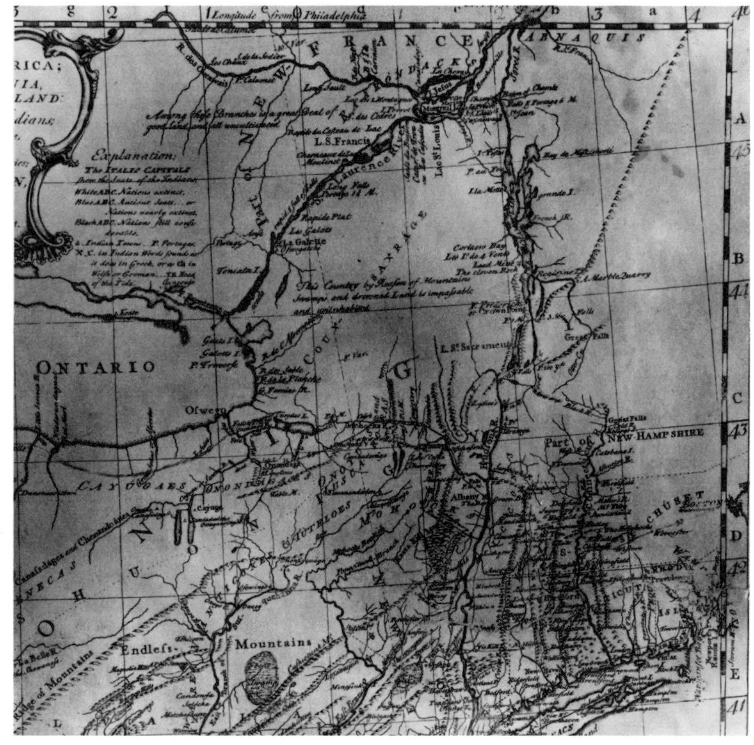

Detail, *General Map of the Middle British Colonies*, 1755. Courtesy American Antiquarian Society.

The first part of the region to be described was the eastern portion. Samuel de Champlain heard tales about a large lake to the south of Quebec during the winter of 1608, which he spent in Quebec. In 1609 he set out with a band of Iroquois and three Frenchmen to explore the lake that now bears his name. His narrative is more informative about the region that became Vermont than about the Adirondacks, whose mountain peaks he only glimpsed. His Algonquin Indian guides were familiar with the fertile valleys to the east of the lake, but not with the Adirondack mountains, which they avoided because their enemies the Iroquois lived to the west.[1]

Champlain witnessed an Indian skirmish at the site of a strategically important spot at the foot of Lake Champlain. Fort Carillon, later to be known as Fort Ticonderoga, was established at this point in 1755 by the French. Of great strategic importance militarily, it was the site of battles between the English and the French during the French and Indian Wars in 1758 and 1759. Colonial forces captured the Fort early in the American Revolution, but General Burgoyne recaptured it in 1777. Its picturesque ruins attracted artists and other visitors of the nineteenth century who were interested not only in its history but also in the scenic qualities of its position on Lake Champlain. During the same year that Champlain explored the northern portion of the region, Henry Hudson sailed the *Half Moon* about one hundred and fifty miles up the river that bears his

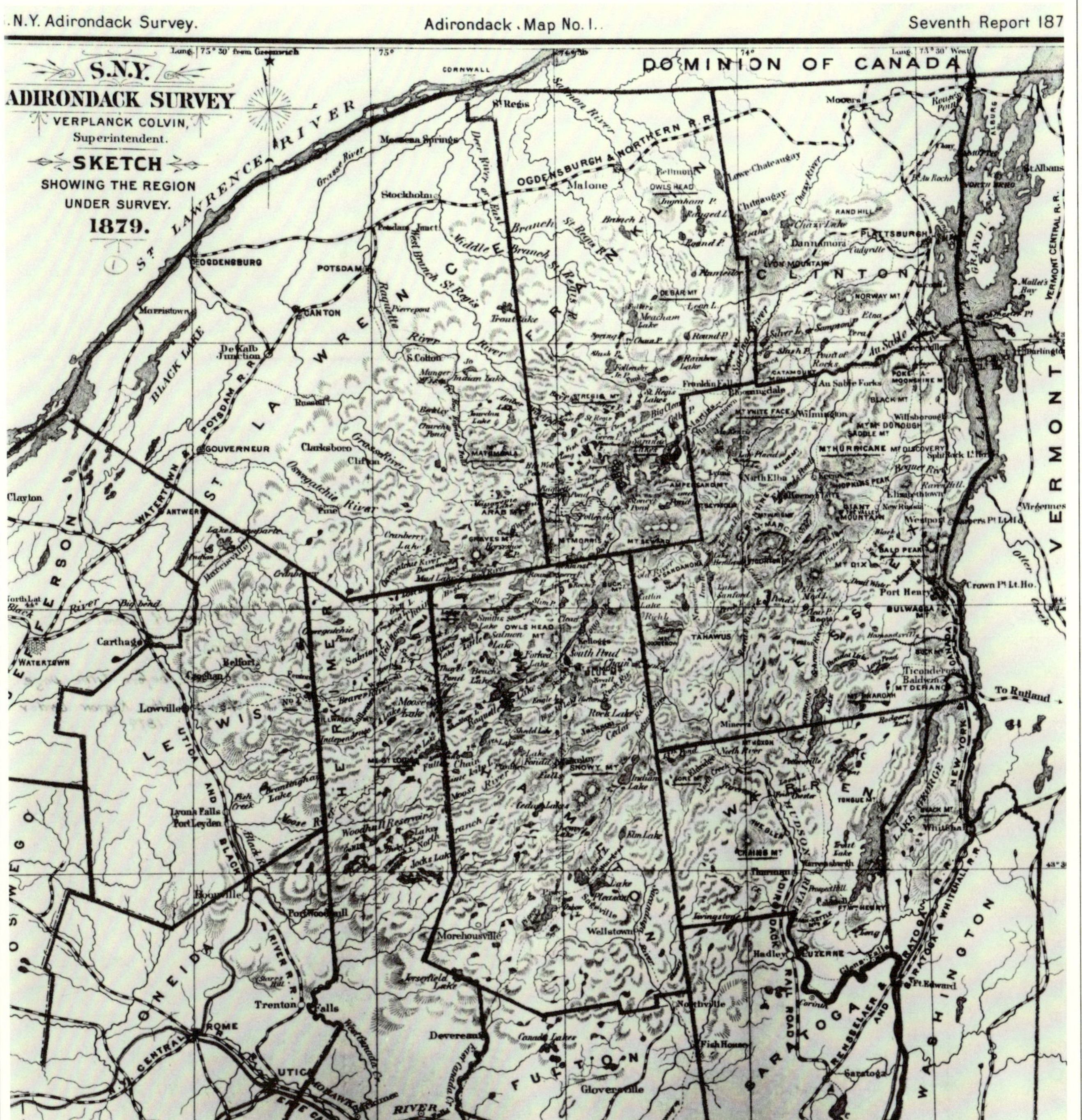

Detail, *State of New York for Spafford's Gazetteer*, 1813. Courtesy American Antiquarian Society.

name, beginning the exploration of the region just south of Lake George.[2]

During the second half of the eighteenth century, the lands of the Adirondacks passed into public then private ownership as the colonial government acquired land from Native American tribes. Settlement of the region was extremely slow and limited; the climate was forbidding, and travel, even by waterways, was difficult. Once the Erie Canal was opened in 1825, it was easier for those leaving the depleted and stony lands of New England to go to western New York State and beyond than it was to travel directly west to the Adirondacks. The diffuse pattern of settlement and development made the region particularly adaptable to its function in the nineteenth century as a "sportsman's paradise."

Settlement of the area can best be described by comparing maps of the eighteenth and nineteenth centuries. On the *General Map of the Middle British Colonies,* published on the eve of the French and Indian Wars in 1755, the region between the St. Lawrence River and the Mohawk River bears the legend: "This Country by Reason of Mountains, Swamps and drowned Land is impassable and uninhabited."[3] This statement implies the land had been explored, but there is no detail on the map west of the ridge of mountains that Champlain had glimpsed in 1609. Almost two hundred years after the first exploration of the region, Simeon DeWitt's *Map of the State of New York,* issued in 1802, shows no settlements in the central portion of the region. There is a road running north from Glens Falls to Plattsburgh paralleling the western shore of Lake Champlain, but no roads run northwest from the Hudson River or the southern tip of Lake George. DeWitt identified the owners of the vast tracts of land by name. However, he labeled few of the lakes or rivers, the main geographic features on the large map.

The map in Horatio Gates Spafford's *Gazetteer of the State of New York,* published in Albany in 1813, uses the term "Wild Country" to describe the region. Indeed, it was sparsely populated. For example, Essex County (1,763 square miles) had eleven towns established between 1799 and 1808 with 9,525 inhabitants. Spafford noted, however, that the land was "rich in ores of iron, with many indications of other valuable metals." He also commented that some sawmills were in operation and the manufacturing of iron had commenced at several locations. Montgomery County bordered the Mohawk River on the south and extended northward almost ninety miles. Spafford wrote that "The settlements can hardly be said to extend beyond 25 miles" north of the Mohawk. The rest "is clothed with evergreens, of an enormous size, and abounds with swamps, small lakes and marshes, little known."[4]

On the maps of the 1830s, most of the larger lakes of the region were named and roads were shown crossing the region. On the maps published in the next two decades, additional roads appeared and more lakes and mountains acquired

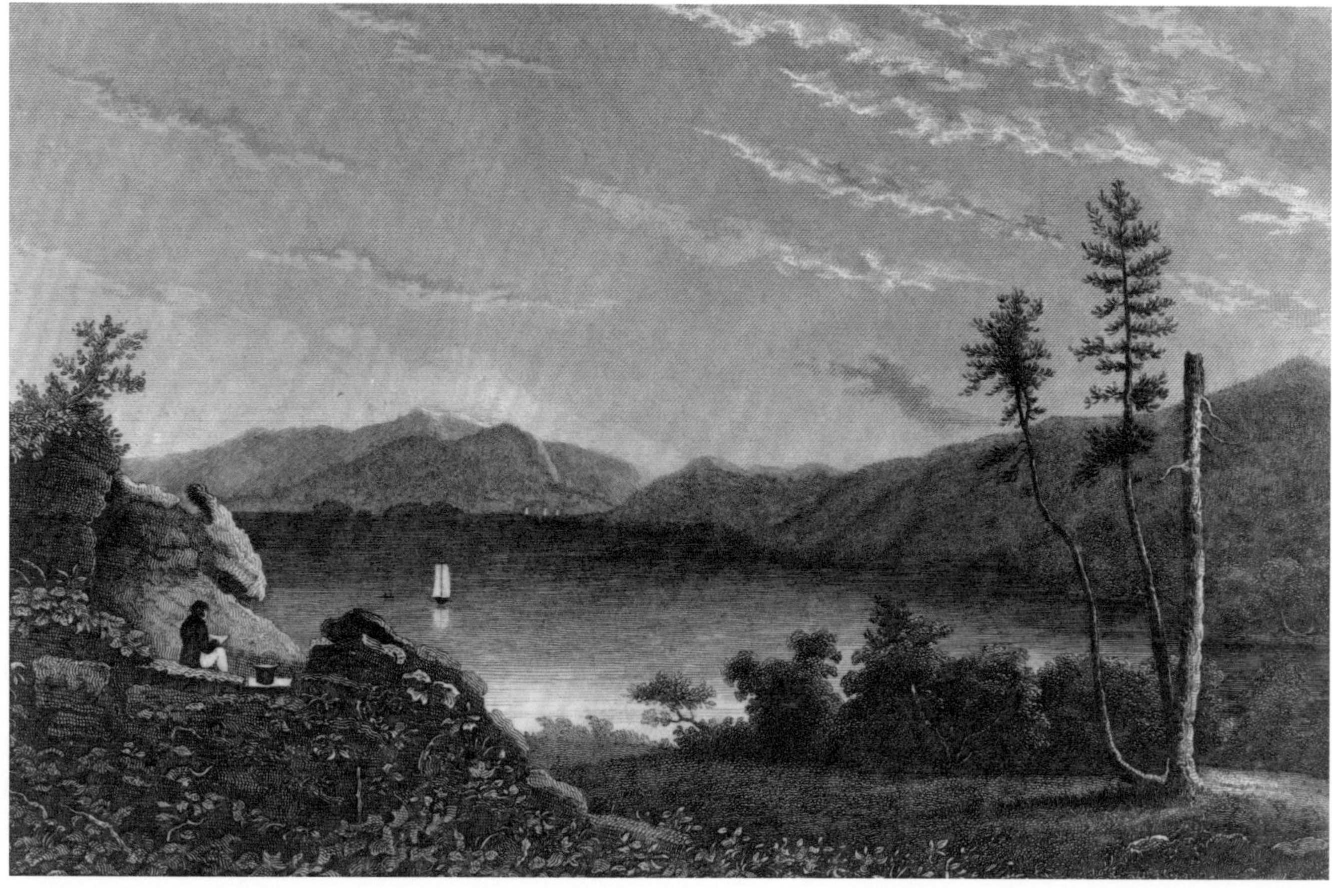

"Lake George, N.Y." (41). *61.53.8.* [Numbers in parentheses refer to the Checklist of Prints.]

names. Railroads and many towns were established on the periphery and several additional settlements appeared in the central portion of the region. By 1880, there were still large portions of the region inaccessible by road, but the region could no longer be called the "Wild Country" as it had at the beginning of the century.

The southern part of the region was described by several travelers during the eighteenth century. Few of their published accounts were, however, illustrated. One exception is Thomas Anburey's *Travels through the Interior Parts of America* published by William Lane in London in 1789. The author was a participant in the Battle of Saratoga as a member of His Majesty's 29th and 24th Regiments serving under the command of General Burgoyne. Anburey was taken prisoner at Saratoga and spent the rest of the war in Cambridge, Massachusetts; Mystic, Connecticut; Charlottesville, Virginia; Frederick, Maryland; and New York City. He was repatriated in November 1781 and remained in the British army for another year before he faded from view.[5] Two illustrations in his book depict a blockhouse (1) and sawmill (2) on Fort Anne Creek, due east of the southern tip of Lake George and just a few miles beyond the current boundaries of the Adirondack Park. Anburey depicted the blockhouse because this type of fortification was unfamiliar to his fellow countrymen. In his text Anburey described the sawmill and blockhouse on Fort Anne Creek as "a very romantic view."[6]

Military service and war drew many to the region. The springs at Ballston and Saratoga also attracted visitors beginning in the late eighteenth century, and illustrations were published in the *New York Magazine* and the *Columbian Magazine* in the last decade of the eighteenth century.[7] William Meade wrote *An Experimental Enquiry into the Chemical Properties and Medicinal Qualities of the Principal Mineral Waters of Ballston and Saratoga in the State of New York,* issued in Philadelphia by Harrison Hall in 1817, to analyze the spring waters. By 1817 hotels had been established in both locations, and the illustrations in the book, drawn by the French naturalist and artist Charles Alexandre Lesueur (1778-1846), depict Ballston Springs from the steps of the hotel owned and operated by Joshua B. Aldridge and the hotel at Congress Spring, one of several in Saratoga Springs. Both towns became renowned resorts. Although Meade's treatise was a form of scientific exploration, the attractive illustrations assured readers that there were substantial hotels to provide accommodations. Lesueur traveled widely throughout the northeastern United States in 1816, and he continued northward from Saratoga Springs to Lake Champlain making sketches of Whitehall, New York, and Lake George.[8]

Another traveler throughout New York State at the same time was William Dunlap (1766-1839), a dramatist, theatrical manager, painter, novelist, and historian. For several years following 1814 he was the assistant paymaster-general of the New York State Militia, a position that required him to travel throughout New York State. In late August 1816 he began a journey from Hudson, New York, to Plattsburgh, located about twenty miles south of the Canadian border. During this trip, Dunlap made at least fifty watercolors of a number of sites including views of Caldwell, at the southern end of Lake George, Fort Ticonderoga, Plattsburgh, and the Saranac River.[9]

Lake George became celebrated for its beautiful sheet of water surrounded by mountains. In the 1820s and later it was part of the American grand tour, along with the Connecticut River, the Hudson River, the Catskills, the Erie Canal, the White Mountains, and Niagara Falls. Towns along the route, such as Saratoga Springs, depended on a steady flow of tourists during the short summer season. The scenic attractions of America's eastern mountains, rivers, and valleys were analogous to the cultural and religious monuments of the European grand tour.[10] Hotels provided more gracious accommodations than the taverns prevalent in previous decades. Tourists who visited Lake George confined themselves at first to the town of Caldwell where the Lake House, established around 1800, lodged tourists and other visitors.[11] The town was named for General James Caldwell to whom 1,595 acres on Lake George were conveyed in 1787 as a result of his service in the American Revolution. By 1821 the town had five to six hundred inhabitants. The shore of the lake, with its forests and dramatic rock faces extending to the water's edge, was particularly appealing to artists. Since Caldwell was unwilling to sell his land, there were no other settlements along the lower portion of the lake, so it remained unspoiled for some years.[12] The beautiful lake and its dramatic vistas were celebrated in the published accounts and views made by early visitors.

Another artist at Lake George prior to 1820 was the English immigrant artist Francis Guy (1760-1820). Trained in the textile trades, he left England in 1795 and settled in New York. Unable to establish himself in business there, Philadelphia, or Baltimore, he determined to become an artist, concentrating on landscapes rather than the more lucrative, but very competitive, portrait trade. About 1817 he painted *Carter's Tavern, at the Head of Lake George,* a depiction of a public house in Caldwell with a view of the lake and surrounding hills. The foreground is dotted with figures. Guy painted additional scenes of Brooklyn, New York, before his death from alcoholism in 1820.[13]

Widely read travel accounts published in the 1820s spread the fame of Lake George. After suffering a physical breakdown while working as a tutor in Yale College, Timothy Dwight (1752-1817) recuperated by traveling extensively on foot and horseback throughout the northeast. His letters describing his journeys were gathered in *Travels in New England and New York* published posthumously in 1821-2. Dwight visited Lake George in 1802 and 1811. His accounts are full of details about the history, topography, and customs of the people. By 1811 travel to Lake George from New York was facilitated by steamboats on the Hudson River as far as Albany and by stagecoach to Caldwell. Dwight had a longstanding familiarity with the region; his first trip to Saratoga occurred in 1792. At that time, he wrote, the springs were surrounded by "an absolute forest, spreading every way to a great distance."[14] In 1802 Dwight noted appreciatively that many of the forests south of Glens Falls had disappeared and were replaced by farms. Between Glens Falls and Lake George, however, the road "crosses a pine ground, generally poor and barren. The road is indifferent, being alternately encumbered with sand, and stones; and the settlements are few, recent, and very unpromising."[15] Of Lake George he wrote: "The water is probably not surpassed in beauty by any in the world: pure, sweet, pellucid, of an elegant hue when immediately under the eye, and at very small, as well as at greater distances presenting a gay, luminous azure, and appearing as if a soft luster undulated everywhere on its surface with a continual and brilliant emanation." He was as rhapsodic about the islands in the lake, the shores, and the mountains that border the lake.[16]

Benjamin Silliman (1779-1864) traveled through the region

and in 1820 published an account of his visit in his *Remarks Made, on a Short Tour Between Hartford and Quebec.* Of the region between Albany northward to Lake Champlain, Silliman wrote: "Indeed, from Albany, upon the course proposed, every part of our way was to be over *classical ground.* History sheds a deeper interest over no portion of the North American States. He who venerates the virtues and the valour, and commiserates the sufferings of our fathers, and he, who views, with gratitude and reverence, the deliverances which heaven has wrought for this land, will tread with awe, on every foot of ground between Albany and the northern lakes."[17] Although Silliman also described the actual, as opposed to the historical, landscape, its place in history was paramount to him. The two engravings in the book—"Lake George, from Fort George" (74) and "Lake George, from the Village of Caldwell"—were drawn by Daniel Wadsworth (1771-1848) of Hartford. His appreciation and enjoyment of the American landscape was perhaps nurtured during trips such as this one with Silliman. Wadsworth's love of landscape found a later and lasting expression in his patronage of artists of the Hudson River School, particularly Thomas Cole.

The renown of the region was clearly spread by published accounts first in books, but also in periodicals. For example, an illustrated article on Fort Ticonderoga appeared in the *Analectic Magazine* in April 1818. The audience for this journal, published in Philadelphia, consisted of the nation's educated elite. The article on Fort Ticonderga was accompanied by an engraving (67) drawn by Hugh Reinagle (1788-1834), a theatrical scene painter and drawing instructor, who was employed in Albany from 1815 to 1817. The text described the history of the Fort, its strategic importance, and the battles that occurred there. The account concludes by noting that the "character of the adjacent country, it will be seen, is mountainous; on the Vermont side it is level. It is remarkably healthy, and many of the inhabitants attain to longevity. The beauty of the situation, and curiosity, excited by a recollection of the events on Lake Champlain, now peacefully navigated by the steamboat, which carries passengers at a very moderate rate, contribute to attract the resort of numerous travelers in the summer season, and to attach something more than an ordinary interest to the scene represented."[18] Many other significant views of American scenery were published in this periodical including two views by Charles Fraser of Charleston, South Carolina, of Haddrils Point, South Carolina, and the Hudson River, both published in 1817. Karol Lawson has argued "Magazine engravings of the post-revolutionary years and the early republic trained Americans to see their native environment as a uniquely patriotic inspiration for an independent culture."[19] In the following decades American artists established their artistic independence from Europe by focusing their talents on the American landscape.

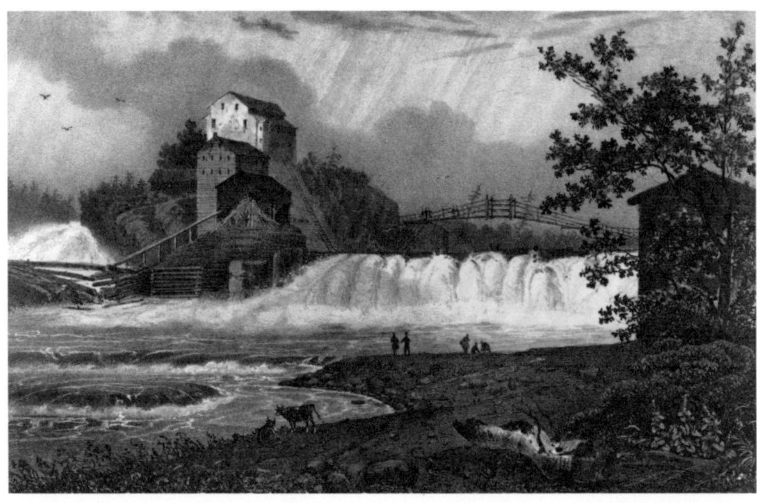

"Mills on the Black River."
(308). *93.12.5.*

In 1815, the French artist and naturalist, Jacques Gérard Milbert (1766-1840), arrived in New York from Le Havre in order to explore the vast land. He found employment mapping a route for the canal between Lake Champlain and the Hudson River and became captivated by the scenery. He determined to return to the wilderness on foot with more leisure to sketch and paint. This opportunity was provided by the French government which commissioned him to collect natural history specimens. He took this assignment seriously; from the time of his arrival in 1815 until his return to France in 1823, he collected over 7,868 specimens of plants, animals, and minerals. It was during the spring of 1818 that Milbert explored the upper reaches of the Hudson River beginning at Lake Luzerne west of Glens Falls. He observed excessive clearing of trees from the slopes of mountains, an activity that would later wreak havoc with the clear waters of the Hudson River.

Milbert took later trips in 1818 and 1821 to explore other parts of New York State—the Finger Lakes Region and the Mo-hawk River Valley westward to Niagara Falls. It was during one of these trips that he drew "Mills on the Black River," (308) just east of Lake Ontario. On his return to France he wrote an extensive and lavishly illustrated memoir of his travels.[20] The drawings that he made of the Hudson River were transformed into lithographs in Paris for a European audience. The lithographs, showing bridges, mills, villages, and groups of tourists, demonstrate that he was interested not just in the dramatic landscape, but in the development of towns as well.[21]

Another artist to explore the Adirondack region to the north and west of Lake George and to paint it was William Guy Wall (1792-after 1863). Twenty of his watercolor sketches were published as *The Hudson River Portfolio* issued by Henry J. Megarey and William B. Gilley of New York and John Mill of Charleston, South Carolina, from 1821 to 1825. This portfolio contains prints engraved by John Hill (1770-1850).[22] Wall, already trained in England as a topographic draftsman, arrived in New York City on September 1, 1818, and quickly became an important member of the artists' community. He was a founder of the National Academy of Design and exhibited there, at the Pennsylvania Academy, and the Apollo Association.

In preparation for the publication, Wall toured the Hudson Valley during the summer of 1820 and traveled farther up the Hudson than previous artists, although he probably journeyed no farther than what is now North Creek, far short of the mountainous area and due west of Lake George. The prints were issued in five numbers each of which contained four prints that cost sixteen dollars per number or eighty

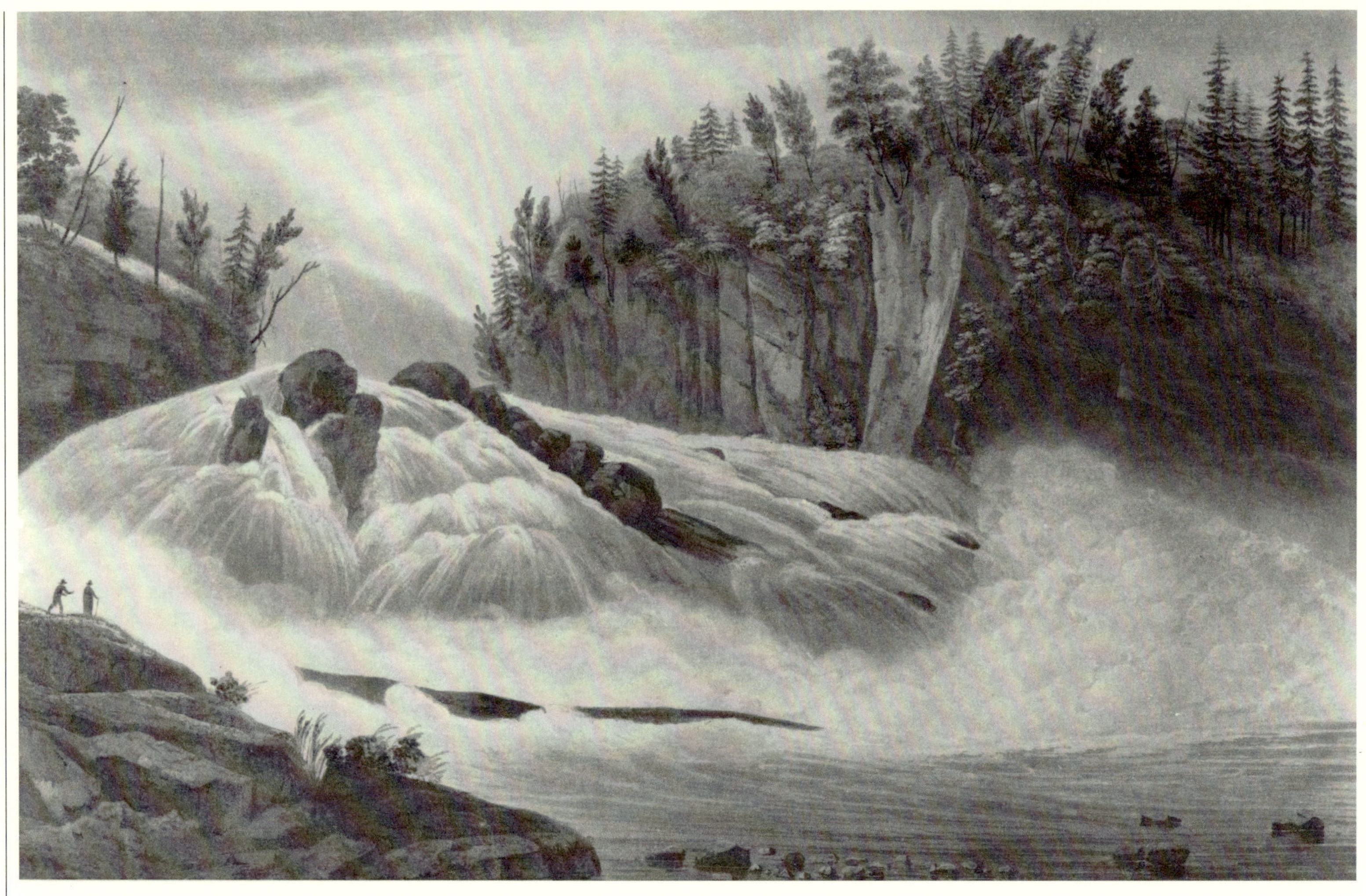

"Hadley Falls. No. 5 of the Hudson River Port Folio." (76). *75.169.2.*

dollars for the entire series. The publishers required people to subscribe in advance to be sure that expenses would be covered.

Wall's watercolors and the prints derived from them are evenly lighted and the landscape is laid out in a rational manner. Careful attention is paid to details, although they are subordinated to the whole landscape. In the tradition already established in England, even the wildest landscapes include

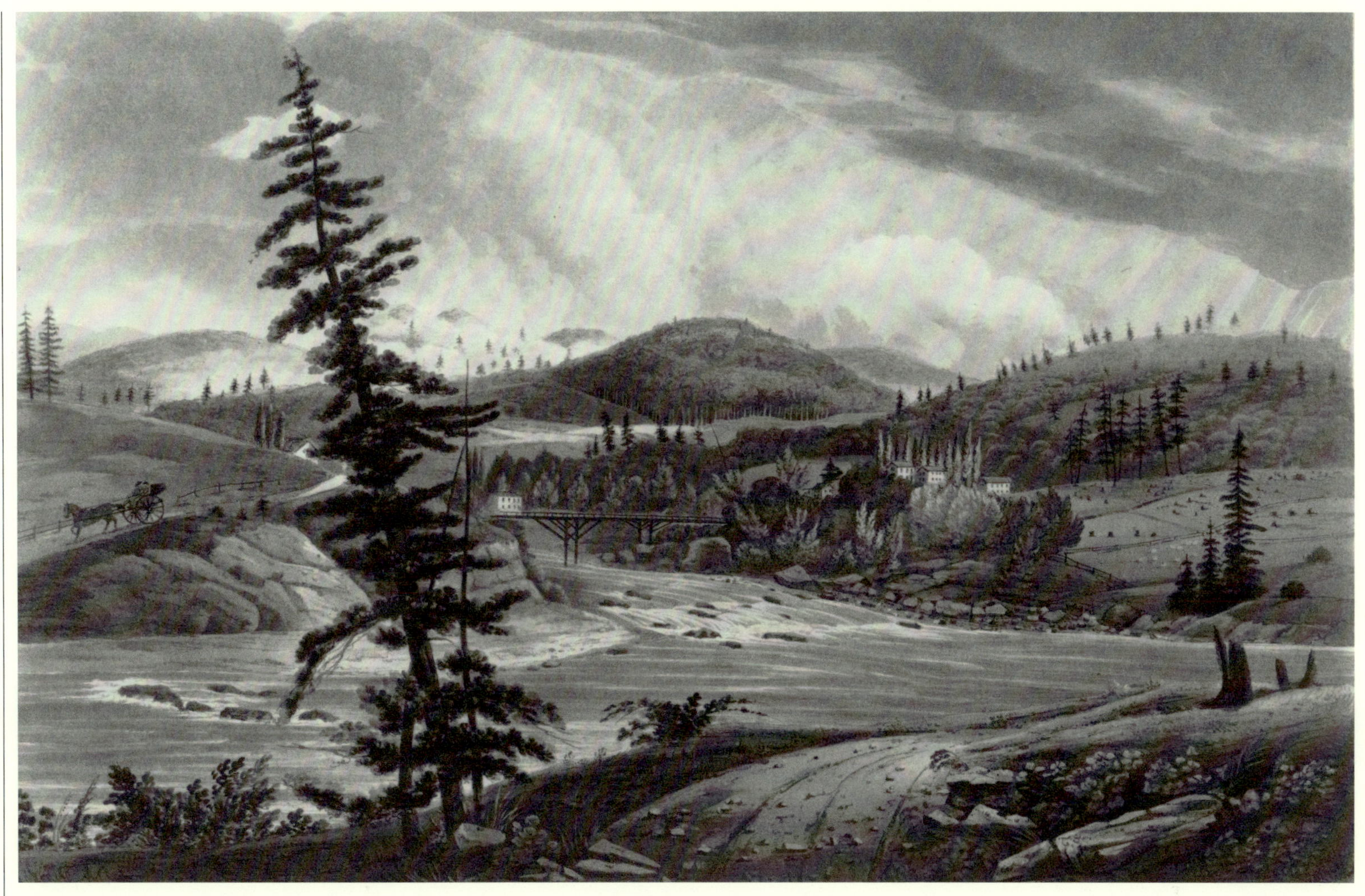

"The Junction of the Sacandaga and Hudson Rivers. No. 2 of the Hudson River Port Folio." (75). *75.169.1.*

a few figures in the foreground, usually dwarfed by the site. In the foreground of "Hadley Falls," (76) for example, two well-dressed figures stand on a rock promontory at the left. Additional Adirondack subjects include "Little Falls at Luzerne," "The Junction of the Sacandaga and Hudson Rivers" (75), "View near Sandy Hill," "Glenns Falls," "Baker's Falls" (77), and "Fort Edward."

Beginning in the 1820s, state governments began to com-

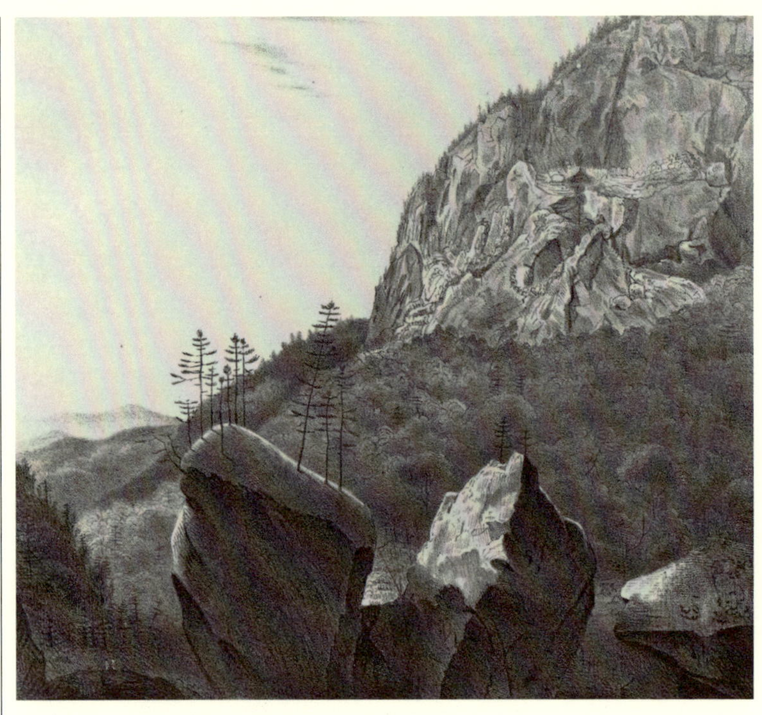

"View of the Indian Pass." (170). *65.35.1.*

mission geological and zoological surveys to provide inventories of mineral, botanical, and animal resources, all of which had economic value.[23] New York State commissioned Ebenezer Emmons of Williams College to explore and survey the mountains of the Adirondack region to determine the extent of iron ore deposits. The land Emmons and his party explored was owned by Archibald McIntyre who later formed the Adirondack Iron and Steel Company. One of the artists invited by Emmons to participate in the survey was Charles Cromwell Ingham. Ingham painted the magnificent *Great Adirondack Pass, Painted on the Spot* (Adirondack Museum collection, 66.114.1) which was reproduced as a lithograph (170) in the *New York State Geological Report for 1837* by Emmons and published by the New York State Legislature in 1838 and again in 1840. The Pass lies between two mountains—Wallface and McIntyre, northeast of Lake Henderson. Emmons wrote eloquently about the Pass: "In conclusion, I remark, that I should not have occupied so much space for the purpose of describing merely a natural curiosity, were it not for the fact that probably in this country there is no object of the kind on a scale so vast and imposing as this. We look upon the Falls of Niagara with awe and a feeling of our insignificance; but much more are we impressed with the great and sublime in the view of the simple and naked rock of the Adirondack Pass."[24]

Unfortunately no small print can capture the awesome nature of such a landscape. The place and the image acquired an iconic status. Ingham exhibited the painting in New York in 1839 and then presented it to Mrs. McIntyre whose descendants in turn presented it to the Adirondack Museum.[25]

The New York State Geological Report for 1837 contains a total of ten lithographs and five maps. Because they were the first published depictions of the high peaks area, they constitute a crucial record of the Adirondacks. They include the "View of the Indian Pass, from Lake Henderson" (171), "Trap Dyke at Avalanche Lake" (165), "View of Mt. McMartin" (167), "Distant View of Mt. Marcy" (161), "View at Lake Colden" (166), "View of the Adirondack Mountains" (168), and "View of the Dial Mountain" (169). Ebenezer Emmons was responsible for several of the views, and the plates were lithographed by the firm of John H. Bufford in New York.[26] These prints are also significant because they depict parts of the region not yet on the traditional tourist's route.

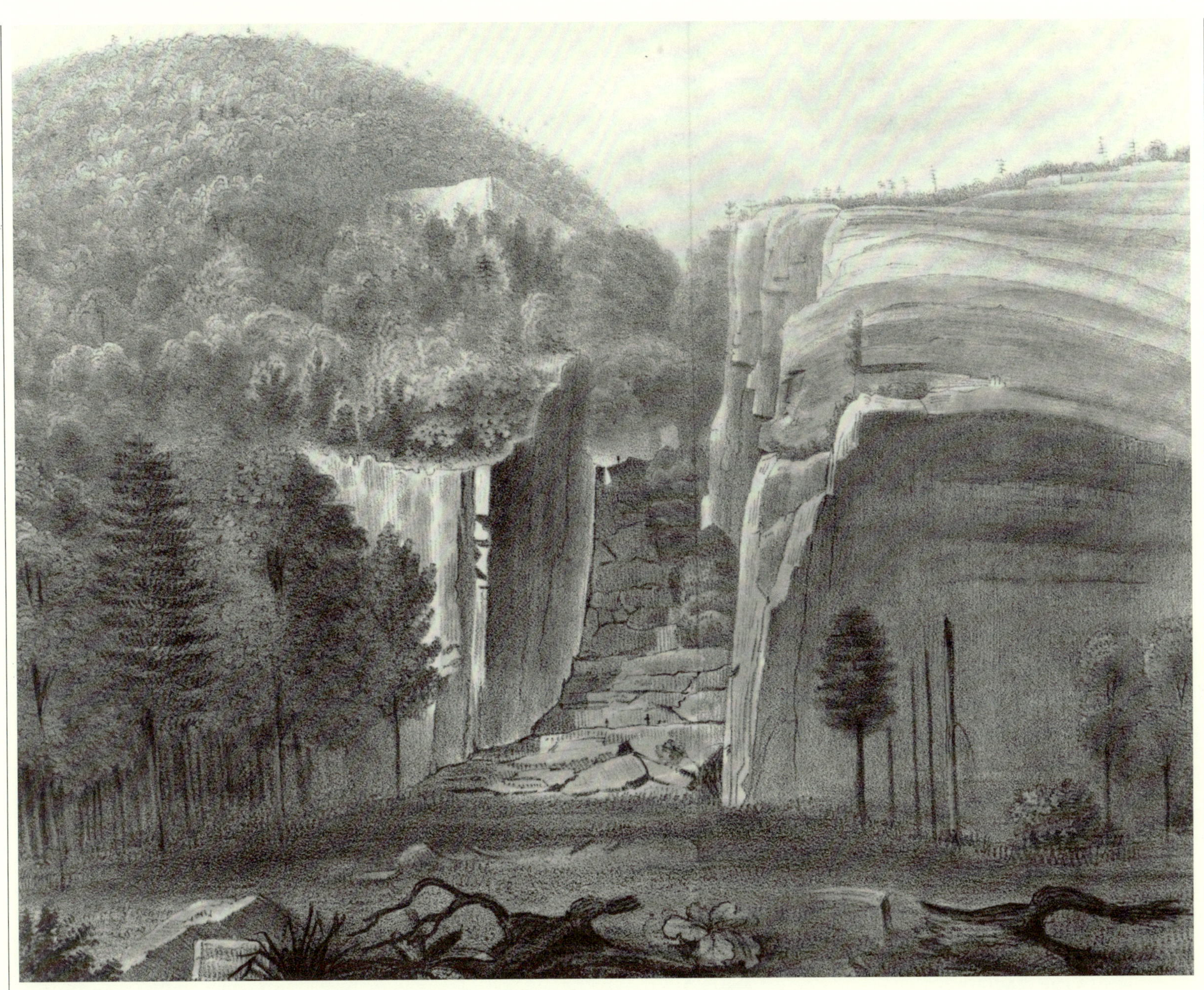

“Trap Dyke at Avalanche Lake.” (164). *58.321.2.*

"Lake Catharine, Hamilton Co."
(276). *66.95.2.*

Emmons' complete report was published in part four of *The Geology of New-York* issued by the New York State Assembly in 1842 with additional lithographs drawn by John William Hill (1812-1879). Hill was the son of the engraver of William Guy Wall's *Hudson River Portfolio.* His mother printed many of the plates for that series and his older sisters helped to hand color some of the aquatints.[27] This family background suggests early training as a topographical artist. Indeed, he made his early reputation in that genre; later, after he came under the sway of the followers of John Ruskin, he joined the Pre-Raphaelite movement. His views of Lake Janet (now Blue Mountain Lake) (278), Lake Catharine (now Eagle Lake) (276), and Cedar River (279) in the central Adirondacks are important because few other artists had penetrated the interior of the wilderness and created works of art that were reproduced for the public. The three prints share a low vantage point and are singularly placid, devoid of the drama that other artists found in nature. Hill was acting as a recorder of the topography and was not interested in the effects of the sublime. Indeed, Emmons noted in his text that "these views were not introduced for the purpose of embellishment, or the exhibition of beautiful landscapes, but solely to convey to the reader what has just been expressed [in the text], a correct view of its surface, or of its general outline."[28] Typically, each image contains several figures to provide a sense of scale to the landscape.

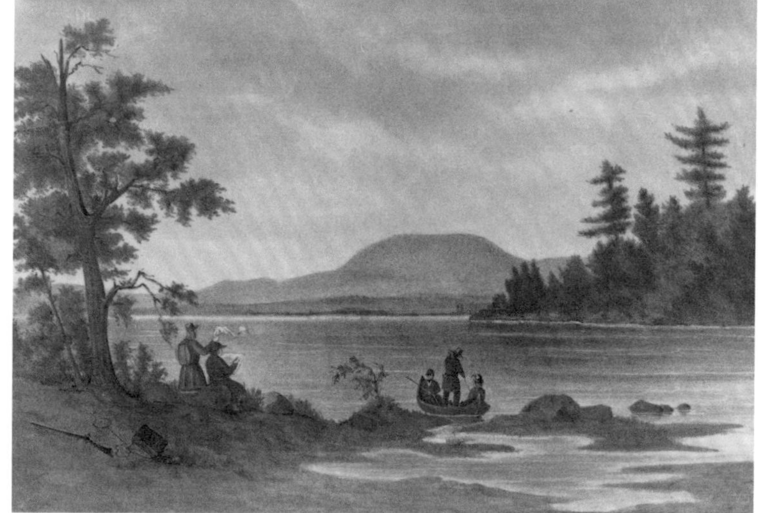

Most of the early prints of the Adirondacks, particularly the elegant and expensive portfolios of Wall and Milbert, were published for limited audiences. Although important as illustrations of previously undescribed portions of the Adirondacks, the lithographs accompanying the New York State Geological Survey were likewise seen by a relatively limited audience.[29] It was not until the establishment of commercial lithographic presses and the reproduction of images by wood engravings in popular magazines that depictions of the Adirondacks were available to the general public. Most of these prints served to promote the region, particularly after the introduction of railroads improved access.

Promotion

Prints in the Service of Tourism

Although the general purpose of prints is to present information in a visual language, they are often published with specific goals in mind. With respect to the prints of the Adirondacks, one can argue that images in the popular press were essential for the success of tourism. Commercially produced lithographs were issued in large numbers because several thousand impressions could be produced from one lithograph stone. Currier & Ives and other firms marketed lithographed prints separately, not as parts of expensive portfolios; and, for the first time, prints could be purchased inexpensively. Promotional prints also appeared as illustrations in widely circulated magazines, such as those published by Harper and Brothers and Frank Leslie. The rise of illustrated journalism occurred simultaneously with the emergence of a growing professional, affluent population that had the leisure to read and travel, and the expansion of transportation networks that facilitated access to new regional resorts, of which the Adirondacks was just one. Considering all these prints in their context of publication and audience is important, for the popular press served a specific function and these images were not created in a vacuum.

The publication and distribution of separately published lithographed prints was most successfully practiced by the firm of Currier & Ives in New York. The firm, beginning with Nathaniel Currier in 1835, issued over 7,000 prints in the following fifty years. Other firms imitated Currier & Ives, but none were as successful. Among their marketing strategies was to issue prints in different sizes. Smaller prints, even though hand colored, obviously cost less than the larger more carefully hand colored folio prints derived from paintings by renowned artists.

The popularity of lithographs issued by Nathaniel Currier was insured by the availability of paintings by the artist Arthur Fitzwilliam Tait (1819-1905). During his childhood spent on a farm outside of Liverpool, he acquired a lasting love of hunting and fishing as well as animals. At the age of twelve he began to work in a store in Manchester selling home furnishings including prints. Experimenting by reading art manuals, he learned to draw and to produce lithographs. In his twenties he began to support himself as a teacher of drawing and as an assistant in an architectural firm. Hoping for greater opportunities in America, he left England in 1850 and arrived in New York City. There he found a ready market for his paintings of hunting and fishing scenes, selling some paintings to the American Art Union and to Nathaniel Currier. He also exhibited at the National Academy of Design, to which he was elected in 1854.

Tait first went to the Adirondacks because his brother had abandoned his family and Tait was concerned for their welfare. After doing what he could for his sister-in-law, Tait visited the Chateaugay Lakes, staying at the boarding house kept by Jonathan Bellows and his sons who were all experi-

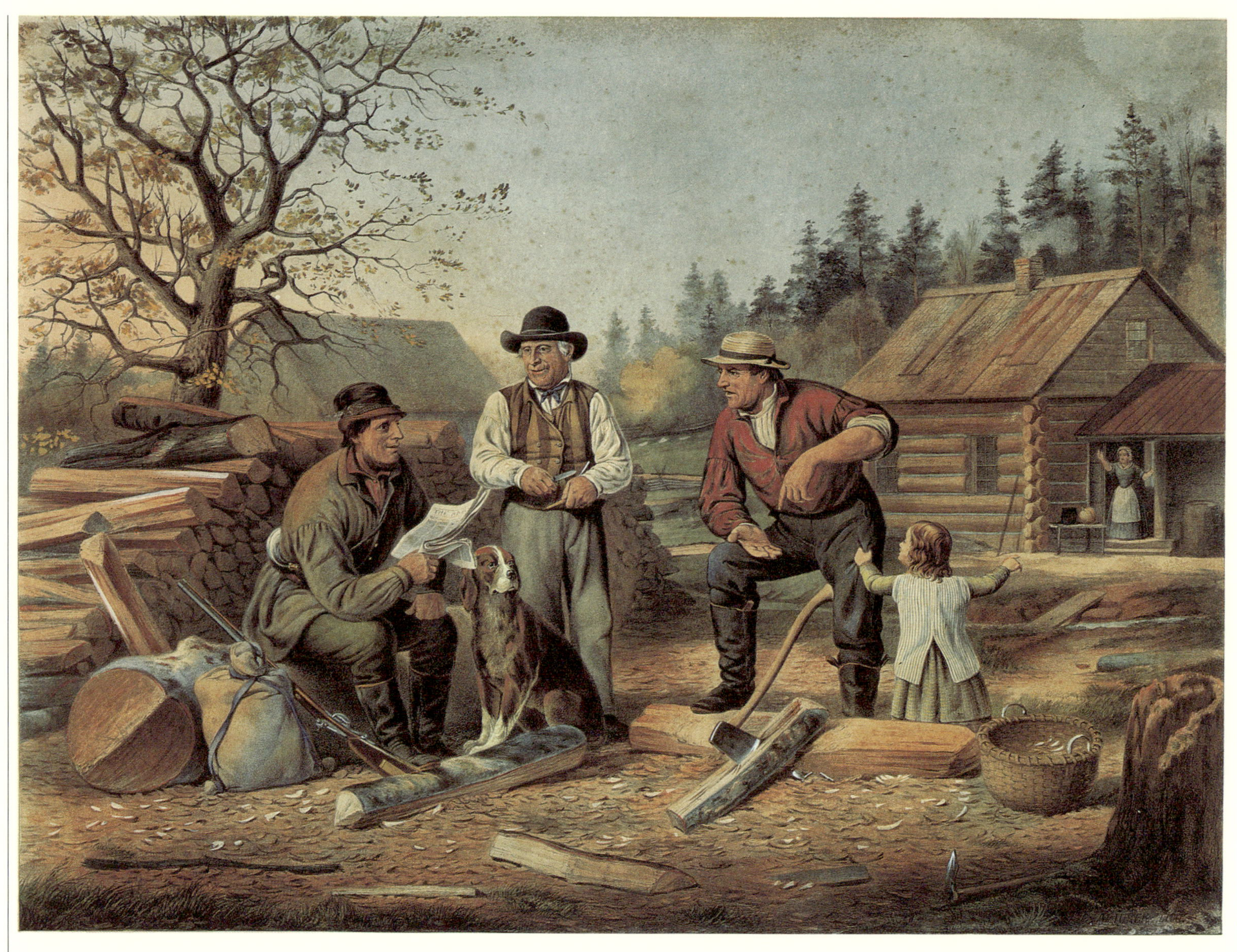

Arguing the Point. (223). 65.42.14.

enced guides. For a sportsman eager for hunting and fishing, this was paradise; Tait had never experienced anything similar in England. He returned to the region during the next few years to hunt and fish and to make sketches that were transformed into full-scale paintings in his New York studio. In the 1860s Tait became so successful that he left the city and moved to Morrisania, a rural suburb outside of New York. He no longer had to sell his own paintings; dealers including Samuel P. Avery and Michael Knoedler had started their own successful businesses as art dealers and were happy to handle Tait's paintings. Just after the conclusion of the Civil War, Tait started to sell paintings to Louis Prang, the publisher of inexpensive chromolithographs in Boston. In the mid-1870s Tait and his family moved to the Adirondacks, on the west shore of Long Lake where they lived year around. Tait sold the house in 1882 and lived in New York City and outlying Yonkers where he worked happily and productively, producing numerous paintings of chickens, sheep, and other domesticated animals until the end of his life in 1905.[30]

One of Tait's earliest Adirondack paintings reproduced by Nathaniel Currier was *Arguing the Point* (223). Although this print can be viewed as a genre print about a woman trying to get the attention of the men conversing by the woodpile, it is a specific rendering of several of the people Tait knew at Chateaugay. A guide, Anthony Sprague, is seated at the left with the newspaper. Jonathan Bellows and his son, Francis Bellows, are standing. Francis's daughter, Georgia, is the child; the woman at the door of the cabin is Sophrone Thurber, a hired girl. Although there was a twelve room boarding house at the site by 1854 when the painting was completed, it is not in evidence in this painting. The work was exhibited at the National Academy of Design in 1856 with the subtitle: "Settling the Presidency." This title would have been appropriate in an election year, and it gives added meaning to the painting that was not particularly pertinent in 1855, the year the lithograph was produced.

Over the next few years, Nathaniel Currier and then Currier & Ives published almost forty lithographs after Tait's paintings.[31] *American Winter Sports. Deer Shooting "on the Shattagee* [*sic*]" (225), derived from a painting titled *Still Hunting on the First Snow: A Second Shot* (Adirondack Museum collection, 65.36.1), shows Tait taking aim at a stag. His companion is thought to be Mathew B. Brady, the New York photographer. *American Forest Scene. Maple Sugaring* (221) of 1856 shows a large group of people making maple syrup in the forest. Like *Arguing the Point,* this is a genre scene rather than a hunting subject. In *American Winter Sports. Trout Fishing "on Chateaugay Lake,"* (222) also of 1856, Tait captures the sensation of the frigid climate by the windblown snow in the background. The mittenless man with a dour look on his face, even as he pulls a fish through the hole in the ice, reinforces the chill. His heavy mittens with the saw

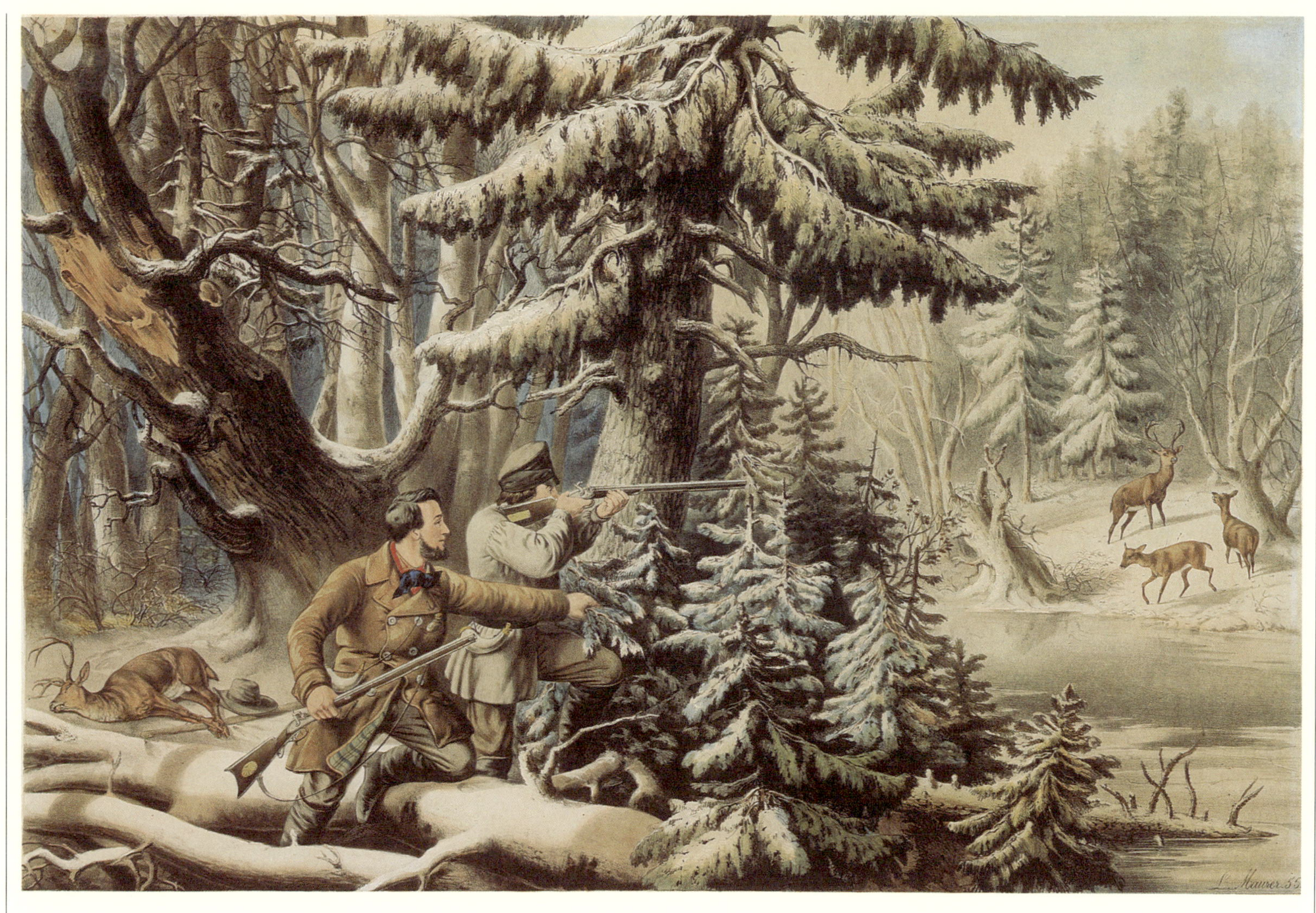

American Winter Sports. Deer Shooting "on the Shattagee [sic]."
(225). *64.152.4.*

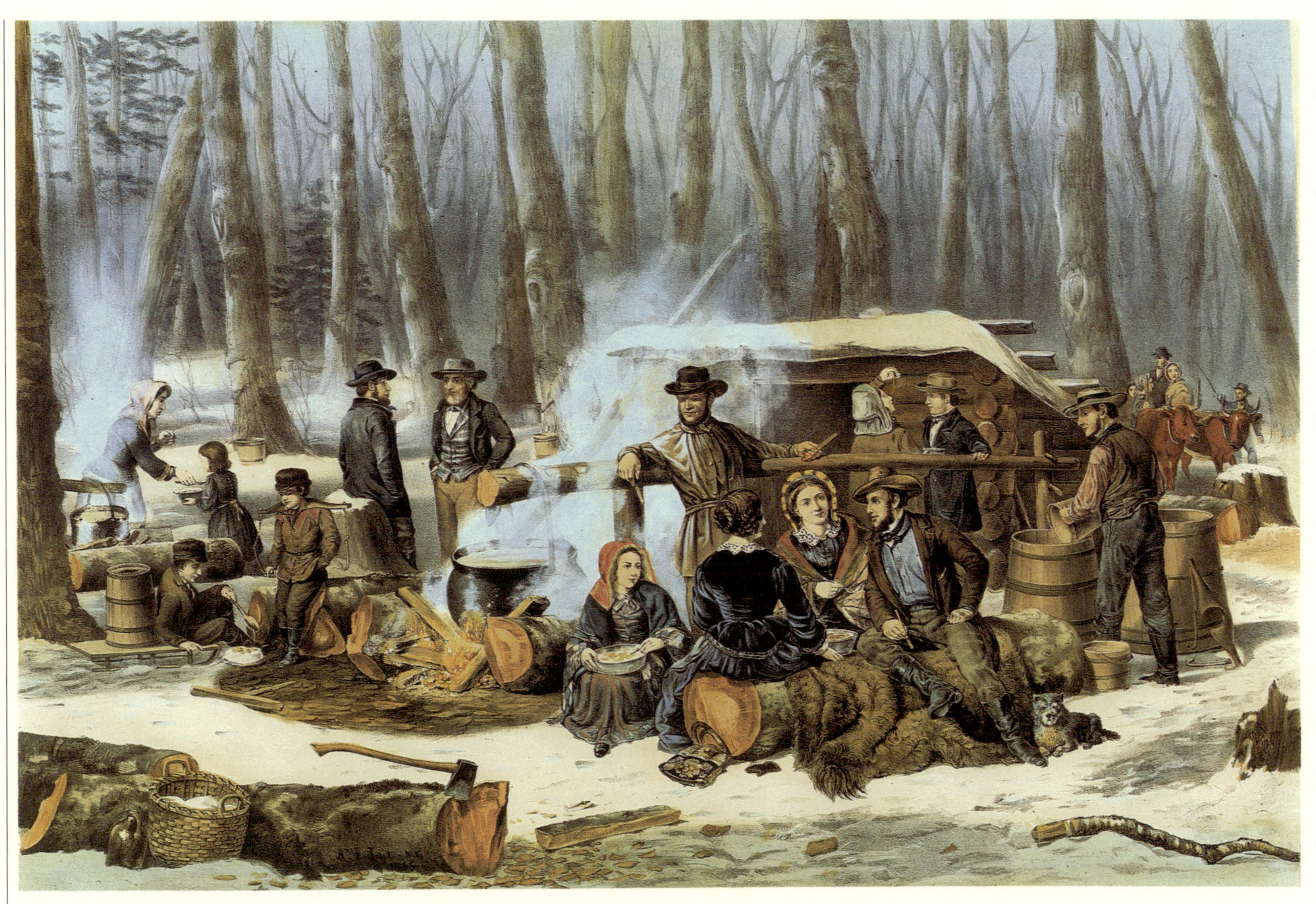

American Forest Scene. Maple Sugaring. (221). *72.137.1.*

American Winter Sports. Trout Fishing "on Chateaugay Lake." (Franklin Co. N. Y.) (222). *65.42.7.*

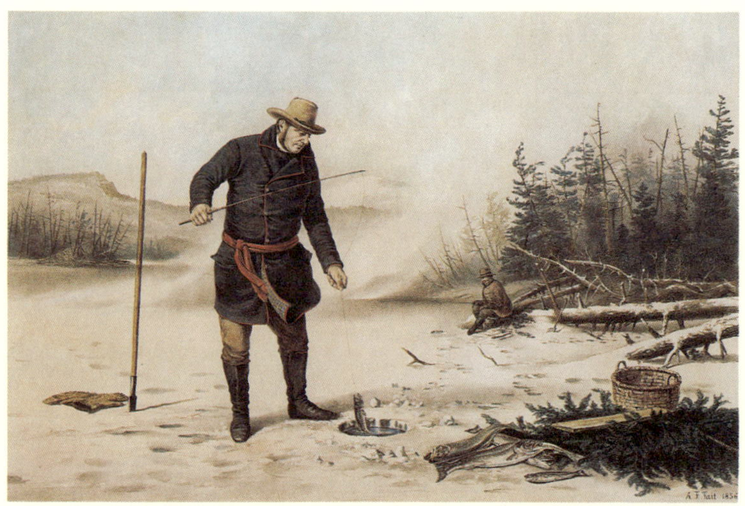

Life of a Hunter. "Catching a Tartar." (238). *64.152.6.*

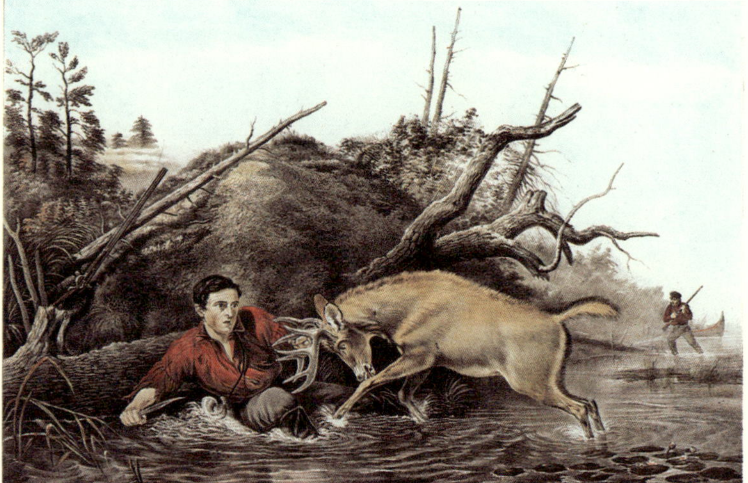

on a pole to cut the hole in the ice are behind him. Such details make Tait's paintings and the prints derived from them valuable documents of life in the nineteenth century.

Halt in the Woods (72) was not published by Nathaniel Currier, but by the firm of Vibert Goupil & Co. in New York City. Goupil was a French dealer in paintings who maintained an office in New York beginning about 1849 to sell paintings as well as to publish and sell prints.[32] The print itself was engraved on steel in Paris by Cottin. It is hand colored, as were the lithographs issued by Currier. This print shows the comradery possible during a hunt. The two hunters and guide are companions sharing a moment of relaxation deep in the woods. *The Life of A Hunter. "Catching a Tartar"* (238) shows a less picturesque moment as the hunter in the foreground struggles to kill the stag. "Tartar" refers to the stag and is used in the sense of a person who proves to be too strong for his assailant.

Camping in the Woods. "Laying Off" (236) was published by Currier & Ives in 1863. This scene of life in camp provides excellent details of clothing and equipment. This print is appealing because it shows how comfortable camps could be and, again, the importance of companionship during the hunt. Tait focuses on the human subject matter because he knew from personal experience the great appeal of hunting

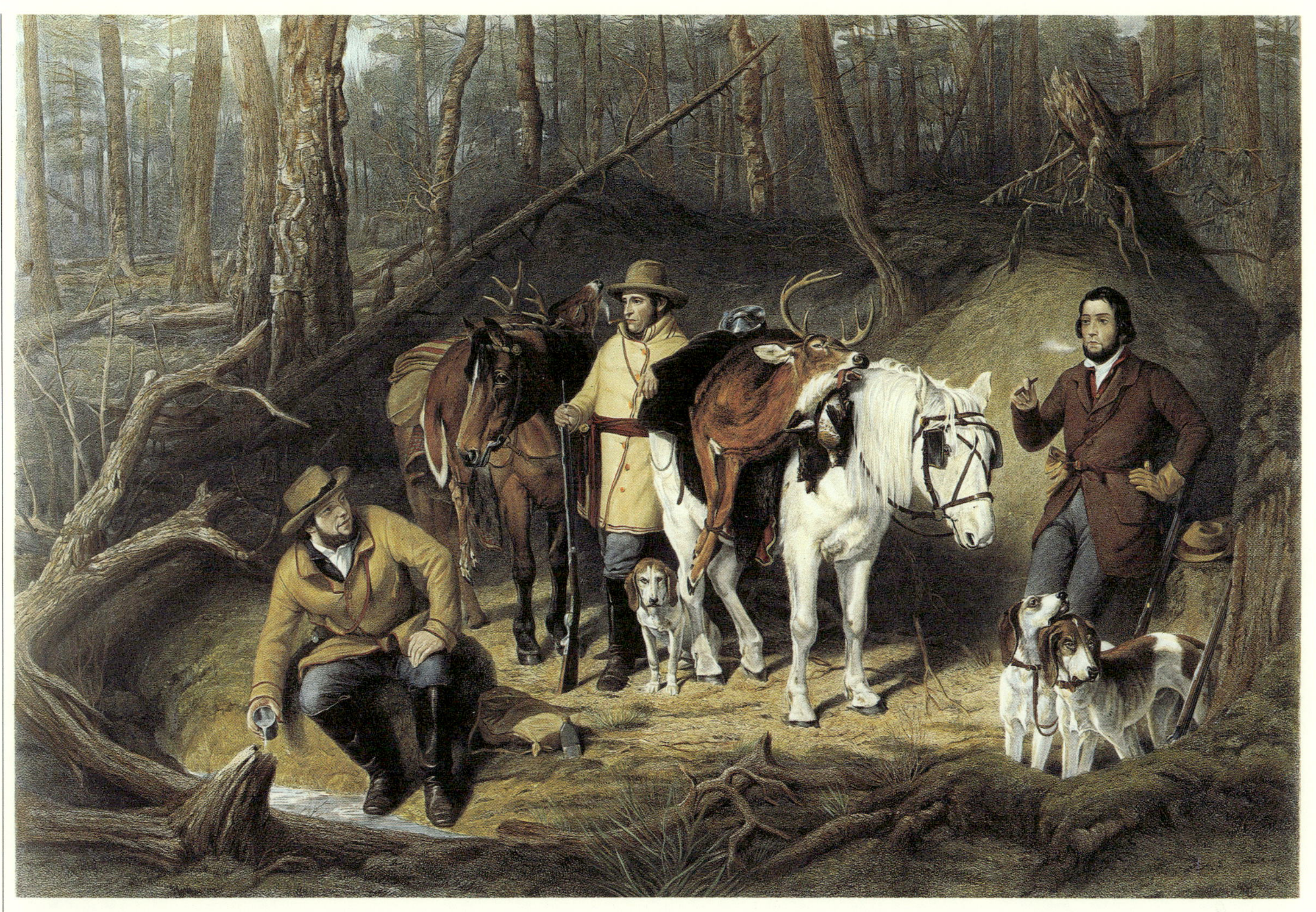

Halt in the Woods. (72). 67.59.1.

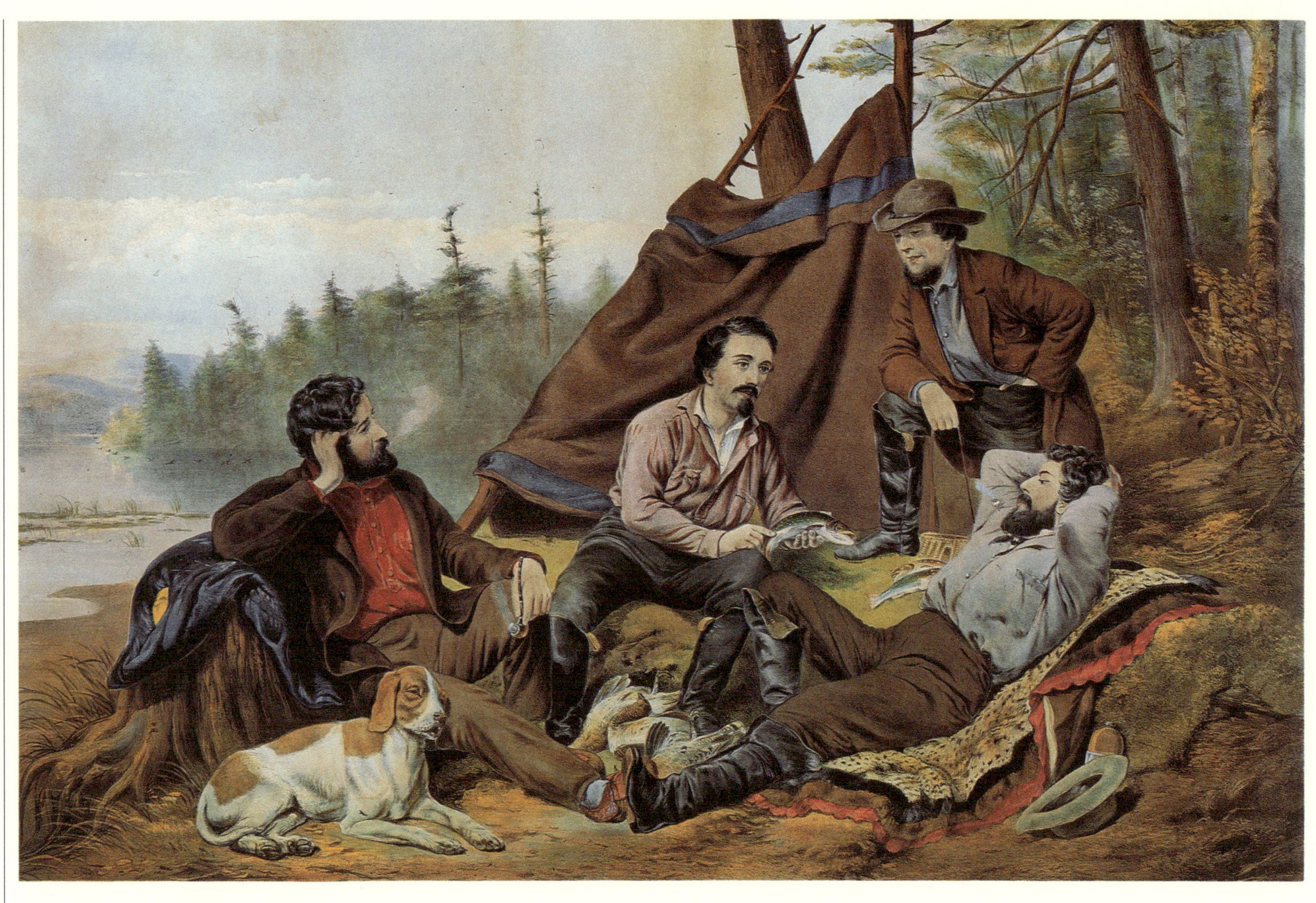

Camping in the Woods. "Laying Off." (236). *64.152.5.*

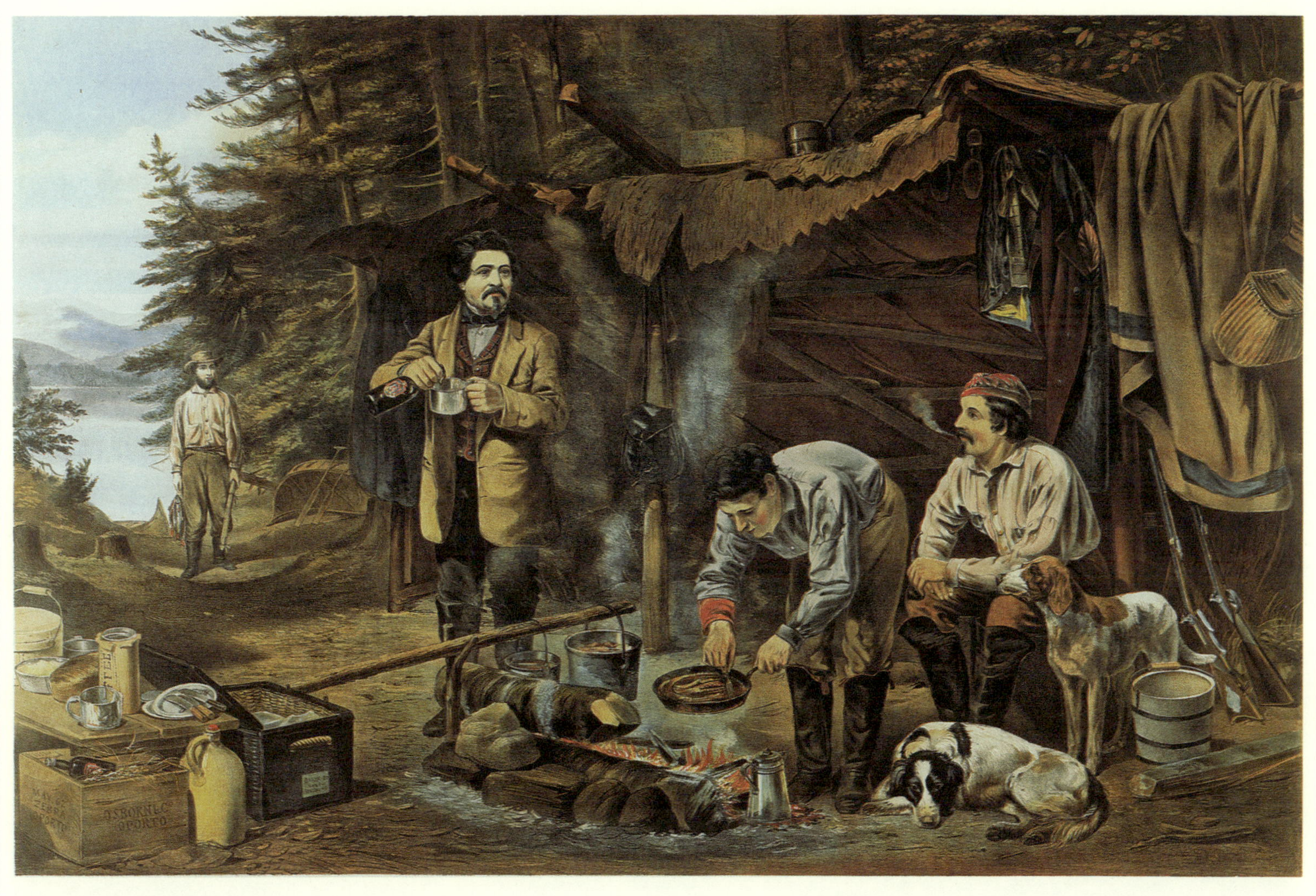

Camping in the Woods. "A Good Time Coming." (235). *63.203.1.*

and fishing. Currier & Ives often marketed their prints in sets. The pendant to *Laying Off* was *Camping in the Woods. "A Good Time Coming"* (235) showing the guides cooking over a fire at a lean-to. A successful fisherman approaches with a string of freshly caught fish for dinner. The camp may be one that Tait frequented on Constable Point on the shores of Raquette Lake.[33] The original painting is in the collection of the Adirondack Museum (63.37.1). *American Speckled Brook Trout*

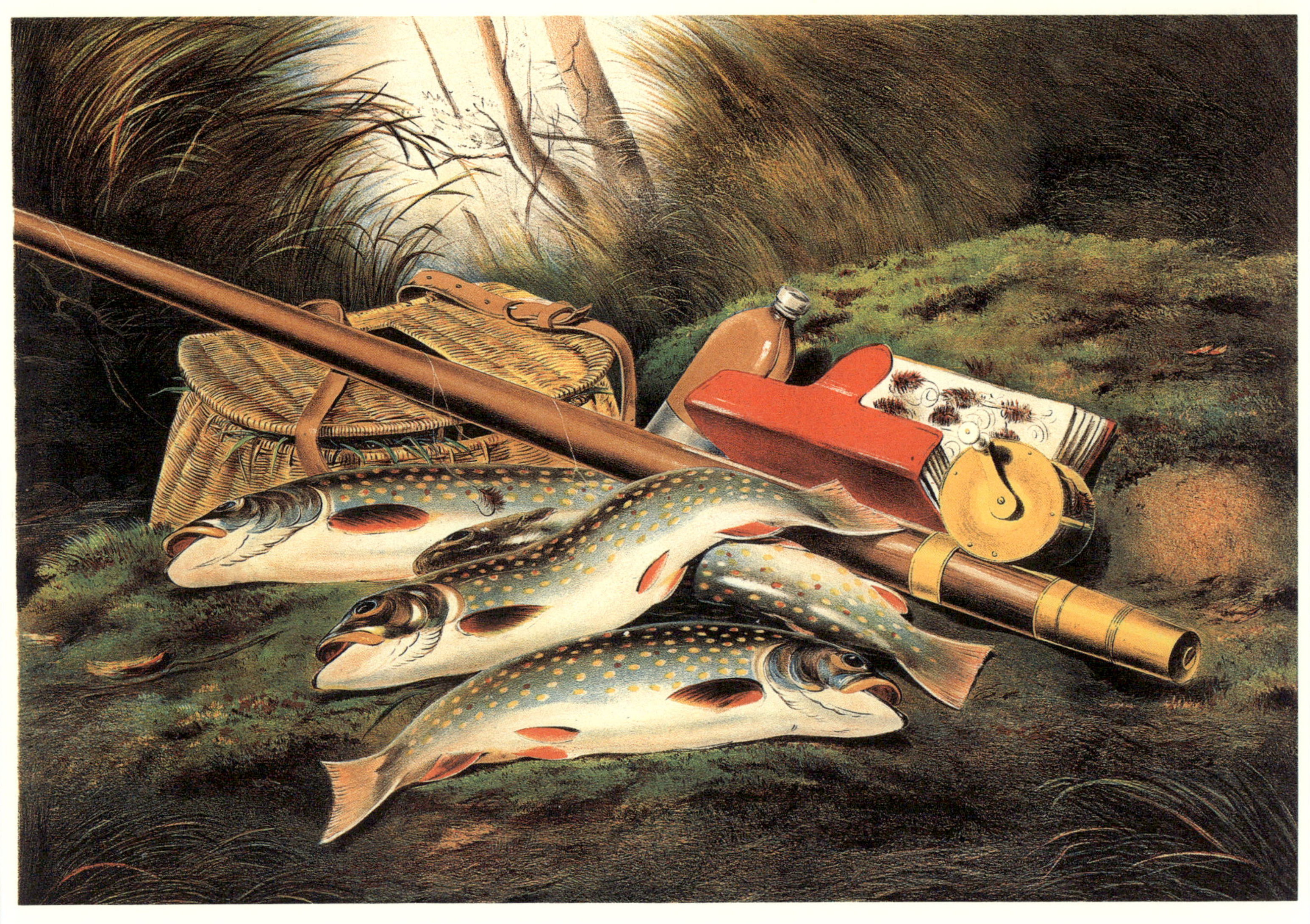

American Speckled Brook Trout. (234). *73.140.1.*

(234) was lithographed in colors by Charles Parsons for Currier & Ives in 1864. This still life would have been a handsome print for the owner's office or study, or appropriate for hanging in a boarding house in the Adirondacks.

Currier & Ives published many other genre scenes and landscapes of the Adirondacks. *Camping Out. "Some of the Right Sort"* (230) was designed by Louis Maurer (1832-1932),

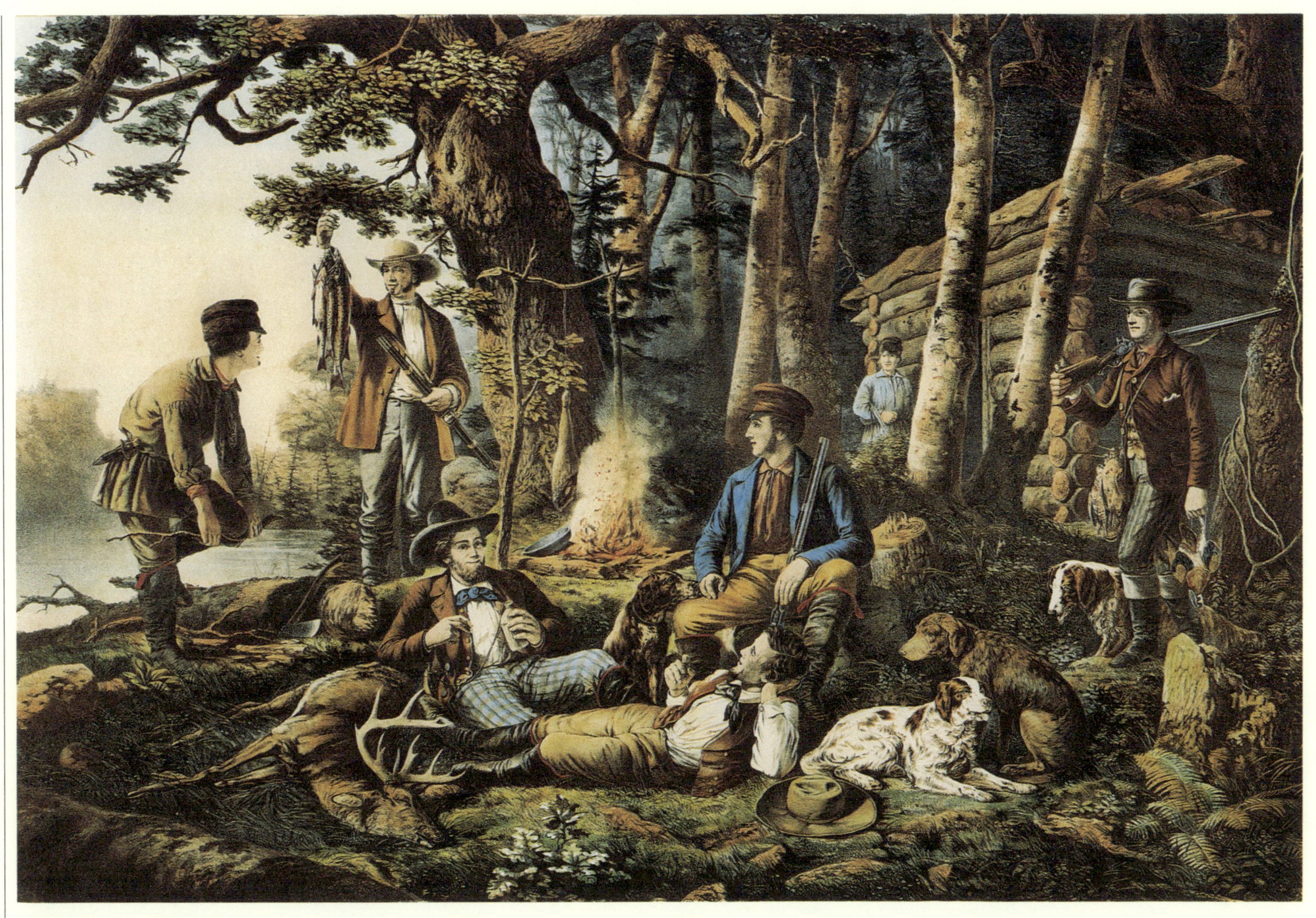

Camping Out. "Some of the Right Sort." (230). *64.152.9.*

the lithographic draftsman who had drawn Tait's *Deer Shooting "on the Shattagee* [*sic*]*"* on stone for Nathaniel Currier in 1855, and was published in 1856. Maurer was German by birth and emigrated to the United States in 1851. An experienced artist prior to his arrival, he quickly found work in the publishing firm of Thomas W. Strong. Later in the year, he began an eight year association with Nathaniel Currier. An

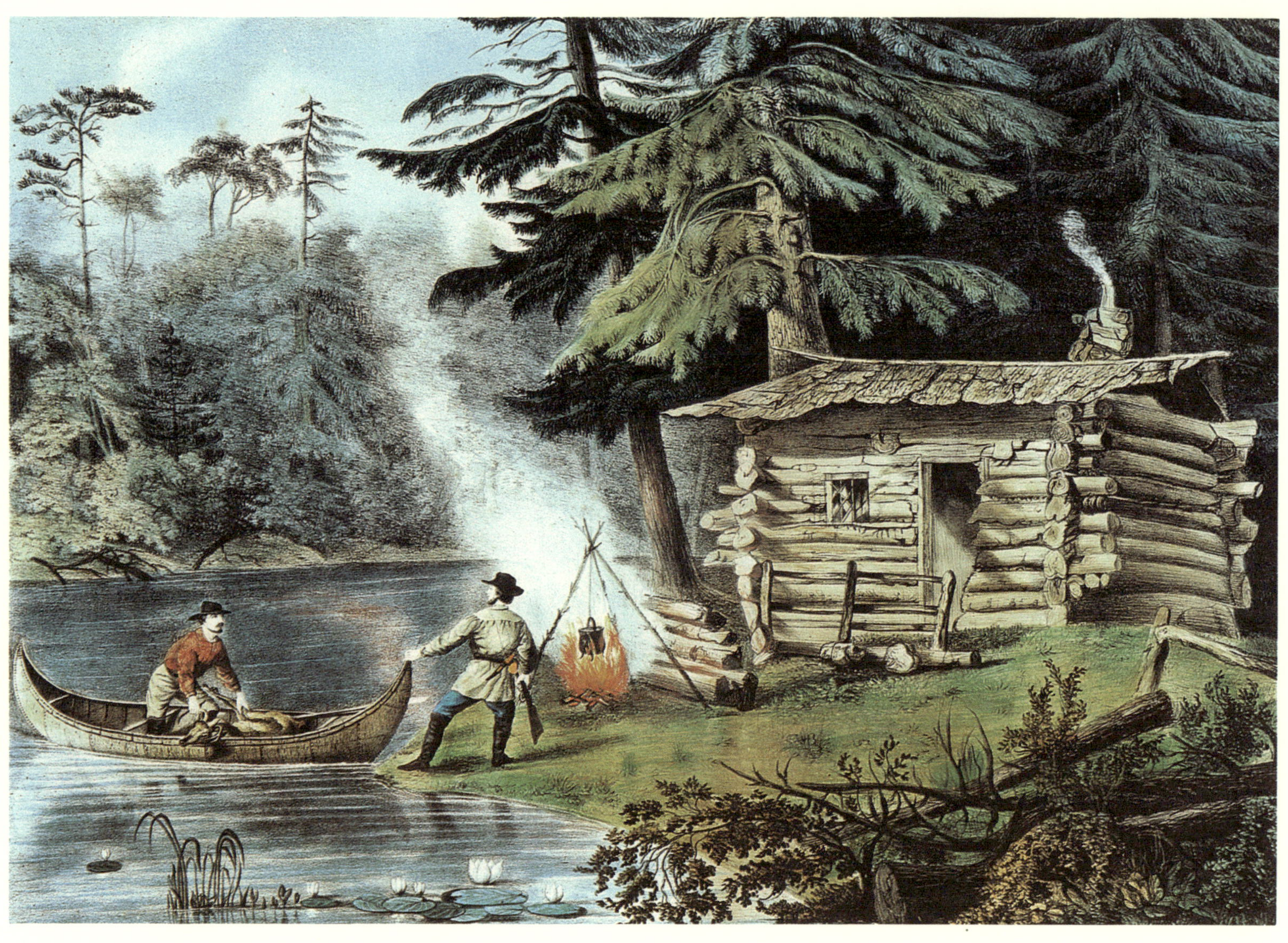

excellent draftsman, he was responsible for many of the political cartoons published by the firm and is known as "one of the ablest artists employed by Currier and Ives."[34] *The Hunters Shanty. In the Adirondacks* (250) was issued in 1861. All of the essential elements are depicted in this print—the log cabin, a blazing camp fire, the slain deer in the canoe

The Hunters Shanty. In the Adirondacks. (250). *62.10.1.*

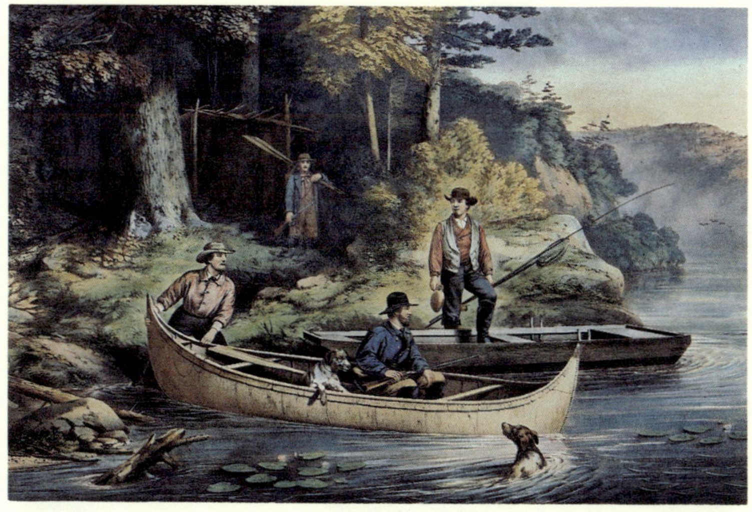

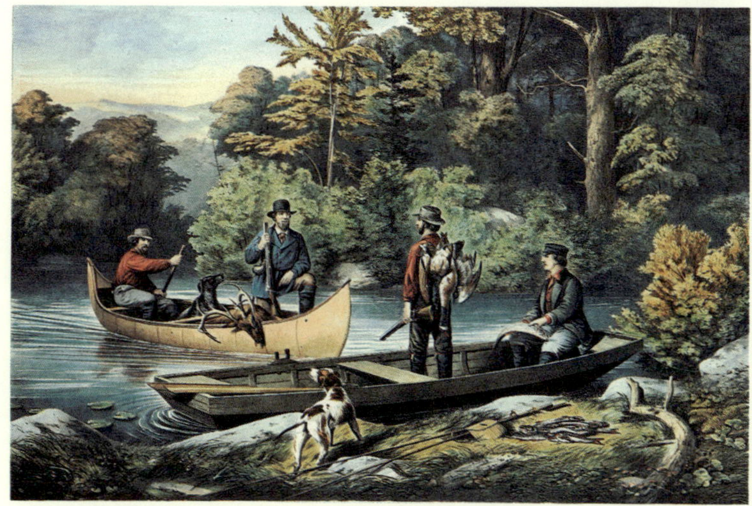

Life in the Woods. "Starting Out." (231). *72.59.1.*

Life in the Woods. "Returning to Camp." (255). *64.152.10.*

being pulled ashore by one of the hunters. Anonymously created, this print derives its elements from the works by Tait whose paintings were widely exhibited in New York. Camp scenes must have appealed to the buyers of prints. In 1860 a pair of prints, *Life in the Woods. "Starting Out"* (231) and *Life in the Woods. "Returning to Camp,"* (255) were issued by the firm. Twelve years later, another series, *Life of a Sportsman* (256–8), depicted similar scenes. Currier & Ives also published prints showing hunters and anglers in action. *Deer Shooting* (245) and *An Anxious Moment. "A Three pounder Sure"* (240) of 1874 are two examples of that genre.

The firm also published numerous landscapes of the region. Unfortunately, with a few exceptions, the landscapes lack the human interest of the genre scenes that makes those prints so successful. Frequently the landscapes, anonymously produced, lack drama and are unconvincing. Missing are the specificity of place and moment that works by recognized artists exhibit. *Sunrise on Lake Saranac* (269) and *Sacandaga Creek* (266) are better than most of these prints.

The lithographs published by Nathaniel Currier and Currier & Ives successfully promoted the Adirondack region. Likewise, popular magazines, illustrated with wood engravings, enjoyed wide circulation, and readers learned much about the wilderness from their pages. Magazines, such as *Ballou's Pictorial, Frank Leslie's Illustrated Newspaper, Harper's Weekly,* and *Harper's New Monthly Magazine,* published many illustrations of places and people in the Adirondacks from the early 1850s to the end of the nineteenth century.

Relatively few illustrations of the Adirondacks appeared in the popular press in the 1850s and 1860s. One of the first illustrations of a place off the beaten track was "St. Jermain's Hotel, Chazy Lake, Northern New York" (459) engraved by

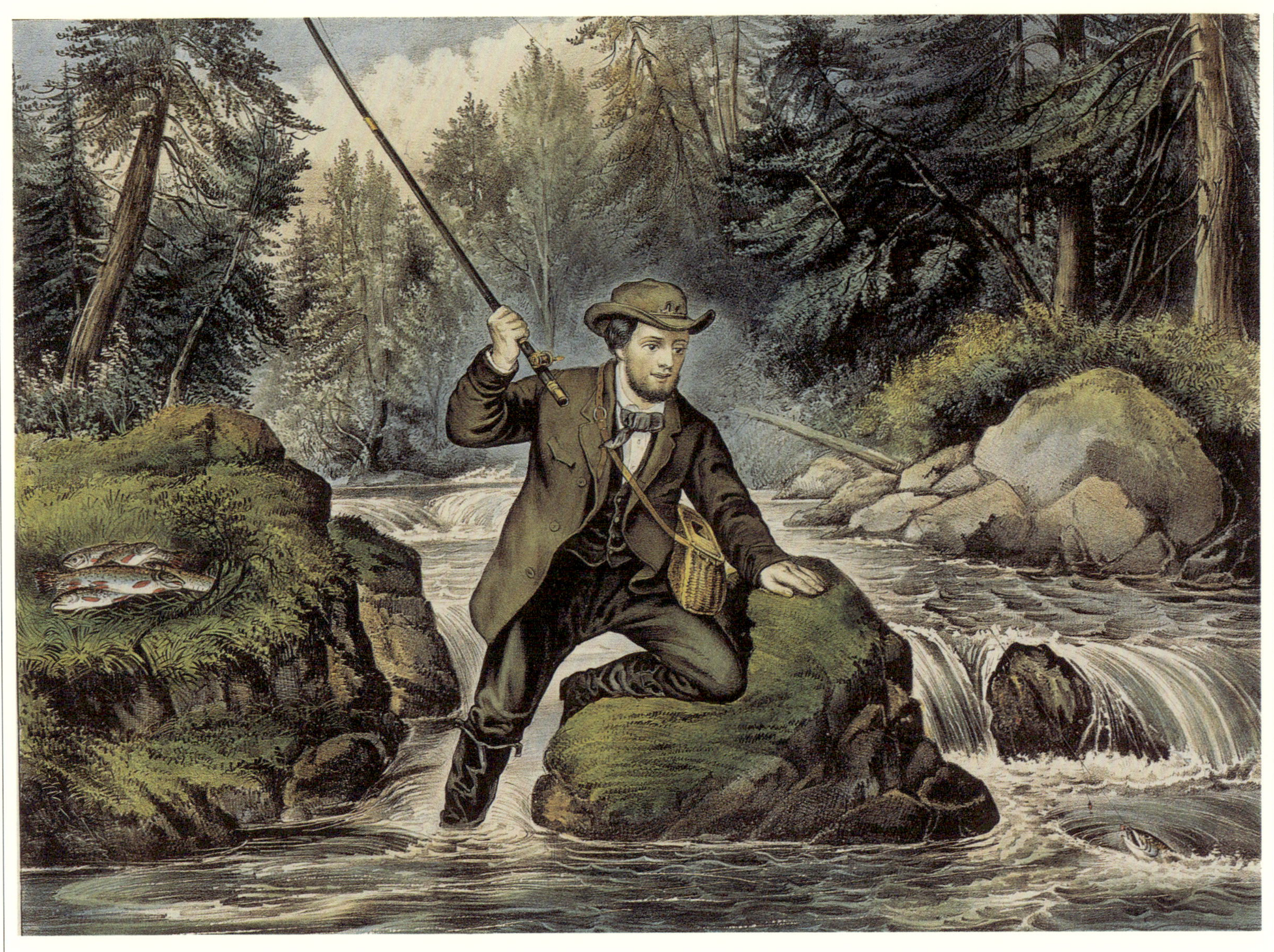

An Anxious Moment. "A Three Pounder Sure." (240). *65.42.11.*

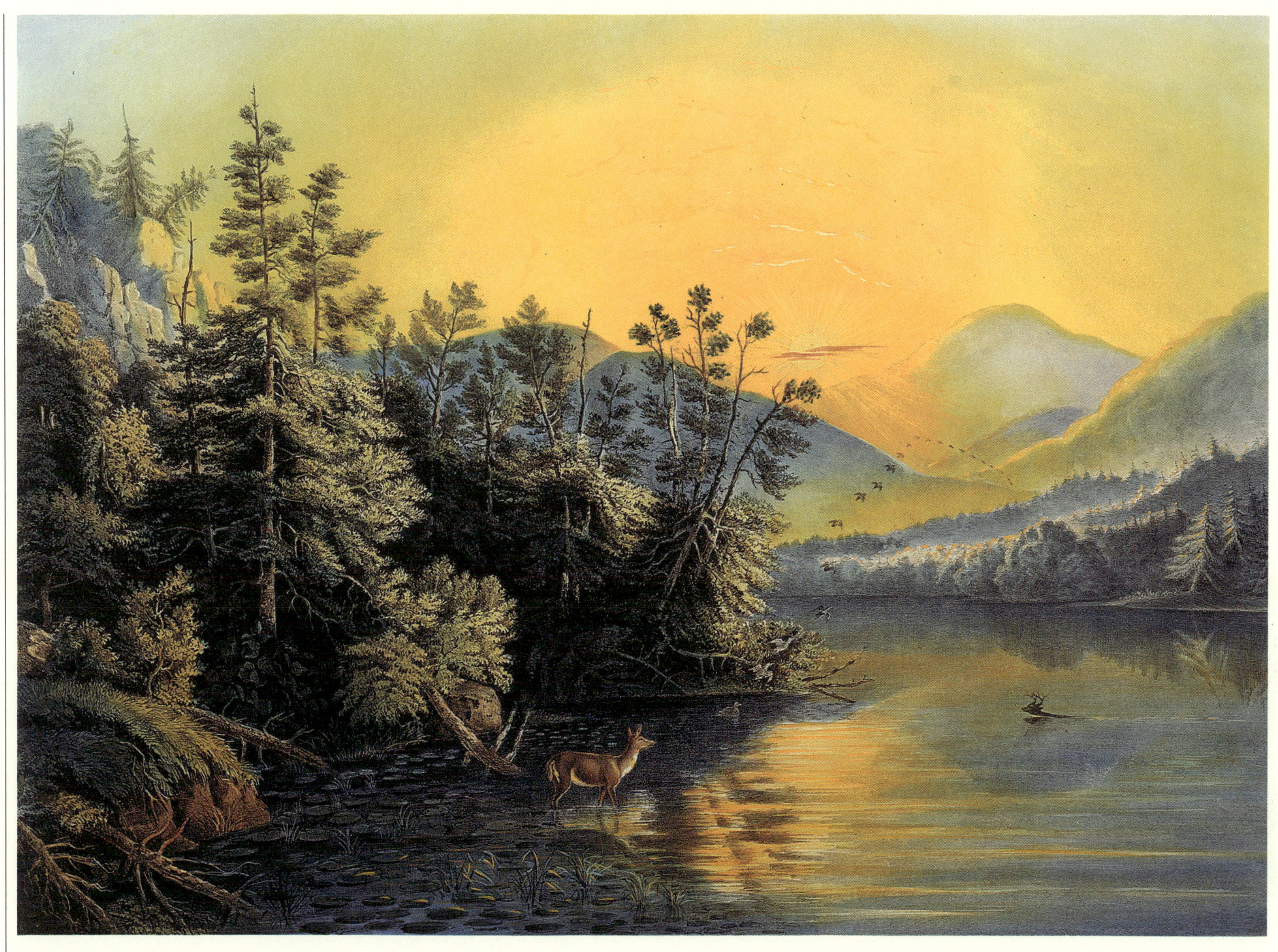

Sunrise on Lake Saranac. (269). *64.152.2.*

"St. Jermain's Hotel, Chazy Lake, Northern New York." (459). *66.112.11.*

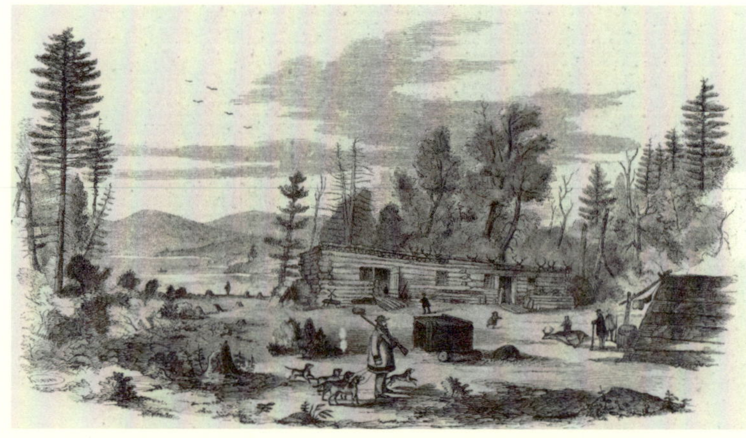

Samuel S. Kilburn after a sketch by Richard P. Mallory. Published in *Ballou's Pictorial* on April 3, 1858, it was accompanied by an anonymous article on St. Jermain and Chazy Lake, "a beautiful and picturesque sheet of water, surrounded by lofty mountains, covered with the original forest, and the haunts of the wild beast and game have never been disturbed by the woodman's axe.... The scenery in this region is magnificent, and will well repay a visit from the tourist or artist, as the whole country is in the state of nature, without the improving (or deforming) hand of man being visible."[35] The author of the article noted that St. Jermain and his sons were experienced guides and that visitors could stay in his "hotel," a long, low log building. On July 17, 1858, another illustration of the Adirondacks appeared in *Ballou's Pictorial*, "Bridge over the Ausable River at Keeseville, New York" (448). The accompanying text stated: "To the artist in search of the picturesque no region affords more material than the wild valley of the Ausable."[36]

One artist who heeded that message was Thomas B. Thorpe (1815-1878), also a lawyer, writer, and journalist, who spent most of his life in the south. As a child, however, he visited Ballston Spa, and probably traveled to the northern woods as a youth.[37] His artistic training, as a landscape and portrait painter, was with John Quidor (1801-1881), the figure painter. In 1859 Thorpe visited the Adirondacks and enjoyed hunting and fishing with two companions whose identities are not revealed in "A Visit to John Brown's Tract" (in the southwestern Adirondacks) published in the July 1859 issue of *Harper's New Monthly Magazine.* Among the illustrations are light-hearted caricatures of neophytes in the woods. Thorpe expressed the opinion of generations of Americans when he wrote in this essay, "Bless the invention of a short trip into the country."[38]

Thomas Addison Richards (1820-1900) illustrated his own article on Lake George for *Harper's New Monthly Magazine* published in July 1853. He also illustrated his essay, "A Forest Story," for the August and September 1859 issues of *Harper's New Monthly Magazine.* Richards, an artist of the Hudson River School, traveled widely and wrote illustrated essays. The first installment of "A Forest Story" focused on "the happy

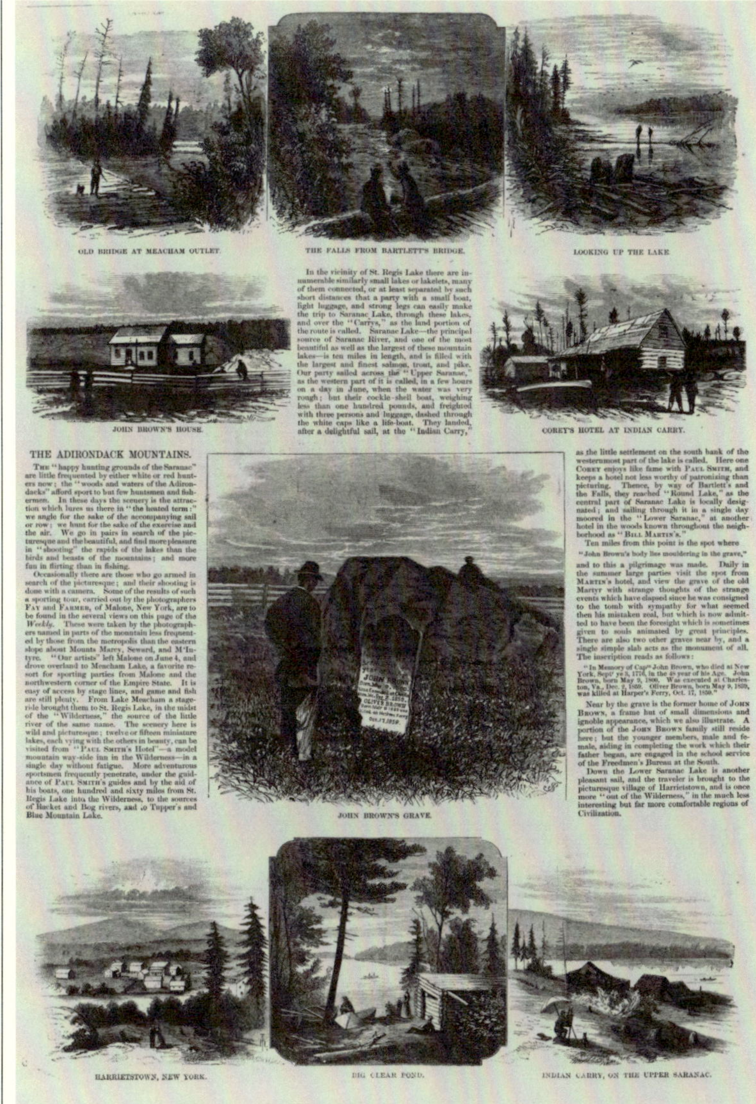

OLD BRIDGE AT MEACHAM OUTLET.

THE FALLS FROM BARTLETT'S BRIDGE.

LOOKING UP THE LAKE.

In the vicinity of St. Regis Lake there are innumerable similarly small lakes or lakelets, many of them connected, or at least separated by such short distances that a party with a small boat, light luggage, and strong legs can easily make the trip to Saranac Lake, through these lakes, and over the "Carrys," as the land portion of the route is called. Saranac Lake—the principal source of Saranac River, and one of the most beautiful as well as the largest of these mountain lakes—is ten miles in length, and is filled with the largest and finest salmon, trout, and pike. Our party sailed across the "Upper Saranac," as the western part of it is called, in a few hours on a day in June, when the water was very rough; but their cockle-shell boat, weighing less than one hundred pounds, and freighted with three persons and luggage, dashed through the white caps like a life-boat. They landed, after a delightful sail, at the "Indian Carry,"

JOHN BROWN'S HOUSE.

COREY'S HOTEL AT INDIAN CARRY.

THE ADIRONDACK MOUNTAINS.

The "happy hunting grounds of the Saranac" are little frequented by either white or red hunters now; the "woods and waters of the Adirondacks" afford sport to but few huntsmen and fishermen. In these days the scenery is the attraction which lures us there in "the heated term:" we angle for the sake of the accompanying sail or row; we hunt for the sake of the exercise and the air. We go in pairs in search of the picturesque and the beautiful, and find more pleasure in "shooting" the rapids of the lakes than the birds and beasts of the mountains; and more fun in flirting than in fishing.

Occasionally there are those who go armed in search of the picturesque; and their shooting is done with a camera. Some of the results of such a sporting tour, carried out by the photographers Fay and Farmer, of Malone, New York, are to be found in the several views on this page of the *Weekly*. These were taken by the photographers named in parts of the mountain less frequented by those from the metropolis than the eastern slope about Mounts Marcy, Seward, and M'Intyre. "Our artists" left Malone on June 4, and drove overland to Meacham Lake, a favorite resort for sporting parties from Malone and the northwestern corner of the Empire State. It is easy of access by stage lines, and game and fish are still plenty. From Lake Meacham a stage-ride brought them to St. Regis Lake, in the midst of the "Wilderness," the source of the little river of the same name. The scenery here is wild and picturesque; twelve or fifteen miniature lakes, each vying with the others in beauty, can be visited from "Paul Smith's Hotel"—a model mountain way-side inn in the Wilderness—in a single day without fatigue. More adventurous sportsmen frequently penetrate, under the guidance of Paul Smith's guides and by the aid of his boats, one hundred and sixty miles from St. Regis Lake into the Wilderness, to the sources of Racket and Bog rivers, and to Tupper's and Blue Mountain Lake.

JOHN BROWN'S GRAVE.

as the little settlement on the south bank of the westernmost part of the lake is called. Here one Corey enjoys like fame with Paul Smith, and keeps a hotel not less worthy of patronizing than picturing. Thence, by way of Bartlett's and the Falls, they reached "Round Lake," as the central part of Saranac Lake is locally designated; and sailing through it in a single day moored in the "Lower Saranac," at another hotel in the woods known throughout the neighborhood as "Bill Martin's."

Ten miles from this point is the spot where

"John Brown's body lies mouldering in the grave,"

and to this a pilgrimage was made. Daily in the summer large parties visit the spot from Martin's hotel, and view the grave of the old Martyr with strange thoughts of the strange events which have elapsed since he was consigned to the tomb with sympathy for what seemed then his mistaken zeal, but which is now admitted to have been the foresight which is sometimes given to souls animated by great principles. There are also two other graves near by, and a single simple slab acts as the monument of all. The inscription reads as follows:

"In Memory of Capt John Brown, who died at New York, Sept ye 3, 1776, in the 48 year of his Age. John Brown, born May 9, 1800. Was executed at Charlestown, Va., Dec. 2, 1859. Oliver Brown, born May 9, 1839, was killed at Harper's Ferry, Oct. 17, 1859."

Near by the grave is the former home of John Brown, a frame hut of small dimensions and ignoble appearance, which we also illustrate. A portion of the John Brown family still reside here; but the younger members, male and female, aiding in completing the work which their father began, are engaged in the school service of the Freedmen's Bureau at the South.

Down the Lower Saranac Lake is another pleasant sail, and the traveler is brought to the picturesque village of Harrietstown, and is once more "out of the Wilderness," in the much less interesting but far more comfortable regions of Civilization.

HARRIETSTOWN, NEW YORK.

BIG CLEAR POND.

INDIAN CARRY, ON THE UPPER SARANAC.

"The Adirondack Mountains."
(536). *76.168.2.*

hunting-grounds of the Saranac." Illustrations in that article include landscapes showing deer by St. Regis Lake, "The Crotchet Mountains—Lower Saranac Lake," "Landing-Place on the Saranac," and genre scenes such as the "Camp-Scene near Round Lake" and "Making a Portage." Illustrations published the next month include "The Storm in the Forest," views of the Indian Pass, Lake Sanford, Echo Mountain, Mount Colden, Mount McIntyre, a deer hunt at Preston Woods, climbers ascending Mount Marcy, and the Santanoni Mountains (483-492).

Harper and Brothers published two very popular magazines during the second half of the nineteenth century. *Harper's New Monthly Magazine* was mainly literary, with no political content. *Harper's Weekly* was highly topical, both in terms of editorial content and illustrative matter. During the Civil War the publisher sent artists to the front who sent back drawings that were reproduced as wood engravings. Illustrators such as Winslow Homer and Theodore R. Davis, employed during the Civil War, continued to provide drawings for the magazine.

In 1867 *Harper's Weekly* published several genre scenes and landscapes depicting the Adirondacks. In the issue of August 31, 1867, was a page containing nine vignettes of scenery: the old bridge at Meacham Outlet, the waterfall seen from Bartlett's Bridge, a view of St. Regis Lake and Big Clear Pond, the Indian Carry on the Upper Saranac, Corey's Hotel at Indian Carry, and views of the abolitionist John Brown's house, his grave, and Harrietstown (536). The vignettes are based not on sketches by an artist but on photographs by the firm of Fay and Farmer located in Malone and Albany, New York. Prints of these photographs are in the historic photograph collection of the Adirondack Museum.

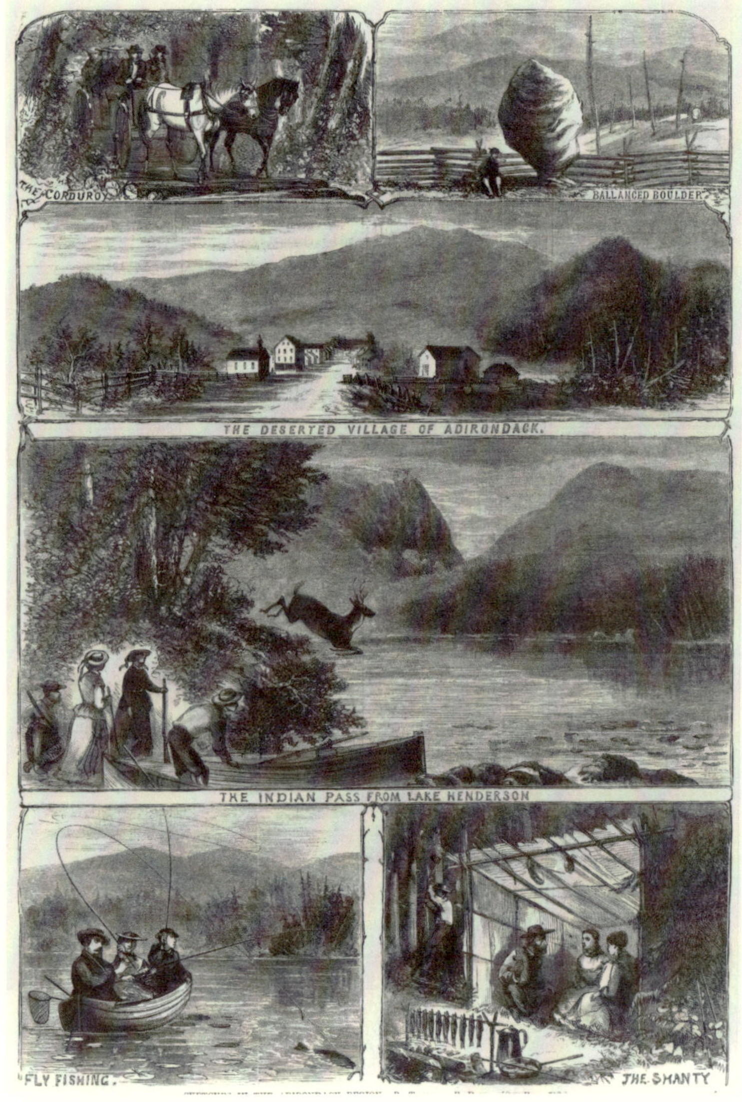

"Sketches in the Adirondack Region." (362). *67.37.1.*

Theodore Russell Davis (1840-1894) provided additional material to *Harper's Weekly* the next year. Gathering honey from wild hives—"Smudging for Bees" and "Working Down the Bee Tree" (359)—was the subject of two illustrations in the September 26, 1868, issue. On November 21, 1868, appeared a group of six vignettes under the title, "Sketches in the Adirondack Region" (362). These images depict the range of experiences that awaited visitors to the Adirondacks, from traveling in an uncomfortable packed buckboard over a bumpy corduroy road to fly fishing.

The year 1869 was an important one for tourism in the Adirondacks. On the first of April, or thereabouts, appeared *Adventures in the Wilderness; or, Camp-Life in the Adirondacks* by William Henry Harrison Murray, a clergyman who initially went to the Adirondacks at the suggestion of one of his parishioners. Their names, along with those of their wives, are inscribed in the Raquette Lake Hotel Register in September 1866.[39] Murray's initial trip led to others and he began to publish literary sketches of his excursions in a Meriden, Connecticut, newspaper. In the fall of 1868 he moved to the Park Street Church in Boston; six months later his *Adventures* was published by Fields, Osgood, and Company, the leading literary publisher of Boston. The success of the book certainly changed the direction of his life and encouraged additional tourism in the Adirondacks.

Murray's income from lectures on the Adirondacks and royalties from his book enabled him to nurture his love of breeding horses. That, in combination with disagreements with his parish over his perceived need for assistance in the pulpit and outreach programs for his church in Boston, led to his resignation from that pulpit. After a series of other activities, he left the northeast and settled in Texas. After a

"'Martin,' shouted I, 'Hang on; that's your deer.'" (366). *70.147.16.*

"'When, high in mid air he shook himself, the crystal drops were flung into my very face.'" (370). *70.147.14.*

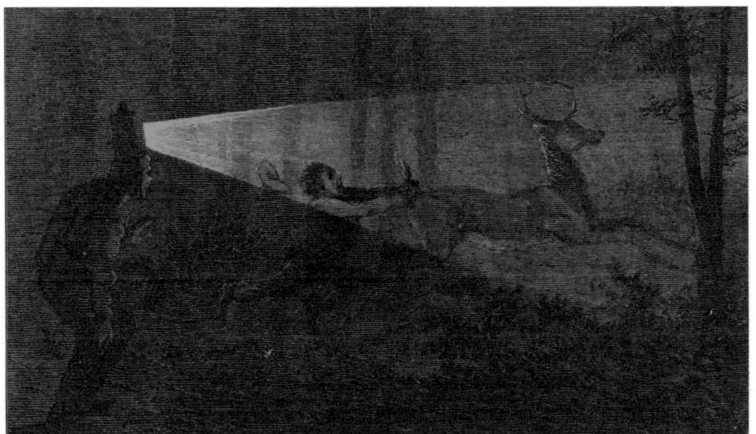

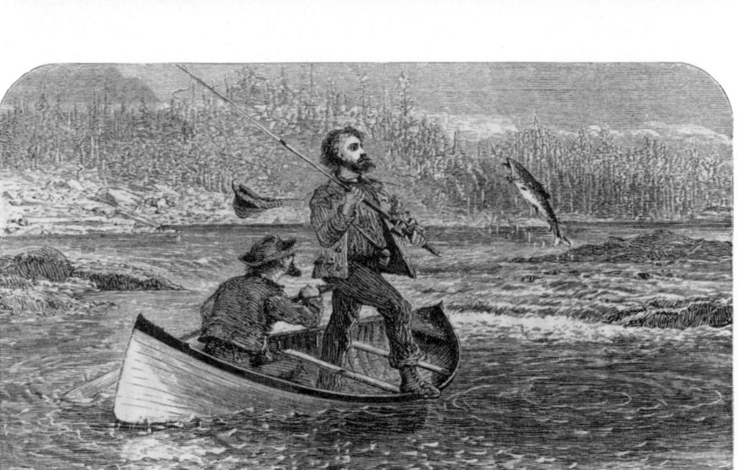

"'It is pleasant for a man, in the position that I was in, to feel that he has something under him.'" (365). *70.147.18.*

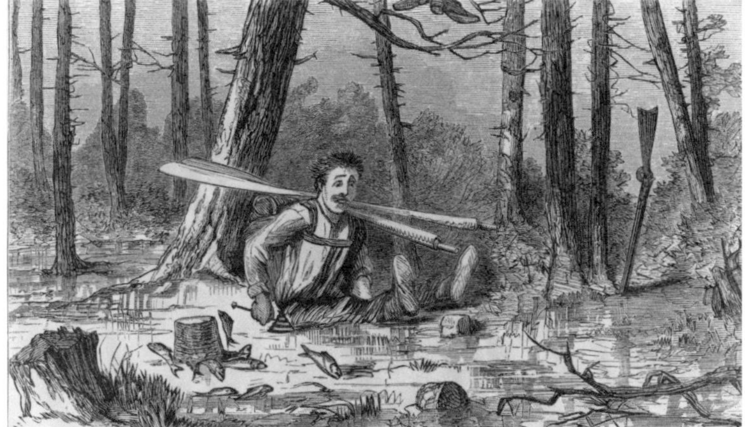

business failure, he moved to Canada, then to Burlington, Vermont. His family's homestead was up for sale about 1890 in Guilford, Connecticut. Murray repurchased it and spent the remaining years of his life there, dying in 1904.[40]

Although other writers had published travel accounts of the Adirondacks, the content and tone of Murray's *Adventures* made it a publishing success and it went through many printings. One edition of Murray's *Adventures* issued by Fields, Osgood, and Company was known as the *Tourist's Edition.* Its introduction provided instructions for travel by railroad from Boston to Plattsburgh and Ogdensburg and gave the history of the towns en route. Time tables for travel from New York were also available. A folding map of New

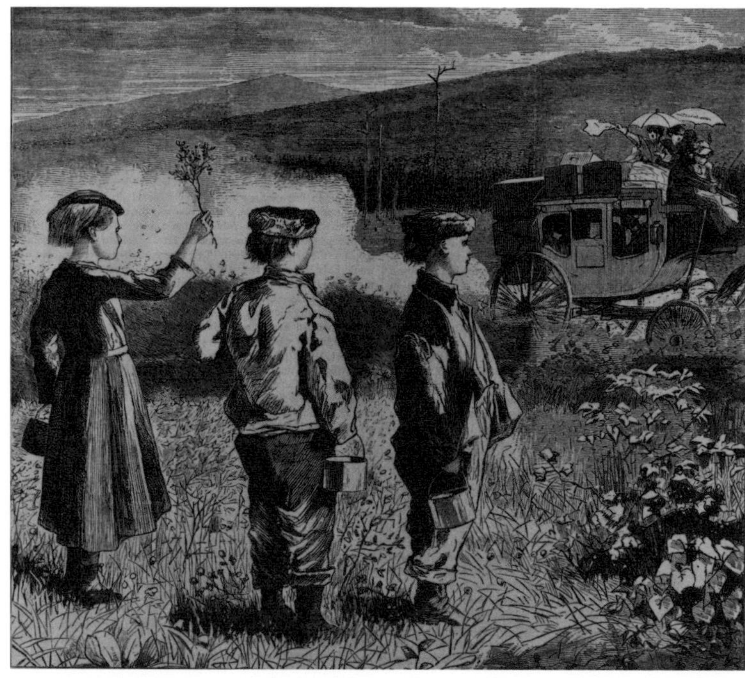

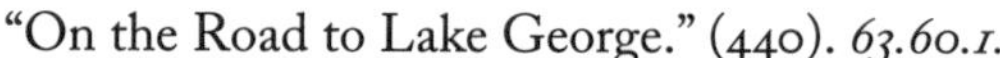
"On the Road to Lake George." (440). *63.60.1.*

England and New York State shows connecting railroad lines from the western part of the state as well as from Massachusetts, Connecticut, and Rhode Island. The linking of Murray's illustrated anecdotes about camping in the Adirondacks with explicit travel instructions suggests that the drove of tourists described in the popular press during the summer of 1869 as "Murray's Fools" was a fact, not hyperbole.

Murray's text was illustrated by Harry Fenn (1845-1911), an English artist who came to the United States about 1863, ostensibly to visit Niagara Falls. He provided designs for many books for the Boston publisher Ticknor and Fields beginning in 1866. There is nothing in the images for Murray's text that suggest that he needed to visit the Adirondacks to design them; illustrators of literature were very accustomed to working from the text. However, Fenn executed the drawings for the section on the Adirondacks for a slightly later publication, *Picturesque America*, and he undoubtedly was familiar with the Adirondacks by 1868 or 1869. His illustrations (364-370) harmonize with Murray's stories perfectly. Murray's book, although not the first book on the Adirondacks, was the first that seized popular attention. Magazine publishers responded to the increased interest in the region by including more images of the Adirondacks in their issues, particularly those that appeared during the late spring, summer, and fall—prime times to visit. Publishers sought out artists familiar with the region to provide illustrations that were usually amplified by a few paragraphs of text.

Among the well-known illustrators in New York was Winslow Homer (1836-1910). The first of his many Adirondack subjects was published on the cover of the July 24, 1869, issue of *Appleton's Journal of Literature, Science and Art.* The illustration, "On the Road to Lake George" (440), demonstrates Homer's skill as a draftsman and his sympathetic portrayal of children. The editor commented that "These little summer scenes, like that of Mr. Homer's sketch, are necessarily abundant all through the season. Everywhere—by the lake-side, on the mountain, at the sea-shore—the country is dotted with pleasure-seekers, and artists find no lack of pleasing groups for their sketch-book."[41] The trip made by Homer to Lake George marked the beginning of his years of work in the Adirondacks. It is curious that the first of his Adirondack subjects was published by Appleton because he had been supplying illustrations to *Harper's Weekly* since 1857. However, *Appleton's Journal* started publication in 1869; per-

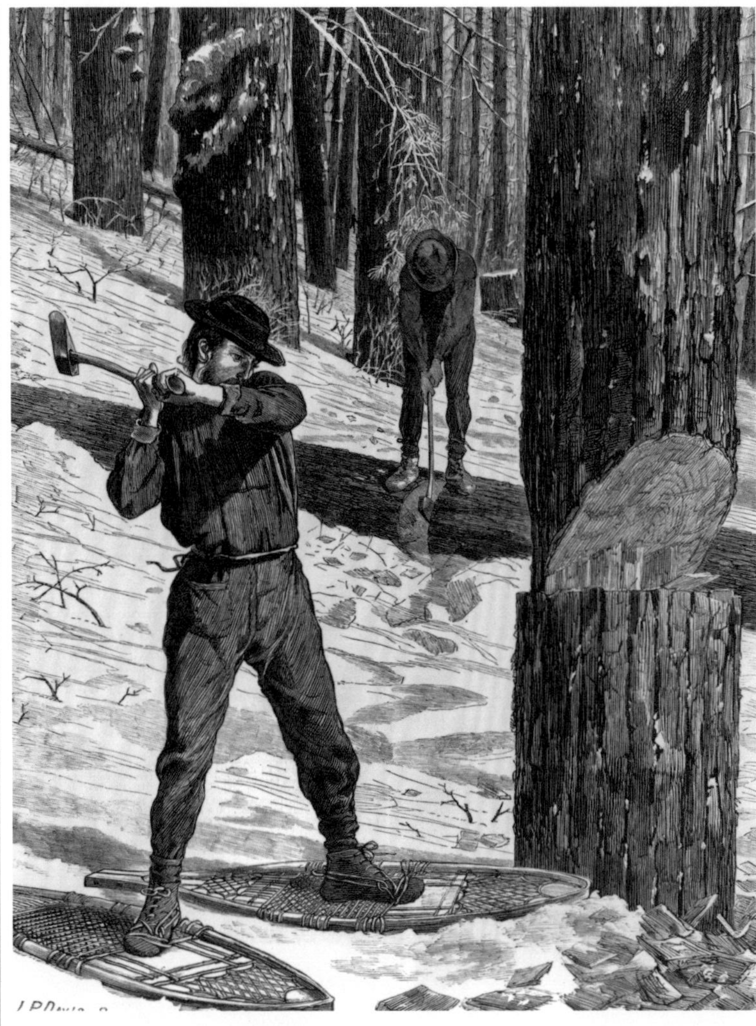

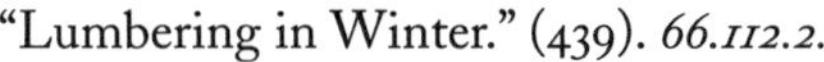

"Lumbering in Winter." (439). *66.112.2.*

haps the editor wanted an artist with a solid reportorial style and established reputation. The publisher commissioned Homer to provide ten illustrations for the journal in the first year of its existence.[42]

Among the best of the illustrations that appeared in the popular press in the decade of the 1870s are Winslow Homer's designs for the periodical *Every Saturday.* Although Homer lived in New York City for over twenty years, from about 1860 to 1880, he did not choose to depict the urban scene; rather, he focused his artistic energies on scenes of rural and resort life. The publisher of *Every Saturday,* Fields, Osgood, and Company included twelve illustrations by Homer in 1870 and 1871. The Adirondack subjects include "Trapping in the Adirondacks" (December 25, 1870) (441), "Deer-Stalking in the Adirondacks in Winter" (January 21, 1871) (438), and "Lumbering in Winter" (January 28, 1871) (439).

In 1870 Homer had visited Keene Valley with his brother, Charles, and another artist, Roswell Morse Shurtleff (1838-1915). Homer returned to the region frequently during the next forty years, creating many works of art. He stayed at the North Woods Club in Minerva nineteen times over a forty year period and produced many significant works based on drawings made there.[43] These illustrations and his later ones for *Harper's Weekly* in 1874 are important in presenting carefully observed details of activities, customs, and dress of both residents of the Adirondacks and summer tourists. Homer worked without sentimentality and the illustrations appear very realistic. Moreover, since Homer worked as an illustrator and a lithographic draftsman for many years and was experienced in transforming the works of other artists into black and white lines, his illustrations for the popular press are excellent compositions, uncommonly bold in their use of black and white.

Harper and Brothers continued to incorporate illustrations of the Adirondacks—or forest scenes suggesting the

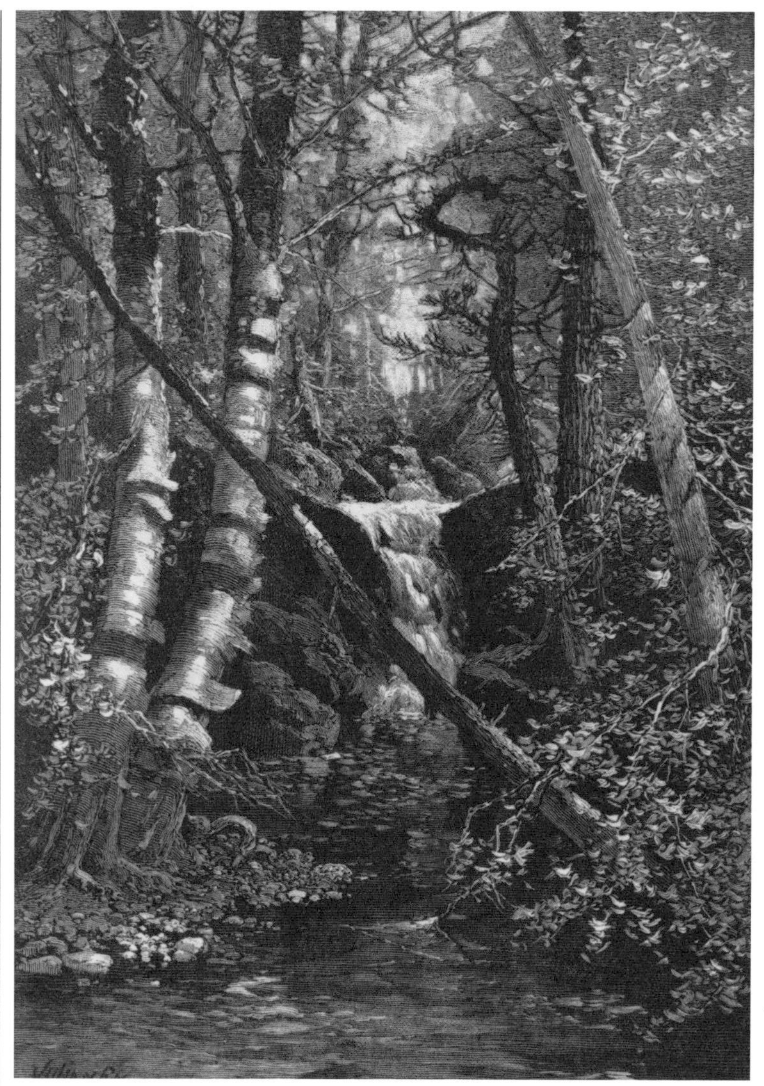

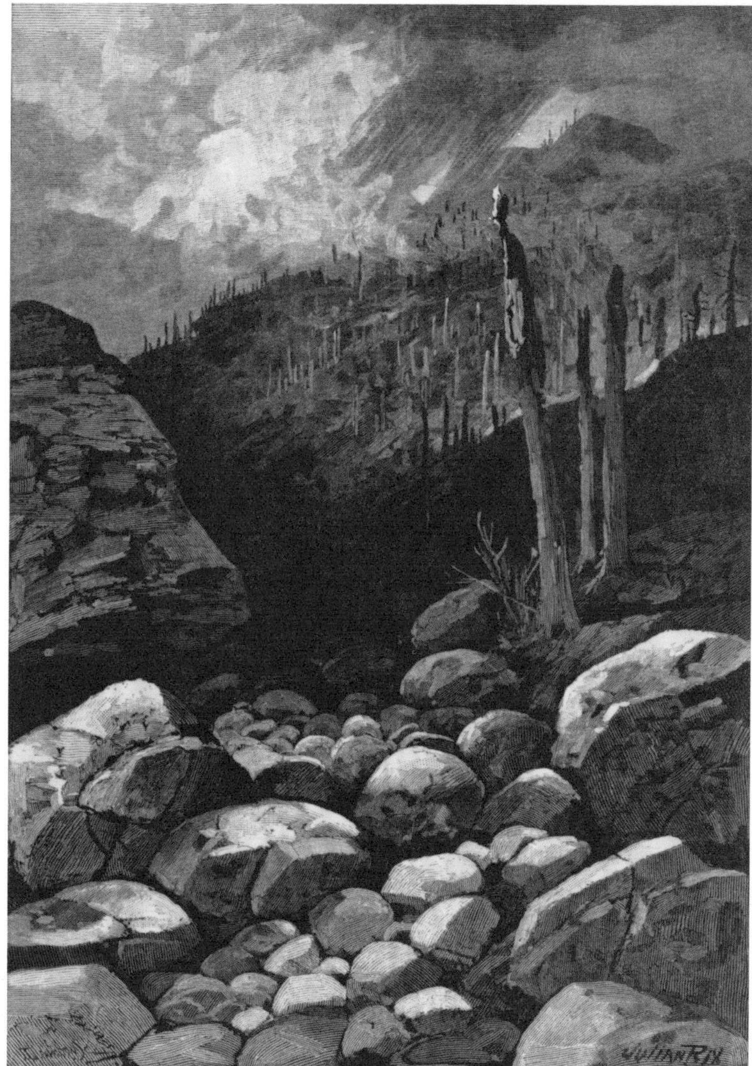

“Forest Destruction in the Adirondacks. The Effects of Logging and Burning Timber. A Feeder of the Hudson—As It Was. A Feeder of the Hudson—As It Is.” (495). *77.196.2.*

Adirondacks—for many years in both their magazines. Theodore Russell Davis provided "The Centennial—The Hunters' Camp" (360) for the October 14, 1876, issue of *Harper's Weekly.* It depicts the camp established by the proprietors of the periodical *Forest and Stream* on the banks of a stream in Landsdowne Valley, Pennsylvania. The text extolled the illustration "as perfect and [a] charming picture of wild life in the woods as could be afforded in a civilized region in the immediate precincts of a great city."[44] Davis had been one of the first to climb Mount Marcy in the Adirondacks in 1859 and his illustrations of the region combine his love of hunting and fishing with his abilities as a draftsman. Between assignments for the Harper firm during the Civil War and afterwards in the West, he spent time in the mountains. He was also an early visitor to the Preston Ponds near Tahawus.

Also published in *Harper's Weekly* were several illustrations designed by Julian Walbridge Rix (1850-1903) and Daniel Carter Beard (1850-1941) that focused on the pillaging of the wilderness by the timber industry. Rix's "Destruction of Forests in the Adirondacks" in the December 6, 1884, issue (493) provided five vignettes showing landscapes spoiled by indiscriminate logging. In the issue of January 24, 1885, an additional pictorial comment by Rix appeared, "Forest Destruction in the Adirondacks" (495). This print recognizes the importance of the Hudson River as a source of drinking water for New York City and suggests the degradation of the watershed caused by logging and the burning of timber. The artist has used the black and white of the wood engraving to good effect in these stark images of a wasted landscape. The article in *Harper's Weekly* by Charles Sprague Sargent explains Rix's images. "We produce upon another page two sketches which illustrate the effect of the excessive forest destruction which is now everywhere going on about the borders of the Adirondack Woods. The first ... depicts a mountain stream—one of the feeders of the Hudson River—bordered by primeval forest. . . . The second ... represents the watershed of the same stream devastated by fire, and reduced to the condition of a desert."[45]

Beard focused his attention on the effects of unregulated hunting. "'Evicted Tenants' of the Adirondacks" (346) in *Harper's Weekly,* February 28, 1885, consists of vignettes of animals no longer found in the region—the moose, elk, wolverine, beaver, panther, and wolf. Such images, with their accompanying articles, were helpful in swaying public opinion about the need for regulation of the once wild region. The role of illustrations in *Harper's Weekly* expanded from pure promotion to preservation of what remained of the wilderness.

Another periodical that featured illustrations promoting summer tourism in the Adirondacks was *Frank Leslie's Illustrated Newspaper.* Typical of this journal's illustrations is "Summer in the Adirondacks" (535) published in the issue of July 28, 1888, and also published that same year in *Frank*

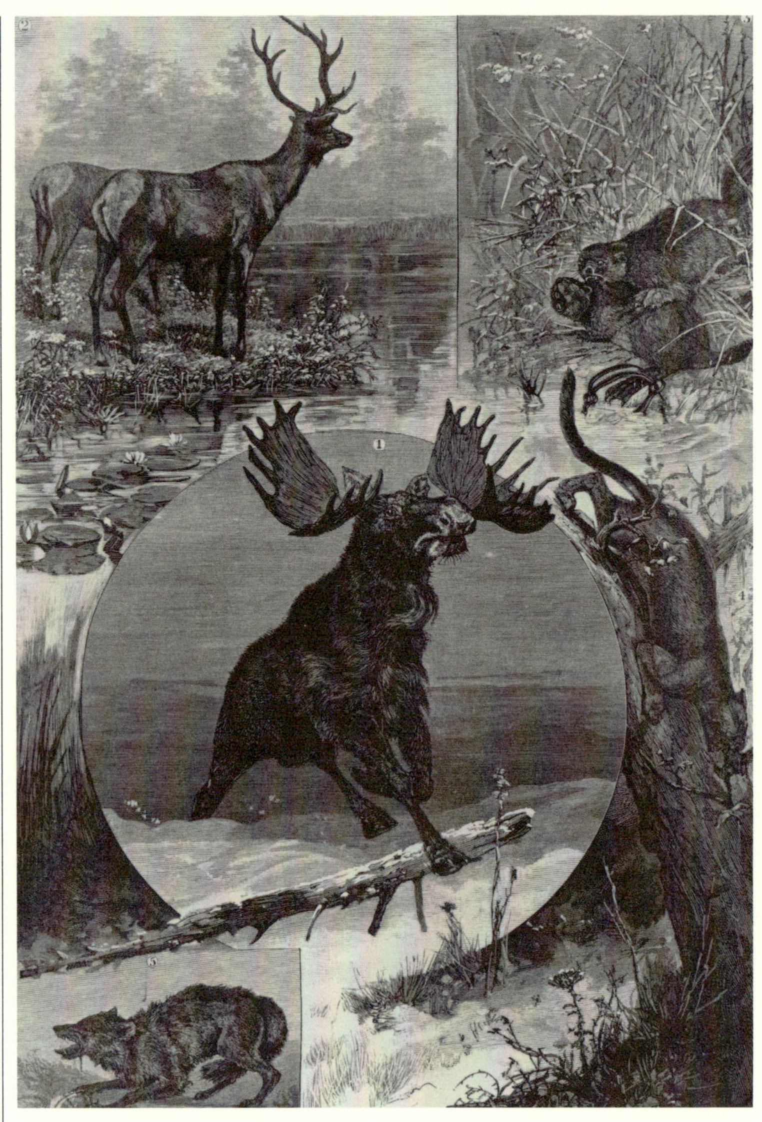

"'Evicted Tenants' of the Adirondacks." (346). *78.8.4.*

"Life in the Woods. A Summer Encampment in the Adirondacks." (545). *78.69.1.*

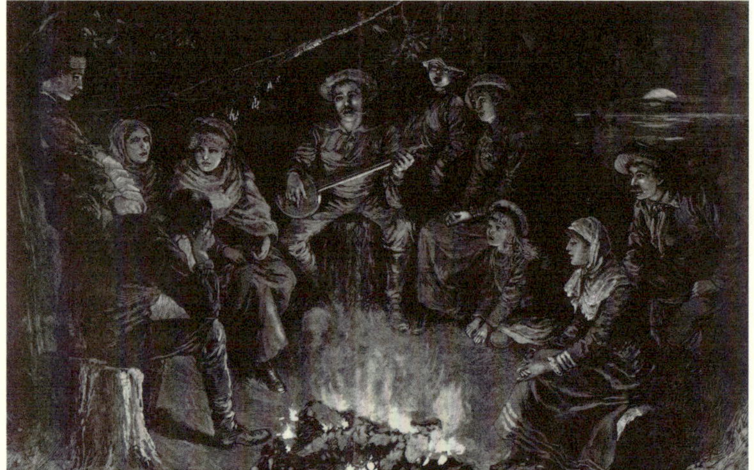

Leslie's Illustrite Beitung circulated to German speaking Americans. Three of the four vignettes feature exceptional scenery; the other shows the legendary, uncomfortable conveyance, the buckboard, needed to get to wilderness areas. These vignettes are copied after photographs, not original drawings. Other illustrations in *Frank Leslie's* focus on genre subjects. "Life in the Woods. A Summer Encampment in the Adirondacks" (545) of July 15, 1882, shows a group of men, women, and children singing to the accompaniment of an accordionist and banjo player. Henry Alexander Ogden's "A Summer Pastime. Drill of the 'Sunflower Brigade,' at Hulett's Landing" (477) of September 15, 1883, shows a line of housekeepers each with a broom and a sunflower at the boat

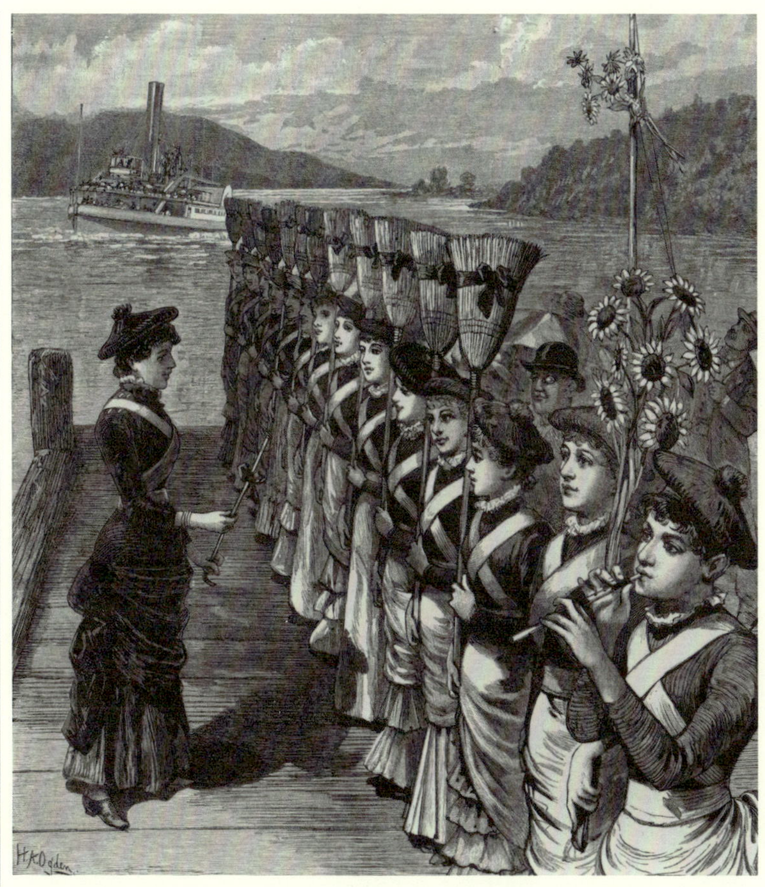

“A Summer Pastime. New York. Drill of the ‘Sunflower Brigade,’ at Hulett’s Landing, on Lake George.” (477). *85.8.1.*

“Summer in the Adirondacks. Glimpses of Lake and Mountain Scenery.” (535). *68.215.2.*

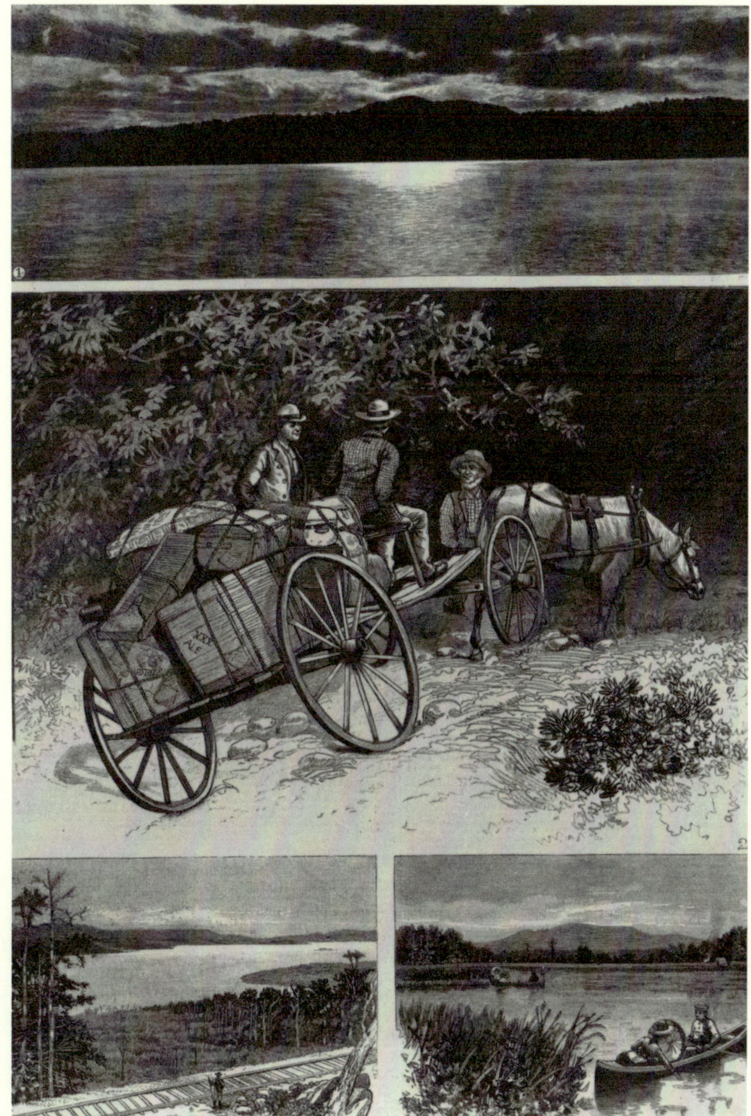

landing on the east side of Lake George. The incoming visitor was assured of a cheerful welcome. “Cottage Life at Lake George” (556) of July 10, 1886, shows a woman relaxing in a hammock while others play music and dance. This is an idyllic life, removed from the rigors of camping on remote lakes and streams.

Celebration

Prints of the Landscape

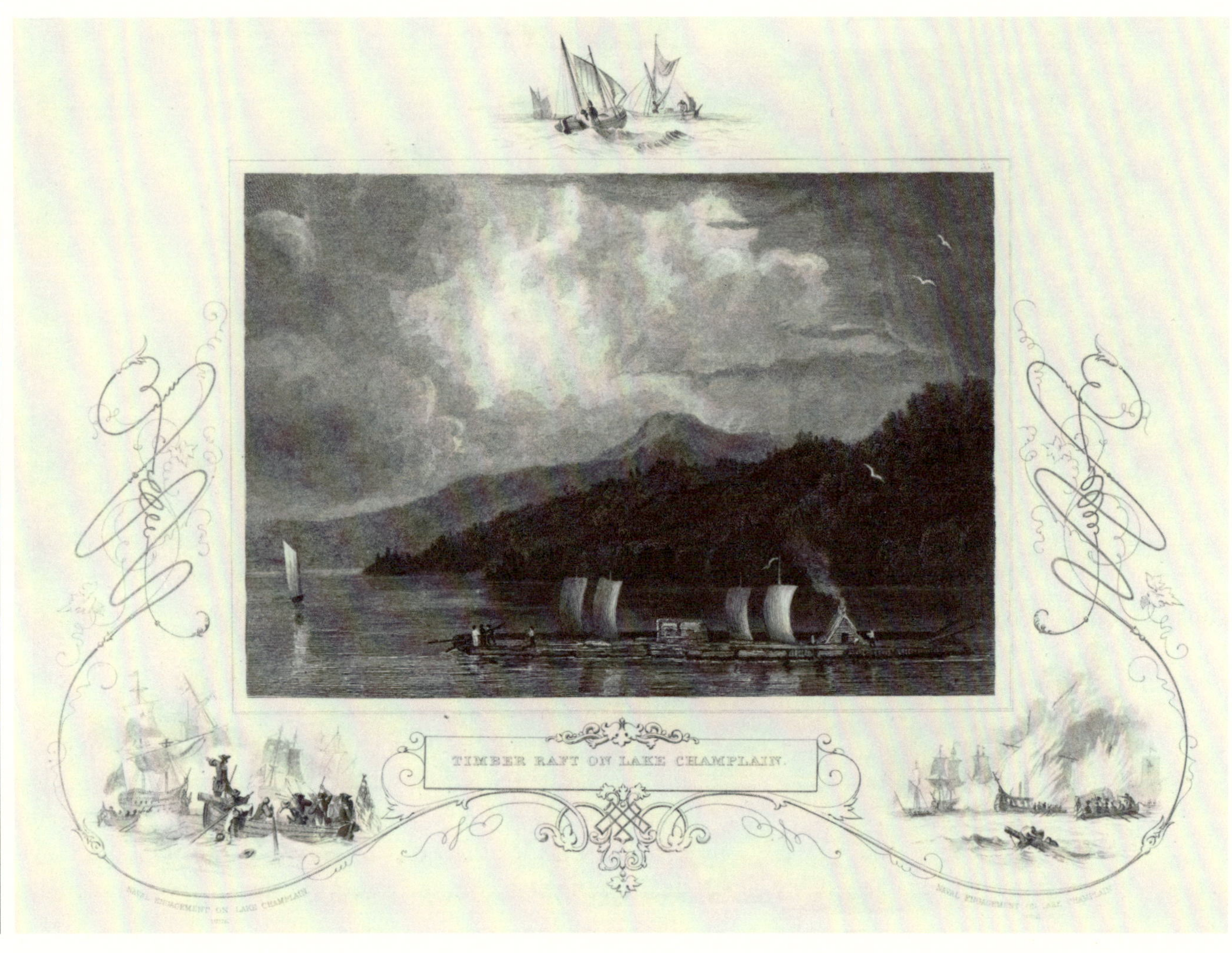

"Timber Raft on Lake Champlain." (44). *68.29.4.*

The appreciation and celebration of the landscape was a phenomenon of the nineteenth century. As the author Edward Bellamy noted in 1874, "that sentimental love of the beautiful and the sublime in nature, the charm which mountains, sea, and landscape so potently exercise upon the modern mind through a subtle sense of sympathy, is a comparatively modern and recent growth of the human mind."[46] Artists of the Hudson River School, beginning with Thomas Cole, found both inspiration and abundant subject matter from the mountains, lakes, valleys, and streams of the Adirondacks and a substantial body of paintings, drawings, and watercolors were produced in the nineteenth century. Many were reproduced as engravings by publishers who recognized that the impulses that drew artists to the region were shared by the population at large, particularly city dwellers who desired elements of a rural existence amid the dirt and noise of major urban centers. Writers, artists, and publishers joined in this celebration of nature.

Thomas Cole (1801-1848) first visited Lake George and Fort Ticonderoga in 1826, just one year after his celebrated sketching trip to the Catskills and the Hudson River Valley.[47] He visited William Ferris Pell near Fort Ticonderoga and made preparatory drawings for *Gelyna (View Near Ticonderoga)* which incorporates a tale from the French and Indian Wars into a sublime landscape.[48] Engravings after Cole's sketches of Lake George (39, 41, 42), Fort Ticonderoga (43), a timber raft on Lake Champlain (40, 44), Congress Hall at Saratoga Springs, Niagara Falls, and the Erie Canal at Little Falls were published in several editions of John H. Hinton's *History and Topography of the United States,* beginning with the London edition published by Simpkin, Marshall, and Thomas Wardle in 1830. Cole had returned to England for additional training as an artist in 1829. In his baggage were his sketches of American scenery. How Cole came to the attention of the publishing firm is not known, but Hinton's *History* was very popular and went through many editions in England and the United States. The plates were copied for the new editions, and these engravings popularized Cole's designs and enhanced his reputation. Cole was pleased to have his sketches reproduced in Hinton's *History,* for at the time of publication he meant to send proofs of the engraving of Daniel Wadsworth's Connecticut estate, Monte Video (also in Hinton's *History*), to his patron.[49]

Beginning in 1835, Cole spent portions of several summers on the shores of Schroon Lake, easily accessible from the road between Caldwell and Plattsburgh. In the summer of 1837, Asher B. Durand (1796-1886), another artist of the Hudson River School, accompanied him. A painting done during the summer of Cole's final trip to Schroon Lake in 1846 is in the collection of the Adirondack Museum (65.3.2).[50] The publisher, George P. Putnam, issued an engraving after another of Cole's views of Schroon Lake in the *Home Book of the Picturesque* in 1852 and reused it in *A Landscape Book by American Artists* in 1868. Other engravings after his earlier views of Lake George and Fort Ticonderoga were published in literary annuals. In *A Landscape Book* the editor describes Cole as the artist who "first gave the American landscape character, and whose genius delighted in portraying the wild and romantic beauty of her forests, lakes, and waterfalls, and who so truthfully presented to the admiring eye the grandeur of her sunsets, tornadoes, and autumn's gorgeous livery. He it was who first taught us that we need not leave our own wild and beautiful scenery for subjects suitable for pictorial embellishment."[51]

In 1836, only a year after Cole's first sojourn at Schroon Lake, an English artist, William Henry Bartlett (1809-1854), traveled to Lake George to prepare illustrations for Nathaniel P. Willis's *American Scenery* published in parts in London from June 1837 through November 1839. Willis, in England from 1831 to 1836 as the foreign correspondent for the *New-York Mirror,* met Bartlett through a mutual friend in 1835. Willis and Bartlett convinced the successful London publisher George Virtue to undertake the publication of a travel book about the United States.[52] They collaborated on two additional travel volumes for the same publisher—*Canadian Scenery* and *The Scenery and Antiquities of Ireland.* The publisher anticipated that *American Scenery* would bring the enjoyment of the American landscape to the "fire-side of the home-keeping and secluded."[53] In all, Bartlett made four trips to the United States to accumulate drawings for the ambitious project. There were 117 engravings and two title page vignettes in the publication, also issued in two volumes in 1840. Dale Roylance has referred to these prints as "an anglicized vision of the American scene."[54] Bartlett took certain liberties with both landscape and the built environment, emphasizing the dramatic qualities of individual views and romanticizing the age and character of buildings to make them less utilitarian and more picturesque. Willis accompanied Bartlett on some of his sketching tours of the United States during the summer of 1836. Among the sketches completed during that first trip by Bartlett were those of Saratoga (8), Glens Falls (6), and Lake George. Other views of New York State, from Albany west to Niagara Falls via the Erie Canal (9, 11), were made in the fall after Bartlett had visited New England.[55]

Although Bartlett did not stray from the established tourist route in making his views of upper New York State, the views of Lake George are of particular interest because of the large number of them. They include views of Caldwell (7), the Narrows (10), Sabbath Day Point (13), Black Mountain (5), Rogers' Slide (12), and "Scene Among the Highlands" (15). In each engraving are elements of genre scenes such as people in boats or on shore that provide a sense of scale and reinforce the concept that Lake George was already

"Sabbath Day Point. (Lake George)." (13). *61.53.6.*

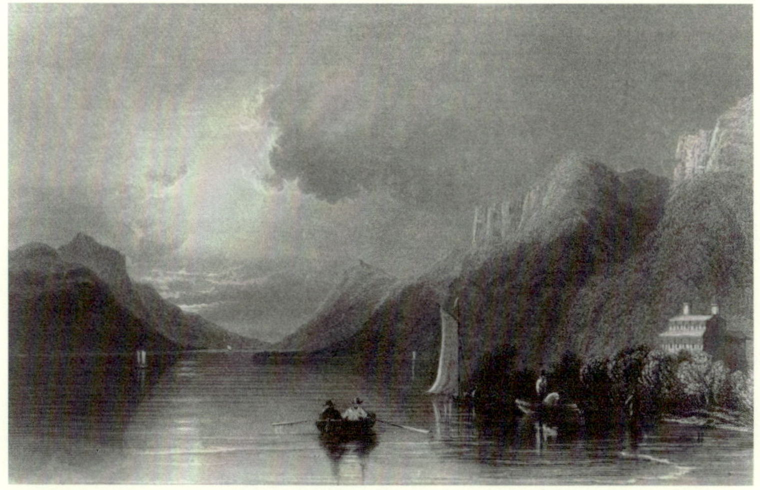

"Black Mountain, (Lake George)." (5). *61.53.4.*

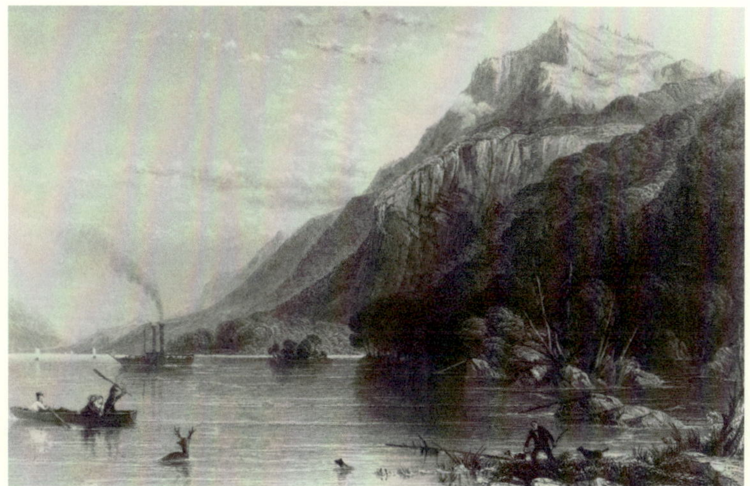

a popular tourist destination, not an untamed threatening wilderness. Bartlett's views are taken from the lake, and water plays a prominent role in the compositions.

George Virtue, the publisher, had a veritable stable of engravers working for him, as he published a number of profusely illustrated books in the 1830s and 1840s. The engravings of Lake George are by different hands, but there is a uniformity of style. The engravings after Bartlett's drawings had a wide distribution because they were frequently copied by American engravers, sometimes without credit to Bartlett as the original artist. Reproductions of the engravings from *American Scenery* can be found in such literary annuals and periodicals published in the 1840s and later as *The Ladies' Companion,* the *Universalist & Ladies' Repository, Family Circle & Parlor Annual,* the *Ladies' Wreath,* and the *New York Illustrated Magazine of Literature and Art.* Some of the Lake George views were also reused by Bartlett in his *History of the United States.*[56]

Although Thomas Cole had ventured away from the beaten track in his search for dramatic landscapes, few artists joined him. Joel T. Headley, the author of *The Adirondack; or, Life in the Woods,* lamented in 1849 that "I could get no sketches of some of the romantic and beautiful scenery of the more central regions but no artist has ever yet ventured into

"View on Raquette Lake." (54). *70.147.4.*

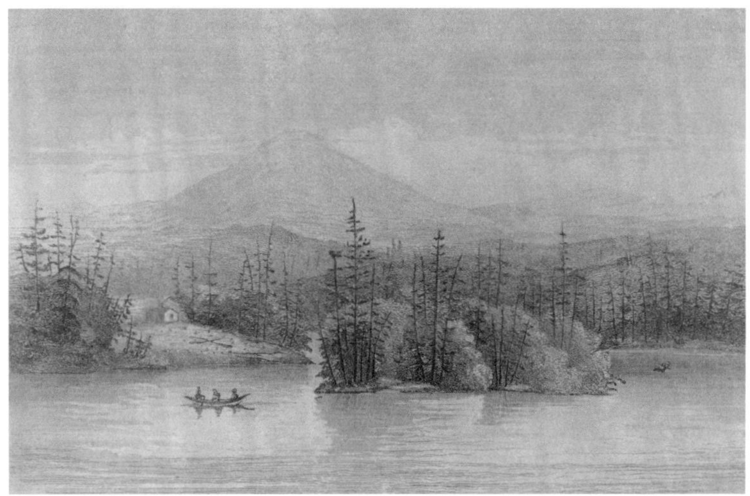

"Lake Henderson." (51). *70.147.5.*

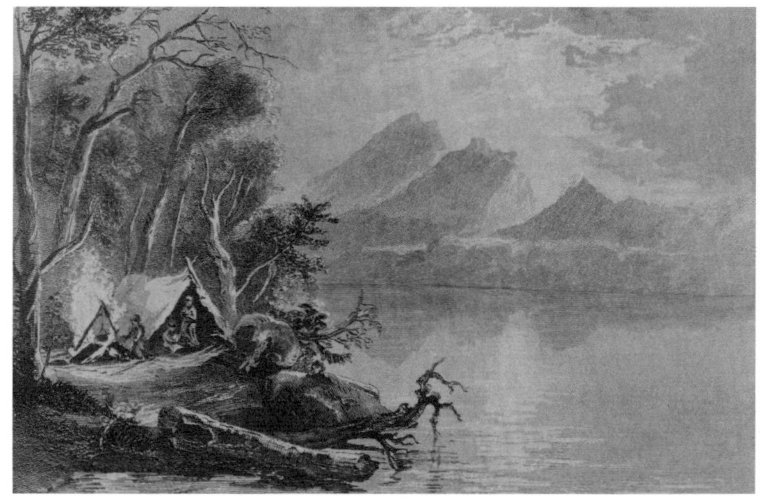

them."[57] The reason few artists found their way to the heart of the Adirondacks was the difficulty of travel. The experience Headley relates, of traveling through the night during a thunderstorm, probably did little to encourage additional visitors at the time. Yet that tale appealed to those in search of sublime experiences and was balanced by anecdotes of superb fishing and the author's return to good health. Engravings in *The Adirondack* reproduce landscapes by John W. Hill of Raquette Lake (54), Régis François Gignoux of Lake Henderson (51), and Charles Cromwell Ingham of Lakes Colden (58) and Sanford and the Adirondack Pass (57). The engraving of Schroon Lake (49) reproduces a drawing by Asher B. Durand, possibly created during the summer he spent with Thomas Cole on the shores of the lake. The frontispiece panorama of the massive high peaks (83) and the scene on Forked Lake (84) are signed only by the engraver, Charles Kennedy Burt. A generation later these engravings reappeared in *The Opening of the Adirondacks.*[58]

By 1850 the custom of presenting elegantly bound books to family and friends as gifts was well established. *American Scenery* with its landscape illustrations was one of the first of the genre. Among the gift books was *The Home Book of the Picturesque* published by George P. Putnam in 1852. It included an engraving titled "The Adirondack Mountains"

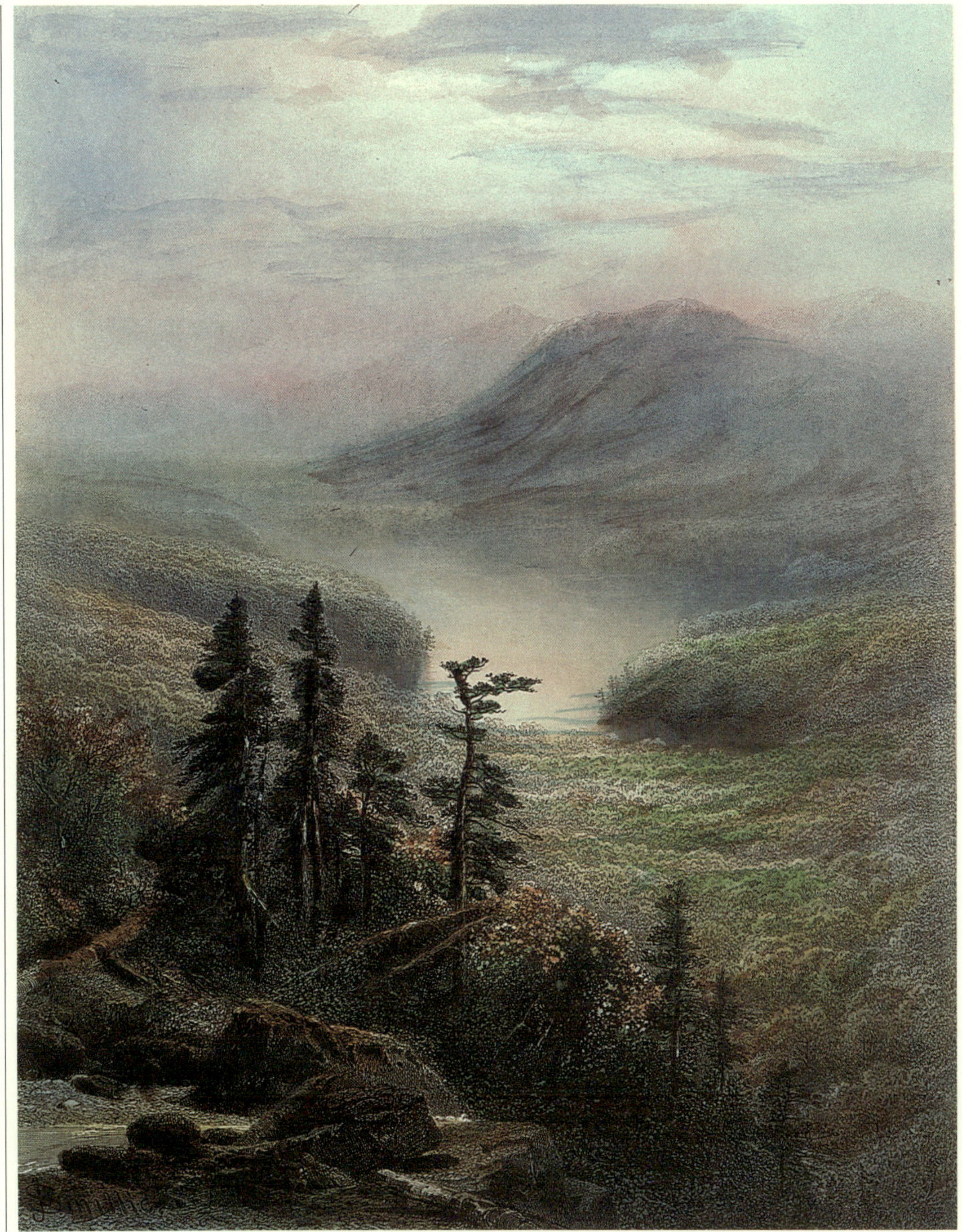

[Upper Ausable Lake]. (71). *64.188.1.*

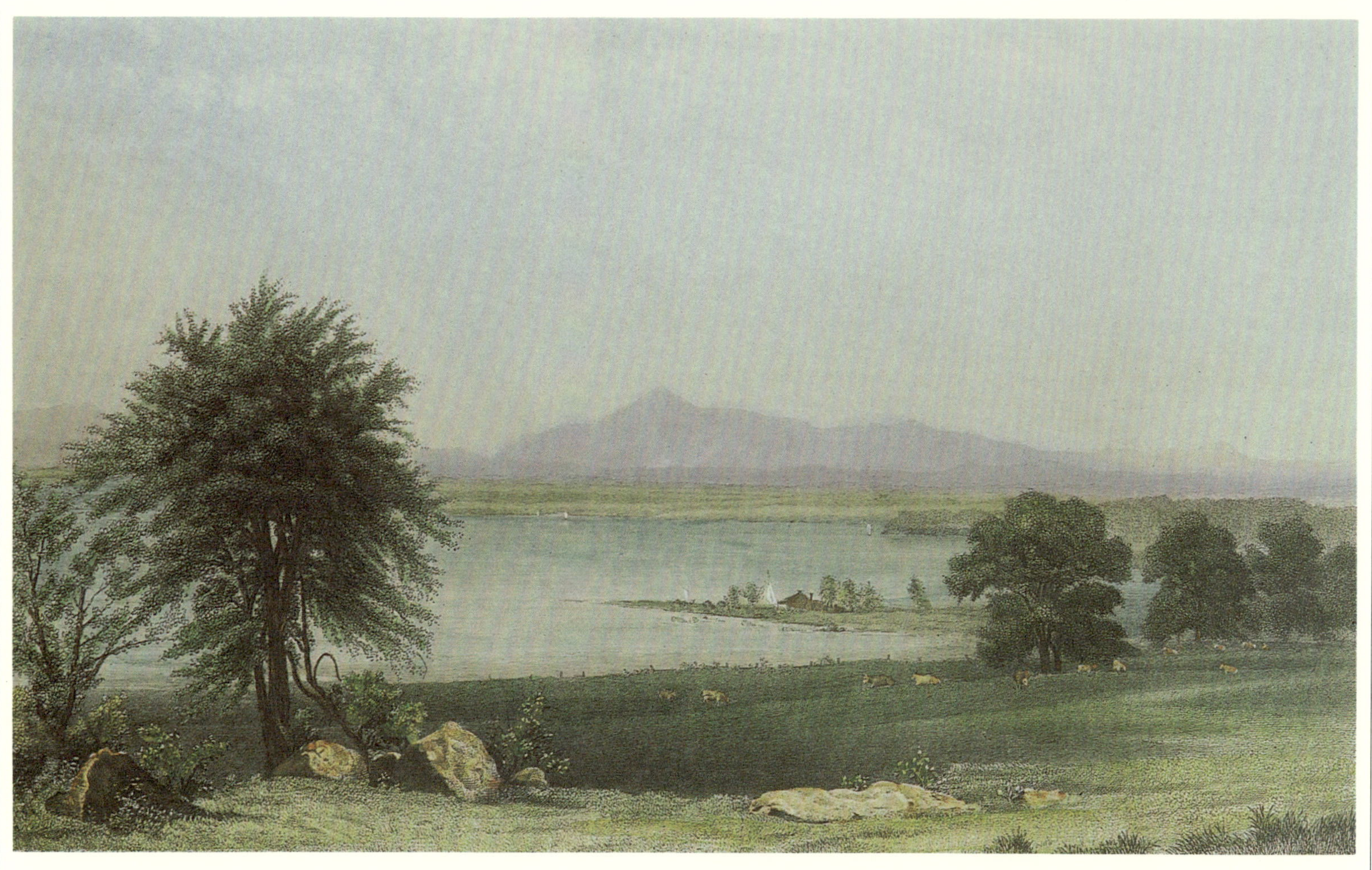

"Lake Champlain, from St. Albans." (56). *72.41.2.*

by Durand. Thomas Addison Richards wrote and illustrated *American Scenery Illustrated* published by Leavitt and Allen in New York in 1854. *A Landscape Book by American Artists and Authors* published in 1868 by George P. Putnam and Company included a view of Lake George (64) by William Rickarby Miller (1818-1893). The *Gallery of Landscape Painters* (New York and London, 1872) included an engraving by James David Smillie (1833-1909) after his own view of Upper Ausable Lake (71), one by Robert Hinshelwood after a view by William Momberger (b. 1829) of Lake George (66), and

"Lake Champlain, from St. Albans" engraved by William Wellstood (1819-1900) after Richard William Hubbard's view (56). These engravings were reused in the *National Gallery of American Landscape* (New York: William Pate & Co., n.d.). Charles A. Dana's *The United States Illustrated*, published in New York by Hermann J. Meyer about 1855, also contained several views of the region including Trenton Falls (95) and "Barhydt's Lake (Near Saratoga)" (23). All of these books, and many others, celebrated the American landscape in text and image.

In contrast to the lithographs of Currier & Ives is the *View on the Raquette River* (314) by Frederic Rondel (1826-1892), the French-born artist responsible for *A Hunting Party in the Woods* painted in 1856 and exhibited the next year at the National Academy of Design, and now in the collection of the Adirondack Museum (65.15.1). The artist was working in Boston in the 1850s, and had moved to New York City by 1860. Rondel's lithograph is particularly delicate in its handling. It was probably based on his painting, *Morning on the Raquette River*, that was exhibited at the National Academy of Design in 1861.[59] In contrast to Currier & Ives' lithographs, however, it was very likely issued in a limited number of impressions by the publisher, Frank F. Oakley. Indeed, it is such a subtle print that its appeal would have been limited. Although the circumstances of the publication of this lithograph are not known, it is possible that it was published in a portfolio with several other lithographs. Such gatherings of prints were issued by American lithographers and publishers at the time. However, often the owners did not retain the covers of the portfolios, but framed the prints individually.[60]

Picturesque America was another major literary and artistic achievement of the nineteenth century, edited by William Cullen Bryant and published in forty-eight parts by D. Appleton and Company from 1870 to 1872. One advertisement reads in part: "The volume will be something more than a gallery of landscapes; it will exhibit our people in their

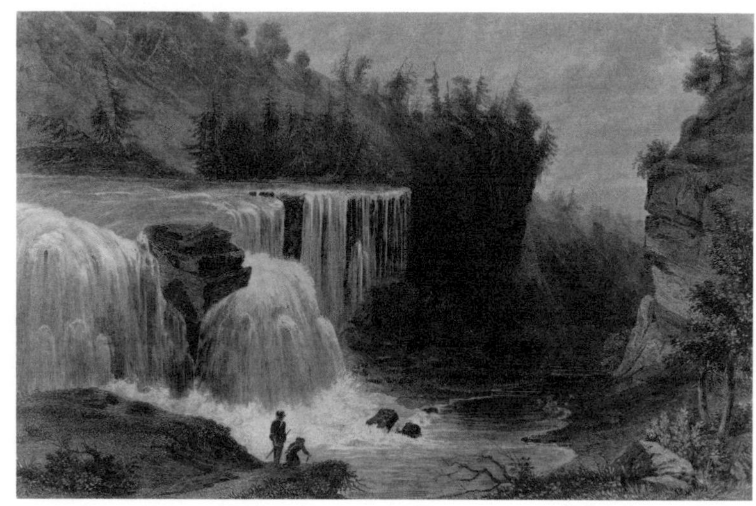

"Trenton Falls (New-York)." (95). *61.53.11.*

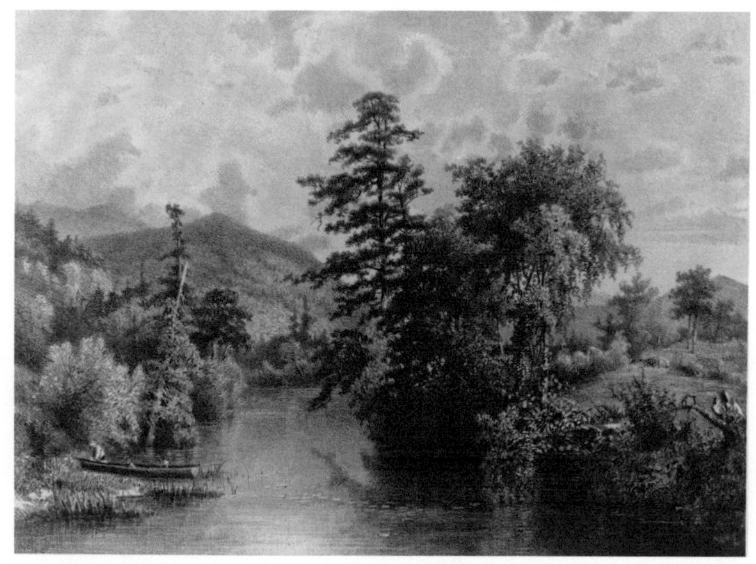

View on the Raquette River, N.Y. (314). *87.9.1.*

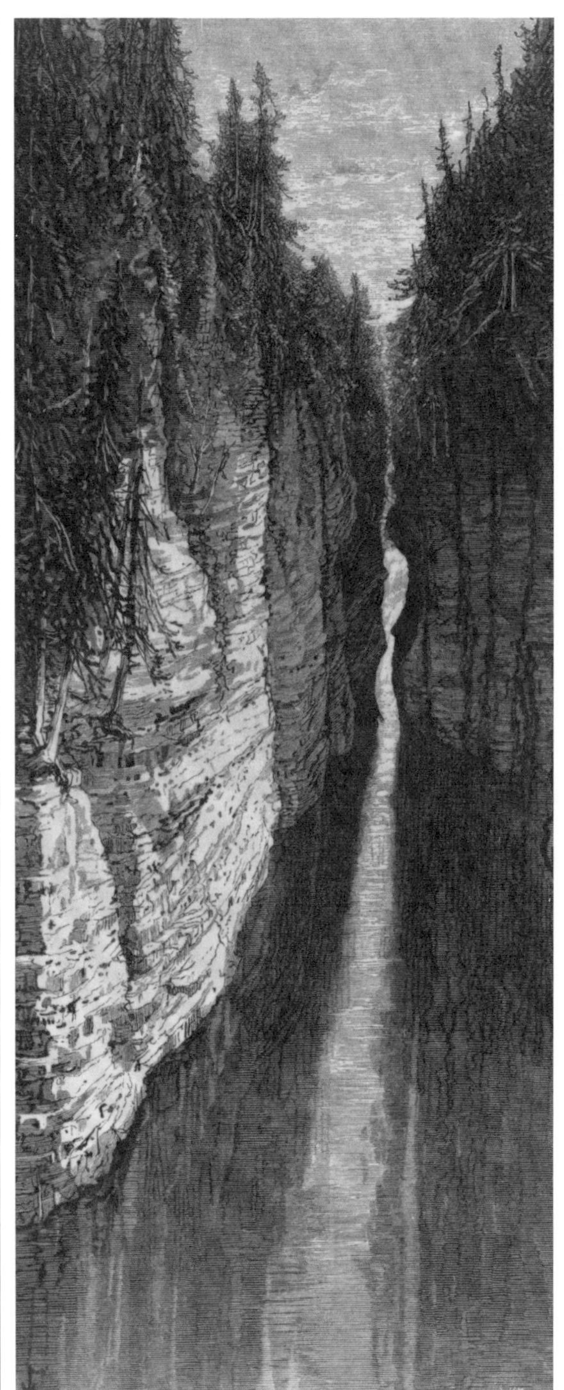

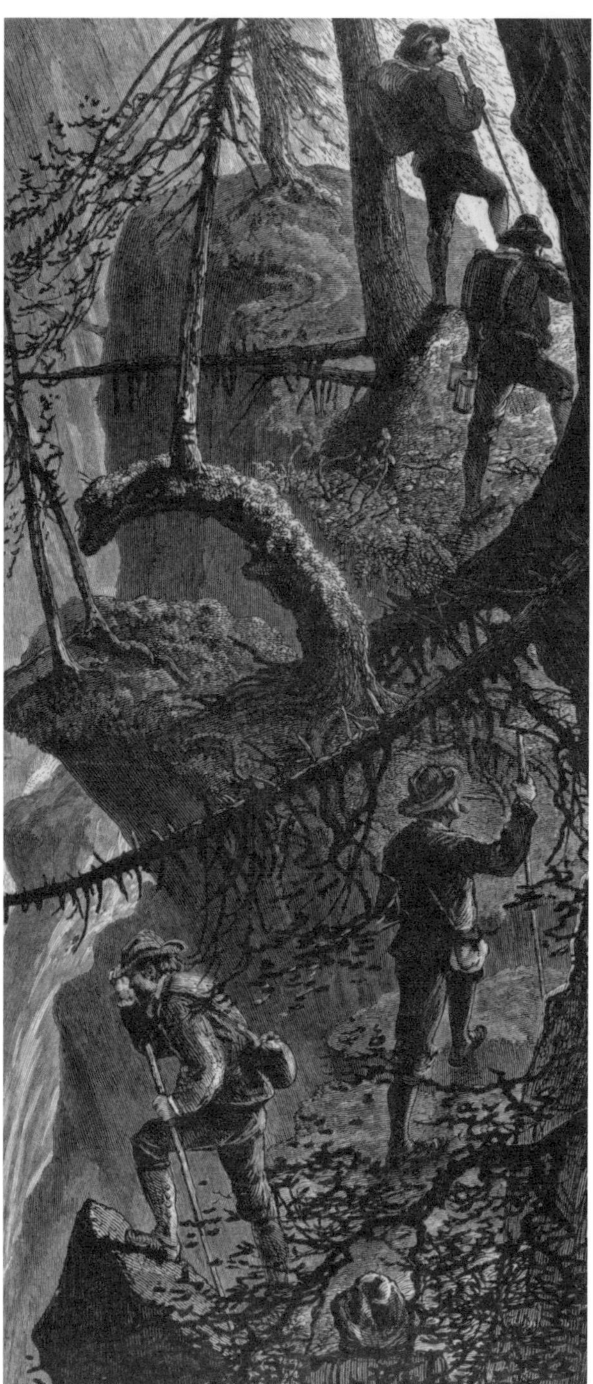

"The Ausable Chasm." (403).
70.147.25.

"The Indian Pass." (422).
74.306.1.

"St. Regis Lake." (412).
70.147.24.

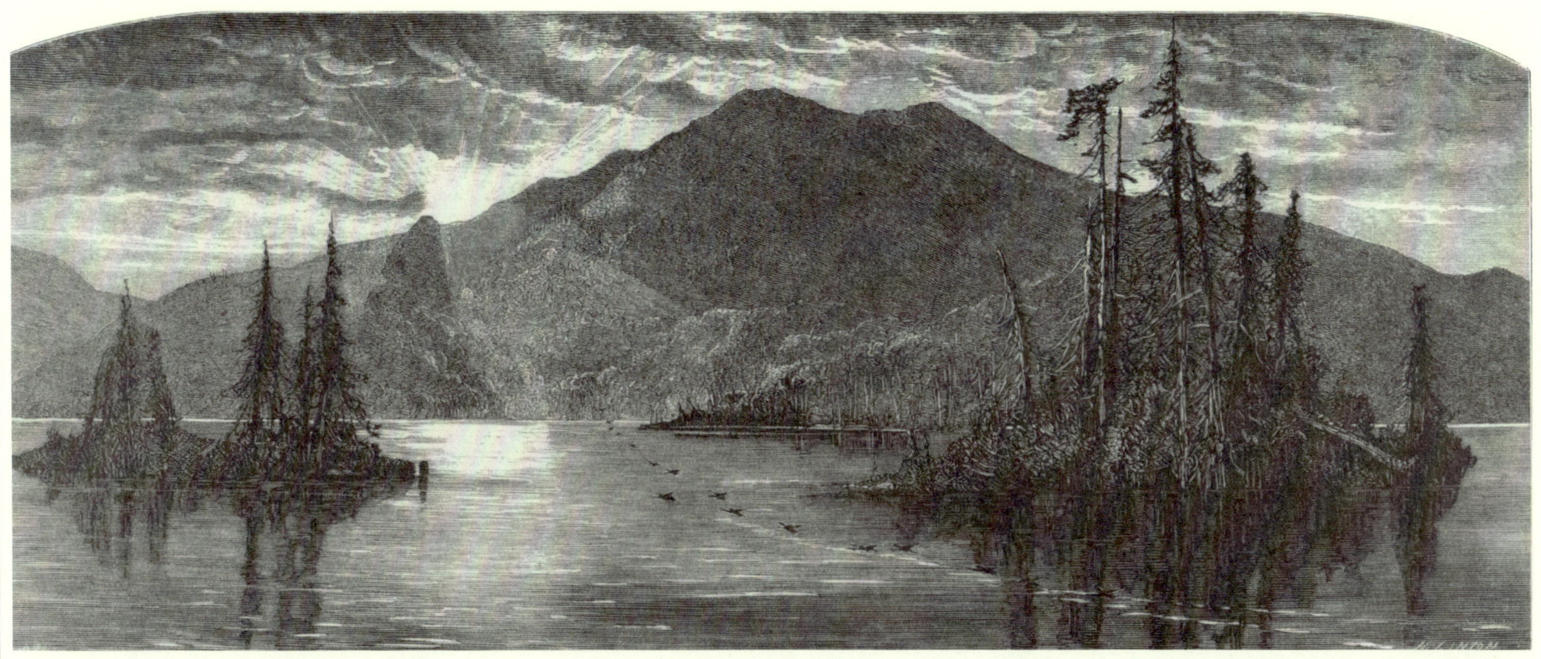

methods of living and travelling, and delineate the picturesque phases of our commerce, as well as the sublime forms of our hills; it will show the often beautiful setting of our cities, and portray the active and brilliant panorama of our bays and rivers."[61] The publication of this monumental work was complex, for there are sixty-five chapters written by twenty-eight authors and illustrated by twelve artists. Although it was ostensibly edited by Bryant, Oliver Bell Bunce (1828-1890) was the individual responsible for the coordination of the publication.[62] The section on the Adirondacks (402-425) was written by Robert Carter and illustrated by Harry Fenn (403, 406 frontispiece, 412, 422), the artist commissioned in 1869 by Fields, Osgood, and Company to illustrate William H. H. Murray's *Adventures in the Wilderness.* Fenn was also responsible for the illustrations of Lakes George and Champlain (378-401) and Trenton Falls (371-377), all of which are in the Adirondack Museum's collection. Bunce wrote the Lake George and Lake Champlain chapters; Rodolphe E. Garczynski wrote the chapter on Trenton Falls.

Two periodicals were particularly important in reproducing for wider audiences the works of artists active in the Adirondacks. The first is *The Ladies' Repository* published by Agents of the Methodist Book Concern in Cincinnati. Modeled after other popular women's magazines of the day, the editors substituted moral essays, articles on history and science, poetry, and book reviews for sentimental fiction. In its second year of publication, 1842, the first of a large number of steel engravings appeared. These prints, accompanied by descriptive texts, were an integral part of the magazine until its demise in 1876. There are seven engravings in the museum's collection that were once part of the periodical. Referring to "Lake Henderson in the Adirondacks" (30) after a painting by T. R. Brown, the editor wrote that the scene had the "look of quiet freshness and coolness ... we would like to sit on the brow of that dark hill and dreamily

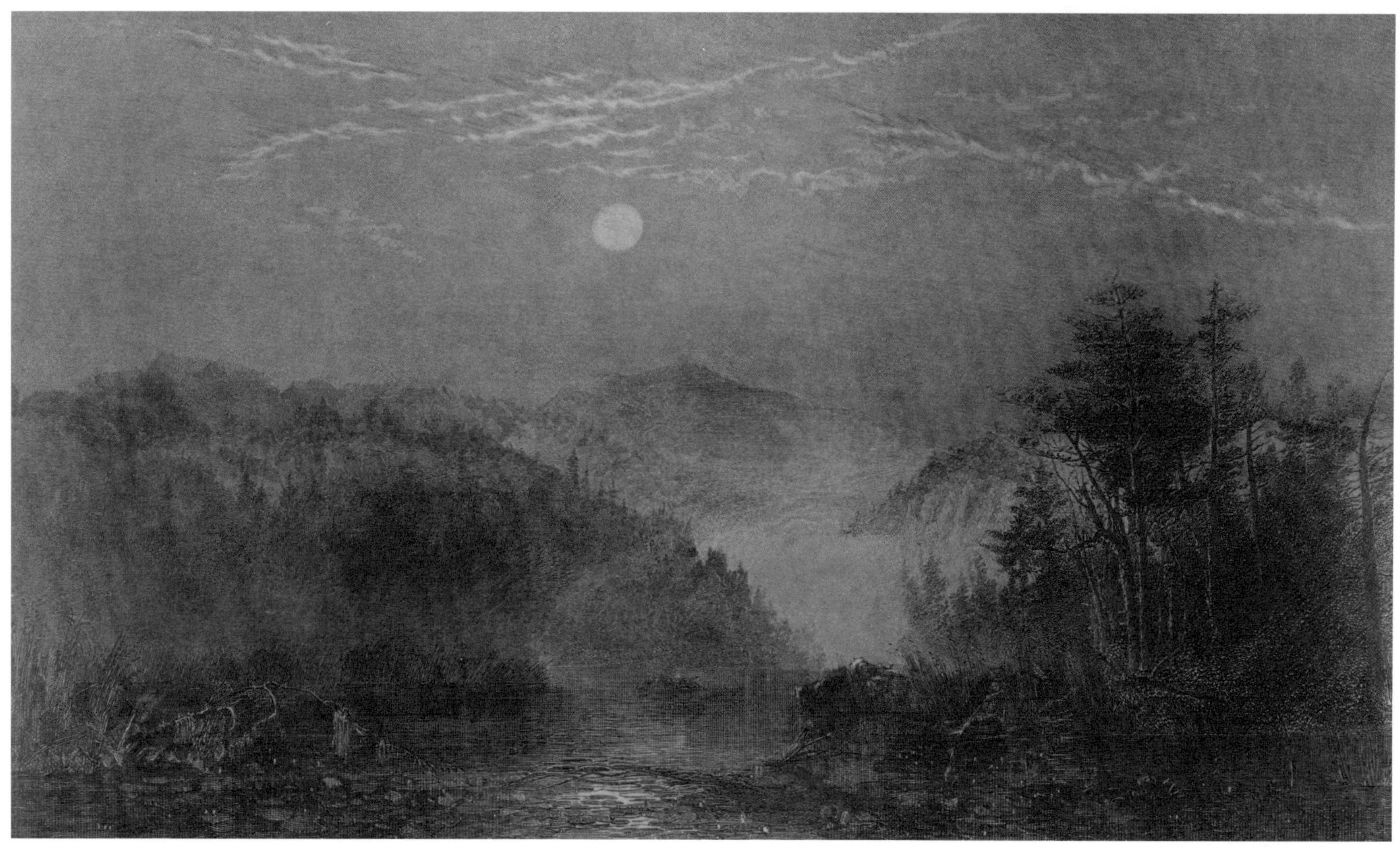

listen to the rustling of the leaves and the play of the wavelets on the shore."[63]

Other engravings reproduce the work of John Casilear (34), Jasper Cropsey (46), William M. Hart (53), Robert Hinshelwood (55), David Johnson (60), and Van Elten (73). The circulation of this periodical must have been national in scope and sufficiently large to support the expense of the engravings. The reproduction of paintings of the Adirondacks is unexpected in a magazine published in Cincinnati. There are equally remarkable engravings after paintings of the Midwest, New England, the deep South, and the West that would have appealed to readers throughout the United States. The editor endowed the reproductions of landscape paintings with religious meaning. "In landscapes, a fine fancy-piece and the well sketched home-stead of our childhood unvisited for years, would excite in us different kinds of admiration. But aside from the power of association, nearly all persons are pleased with *pictures.* It is in human nature to be thus pleased. He who gave us a taste for music and poetry, gave us also a relish for the productions of the pencil; and no matter what objects are skillfully represented, the art which shadows them forth to the eye does of itself demand our

"Lake Henderson at the Adirondacks." (30). *77.109.1.*

"Cat Mountain. Lake George (From a Point Opposite Bolton)." (60). *69.226.4.*

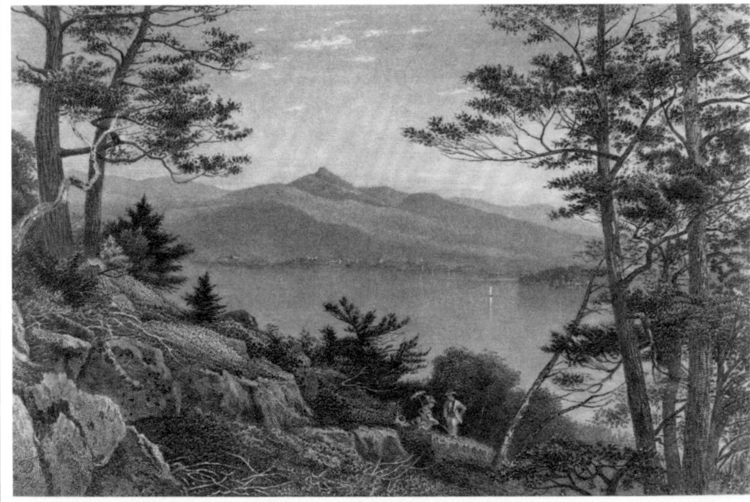

delighted homage. Indeed, so delicate a mechanical use of light requiring an eye and a hand almost divine, ought to excite our admiration—not only of the genius of the artist, but of that wisdom, and power, by which man is so fearfully and wonderfully made."[64]

Hinshelwood's engraving, "Heart of the Adirondack (Morning at Calamity Pond)" (55), depicts a primitive camp, providing a glimpse of the funerary monument erected in memory of David Henderson, an early entrepreneur in the Adirondacks who invested money in a large iron ore deposit in the 1820s. The Adirondack Iron Works, located between lakes Sanford and Henderson, produced iron that was converted to steel at the company's other works in Jersey City, New Jersey. In the 1840s three to four hundred men worked at the forge in the Adirondacks. During a trip in 1845 to locate additional water for the works, David Henderson was killed accidentally. He was commemorated by the monument erected by his children on the shore of the pond. The iron works were abandoned in the 1850s; the problem of transporting the iron through the wilderness was never successfully solved.[65]

David Johnson (1827-1908) painted in the Adirondacks as early as 1859. In 1870 he visited John Henry Hill on Lake George and painted a number of scenes of Buck Mountain, Cat Mountain (opposite Bolton), and Roger's Slide. The engraving of one of his Cat Mountain paintings (60) was printed in *The Ladies' Repository* for 1873. The accompanying text described him as "gifted."[66]

Larger format, wood-engraved reproductions of numerous paintings of the Adirondacks appeared in the pages of *The Aldine,* a periodical issued by a firm of printers in New York City, Sutton, Bowne and Company. It began as an advertising circular in 1868, but it became a more significant publication beginning in 1871 under the editorship of Richard Henry Stoddard, a major literary figure in New York. Among the monthly features were well-engraved reproductions of paintings of both European and American origin. The publisher commissioned the best of American engravers to work on the prints, including William J. Linton, and also used blocks imported from Europe. In contrast to the wood engravings in the popular press, completed under the duress of weekly deadlines, the engravings in this journal are the works of single individuals and are considered to be the best of their type. Linton felt that he had done his best work for the journal, particularly his "Pines of the Racquette [*sic*]" (444) and "White Birches of the Saranac" (445), both after drawings by John Augustus Hows (1832-1874).[67] "The Pines of the Racquette [*sic*]" is a dramatic view showing the kind of natural chaos so typical of forest streams. The engraver reproduces the atmospheric effect of Hows' original by the delicate handling of the lines. "White Birches of the Saranac," issued in March 1873, exchanges the dark of the pines for white birch bark. Hows trained for the ministry and studied law before starting to write and illustrate his own work. One of his early commissions as an illustrator was *Forest Scenes by William C. Bryant, Henry Wadsworth Longfellow, Fitz-Greene Halleck, Alfred B. Street.*[68] From the start of his career, he had a sympathy for landscape.

Linton was justifiably proud of his own work for *The Aldine*. Of the work of another of the engravers, the Frenchman Charles Maurand, Linton wrote, "Maurand's landscapes are capital, daring, and with more drawing as well as decision than is usual in American or English engraving."[69] Maurand engraved Arthur Parton's "Rapids of the Au Sable"

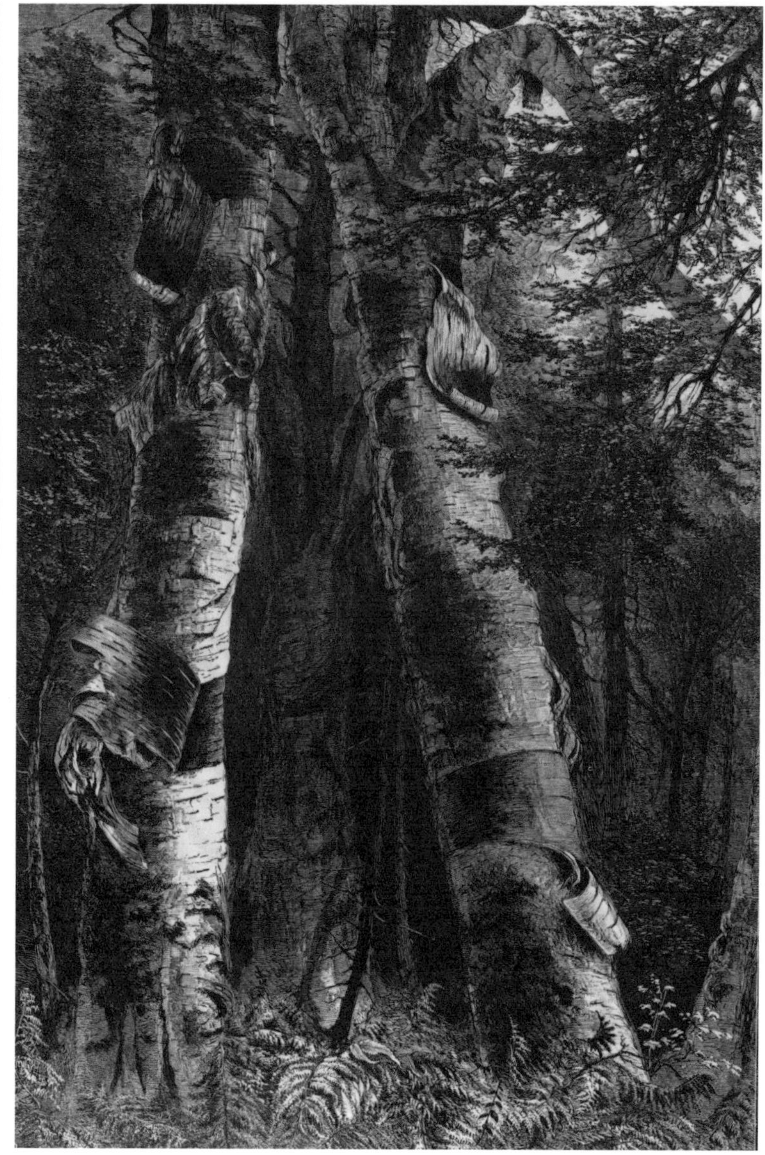

(478) for the October 1874 issue. The accompanying text amplifies the image: "Pen pictures of the scenery of the Au Sable rapids and chasms give but a faint idea of the grandeur and wildness, the sunny nooks and dismal caverns of this wonderful section of the country.... Mr. Arthur Parton

"White Birches of the Saranac." (445). *66.45.11.*

"Adirondack Scenery—Morning on the Ausable." (506). *66.45.14.*

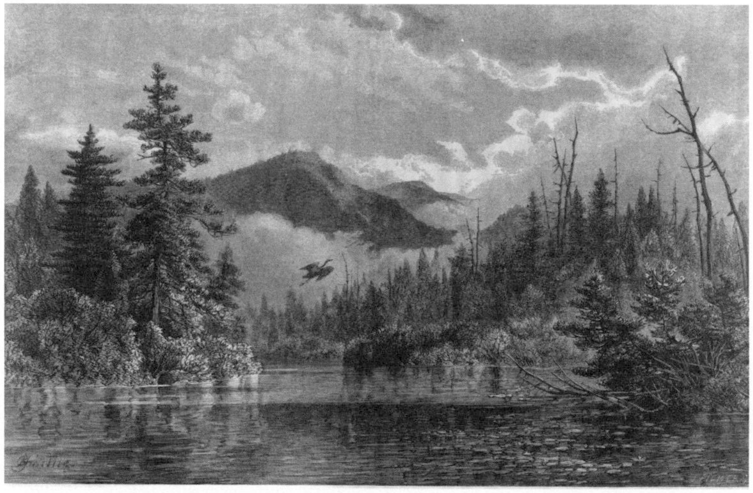

shows us, in his large and noble picture, the Au Sable River in one of its wild and boisterous moods."[70]

Reproductions of at least a dozen Adirondack paintings by seven artists appeared in the pages of *The Aldine* from 1872 to 1874. George Henry Smillie's "Adirondack Scenery—Morning on the Ausable" (506) shows a heron rising from the water's surface. Morning fog and mist hover around the mountain in the background. The journal is careful to locate the view "on the Ausable River, near where it enters the Upper Ausable Lake."[71] Smillie had painted on Ausable Lake in 1868 producing a painting in the collection of the museum (74.292.2). Another trip resulted in a painting *AuSable River* of 1870. A second view "Adirondack Scenery" (505) appeared in the May 1872 issue of *The Aldine.*

The Aldine published a lengthy account of traveling in the Adirondacks in the October 1872 issue. Titled "The Heart of the Adirondacks" it was accompanied by illustrations of Preston Ponds, Lake Henderson, and The Glen. The writer and his party spent "days and days" on Lake George before journeying by wagon from Fort Ticonderoga to the northern end of Schroon Lake. Their guide, Max Tredo, took them to the deserted Adirondac, once the site of a prosperous iron mine, on Lake Sanford. From there they went to Lake Henderson, "a lake of wonderful darkness and beauty." After another carry, the party arrived at Preston Ponds. Their destination was the farther of the two, Lower Preston Pond. There, "with a cold, rippling stream beside us, with mountains and the dense fir forest all around, we lived for weeks in the highest physical and spiritual enjoyment. Trout and venison never failed us; the days flew serenely by; at night we gossiped before a roaring campfire, and, when the logs had changed to glowing embers, lay in our blankets upon couches of fragrant balsam twigs, and watched the August stars."[72]

Fred T. Vance (ca. 1840-1892) provided an illustration of Avalanche Lake (524) for the August 1873 issue. Once part of Lake Colden to its south, Avalanche Lake was formed by massive rock slides. It is described in *The Aldine* as "perhaps the most impressive scene in the whole Adirondack region. It lies walled between precipitous mountains which rear their granite sides thousands of feet directly out of the water."[73]

Among the artists attracted to Keene Valley through which the East Branch of the Ausable River flows was Alexander Lawrie (1828-1917). William Trost Richards introduced him to the area in 1863. Richards and Lawrie had shared a studio in New York and visited Europe together before Lawrie entered the Union Army in 1861. His view of "Elizabeth Valley, Essex County, New York" (451) was published in the October 1873 issue of *The Aldine.*

Thomas Moran (1837-1926) was one of a family of artists. He lived in Philadelphia until 1872 and then moved to Newark, New Jersey, and to New York City shortly thereafter. Acclaimed for his paintings of dramatic western landscapes, he was also active in the Adirondacks. A large number of his drawings were reproduced in guide books such as *The Hudson River Route* published by Taintor Brothers and Company in 1869, J. Bonsall's *The Northern Tourist, an Illustrated Book of Summer Travel* (Philadelphia: John E. Potter and Co., 1879), F. Hastings Bryant's *Nooks in the North* (New York: New York News Company, 1887), and Charles H. Possons's *Lake George and Lake Champlain* (Glens Falls: Charles H. Possons, 1887). His view of Lake George (471) was published in *The Aldine* in April 1874.

Generally artists came to the Adirondacks for the summer or even a shorter period to make sketches that served as inspiration for full-scale paintings that they completed during the winter in their studios. One exception was John Henry Hill (1839-1922). Hill was the grandson and son of artists, both of whom produced Adirondack imagery. His grandfather, John Hill, was the aquatint engraver who reproduced the watercolors of William Guy Wall for *The Hudson River Portfolio.* His father, John William Hill, was one of the artists on the Emmons expedition who produced the early views of Lake Catharine, Lake Janet, Cedar River, and the *View from Prospect Hill, Near Lake George* (276-280). From 1870 to 1874 John Henry Hill lived on Phantom Island in Lake George, rather like a hermit, although fellow artists, including his

"Elizabeth Valley, Essex County, New York." (451). *66.45.9.*

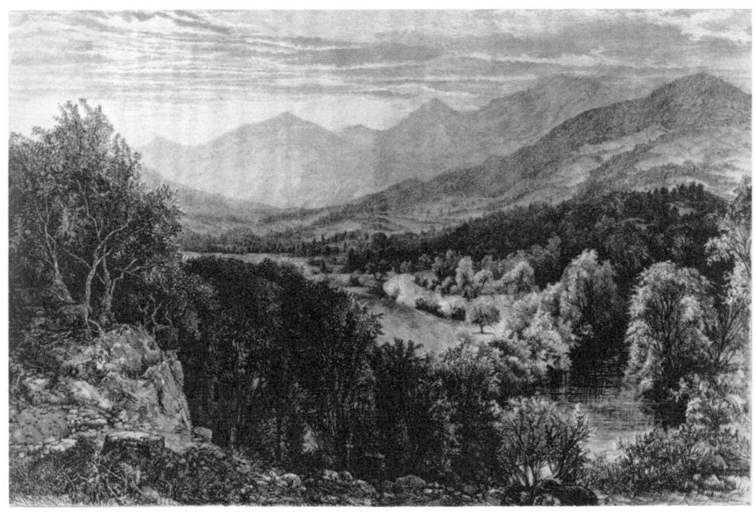

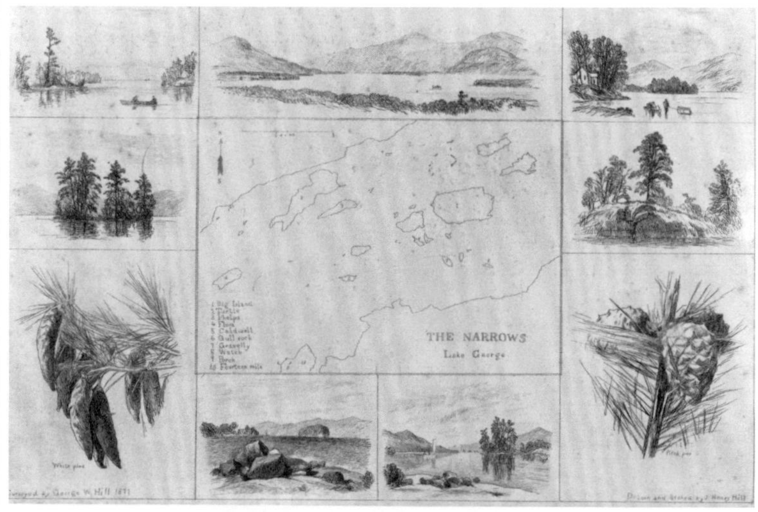

The Narrows Lake George. (129). *57.132.6.*

father, did visit from time to time. He had earlier painted at Long Lake, producing two watercolors in 1867 (Adirondack Museum collection 57.132.1 and 58.34.2).

Hill was among the first generation of American artist-etchers, producing three etchings in 1857. His entire oeuvre included about seventy plates. In 1867 he published a portfolio of his etchings, *Sketches from Nature,* containing twenty-five plates. He was an ardent member of the Pre-Raphaelite movement and recommended the study of Ruskin's *Elements of Drawing* and *Modern Painters* in the preface to the portfolio. During the four years he spent on Phantom Island, Hill produced many etchings, three of which are in the museum's collection.[74] *The Narrows Lake George* (129) combines a survey of a portion of Lake George by his brother, George W. Hill, with small studies of natural objects that are particularly charming and demonstrative of the philosophy of the Pre-Raphaelites whose works aim to be faithful studies of nature based on careful observation of the smallest details. The views depict islands that are situated in the part of Lake George known as The Narrows. The museum owns the watercolor upon which the studies of the pine trees are based (57.132.4).

While at "Artist's Retreat" on Lake George, Hill kept a diary in which he recorded his daily activities, including gathering firewood, traveling over to Bolton Landing for supplies, and working on his etchings and paintings.[75] Many entries concern the weather and particularly the light at different times of day and under varying climatic conditions. *Upper Cascades of Shelving Rock* (130) was etched in October 1871. The solitary figure on the right bank of the cascade provides a sense of scale in the deep woods. Hill has captured the effects of dappled light filtering through the trees. In a contemporary guide book, Shelving Rock is described as "a bold semi-circle of palisades, famed for its dens of rattlesnakes and its good fishing."[76] His etching of Lake George from Bolton (131) is a light-filled panorama of a view that had become very familiar to the artist.

Stephen Parrish (1846-1938) learned to etch from Peter Moran, a fellow Philadelphia artist, in the fall of 1879.[77] He

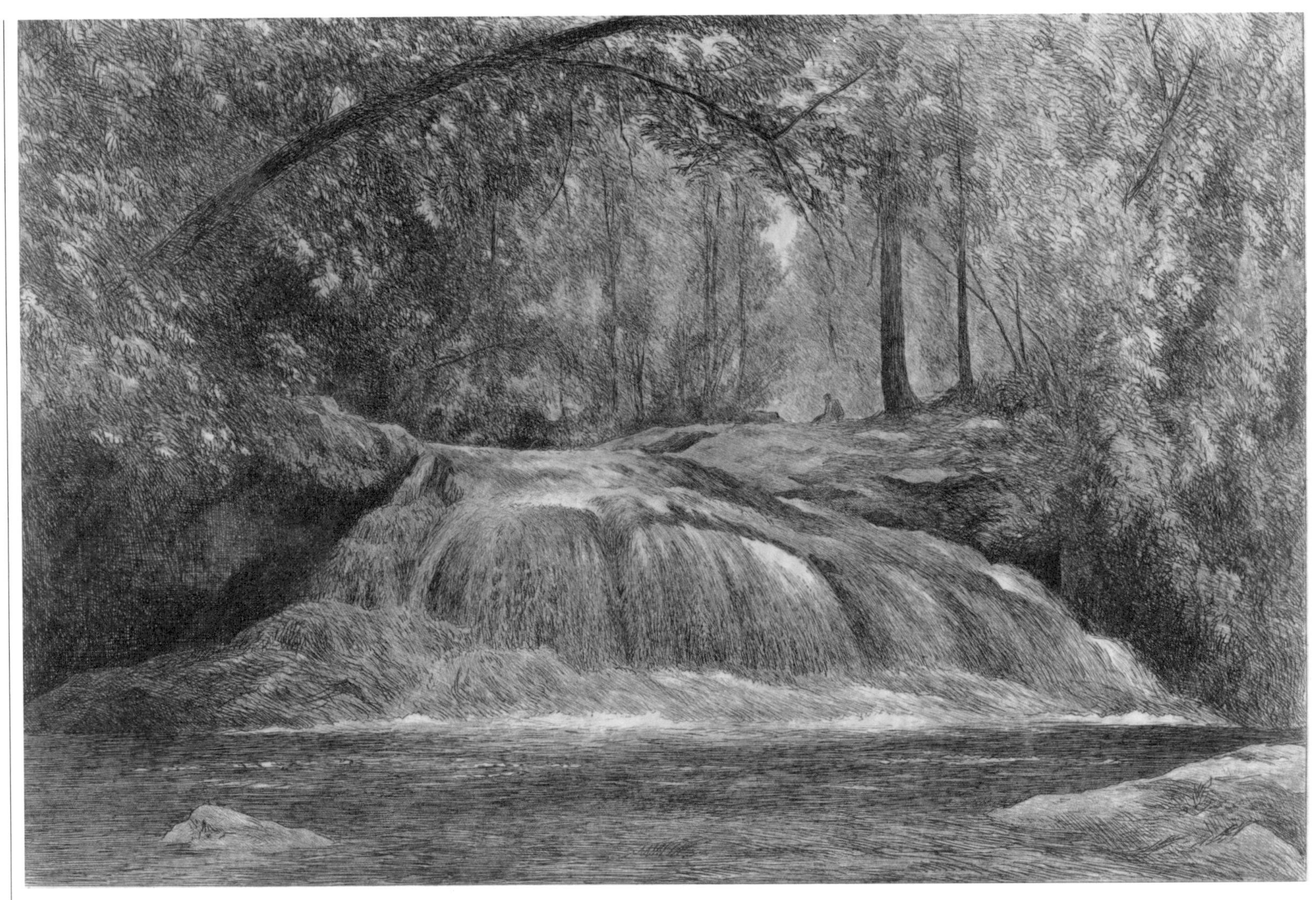

Upper Cascades of Shelving Rock. (130). *57.132.7.*

produced ninety-six etchings within four years, establishing his reputation as an etcher. After etching another sixty plates by the early 1890s, he returned to his career as a painter. His preferred subject matter was landscape and he worked in the Northeast and Europe. Parrish apparently visited the Adirondacks in the late 1870s, for his etchings of Adirondack subjects are dated 1879 and 1880. Parrish's style varies significantly from Hill's. Gone is the tendency towards a topo-

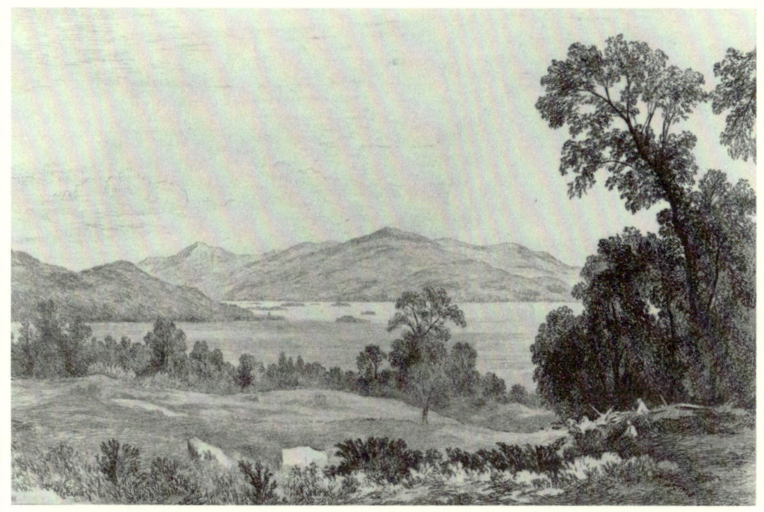

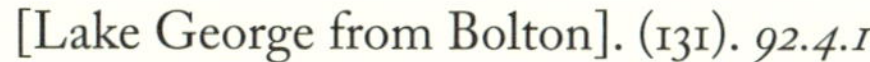

[Lake George from Bolton]. (131). *92.4.1.*

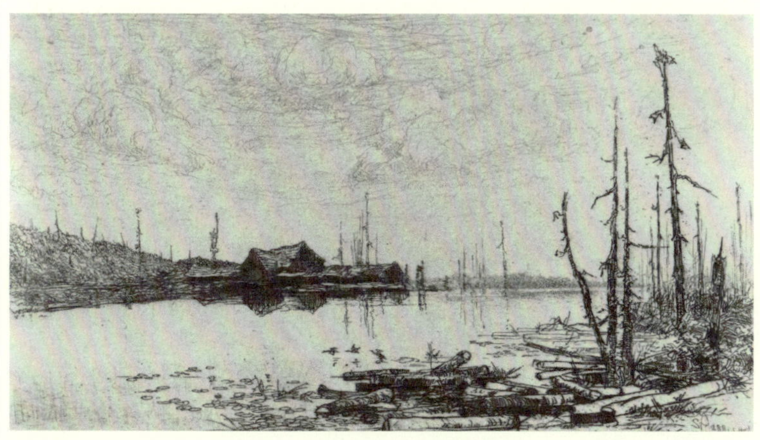

[Flooded Lands—Adirondacks]. (149). 82.131.2.

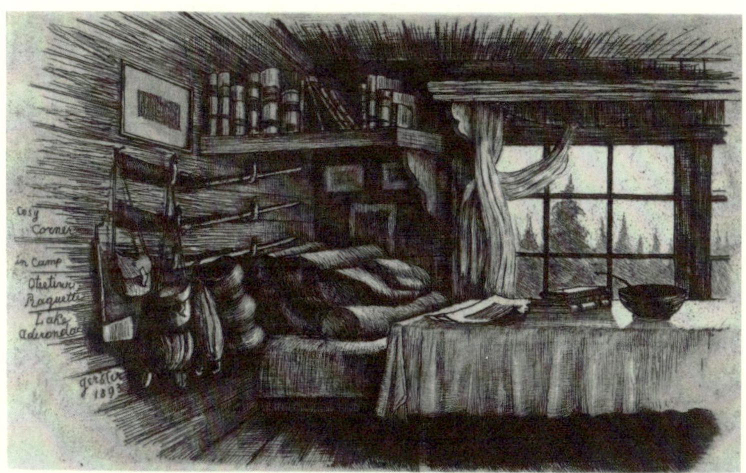

Cozy Corner in Camp Oteetiwi Raquette Lake Adirondacks. (117). *58.273.14.*

graphical description of a broad landscape of typical scenic beauty. Parrish provides several views of the built environment, such as it was, and uses dark tones to create areas of dark shadow. Representative of his work is *Flooded Lands - Adirondacks* (149) of January 1880. The etching can be compared to the painting of the same subject (Adirondack Museum collection 82.131.10). Patricia C. F. Mandel suggests that the etching exhibits greater acuity through the use of delicate line than the painting does with its broad brush strokes. Both show Parrish's interest in the dramatic effect of the contrast between light and dark.[78]

Born in the same generation as Parrish was Arpad G. Gerster (1848-1923). A native of Hungary, he came to the United States and became a successful surgeon in New York City. He was a man of many talents, for his avocations included writing, playing the violin and organ, and etching. He spent sum-

Adirondack Campsite. (136). *68.168.2.*

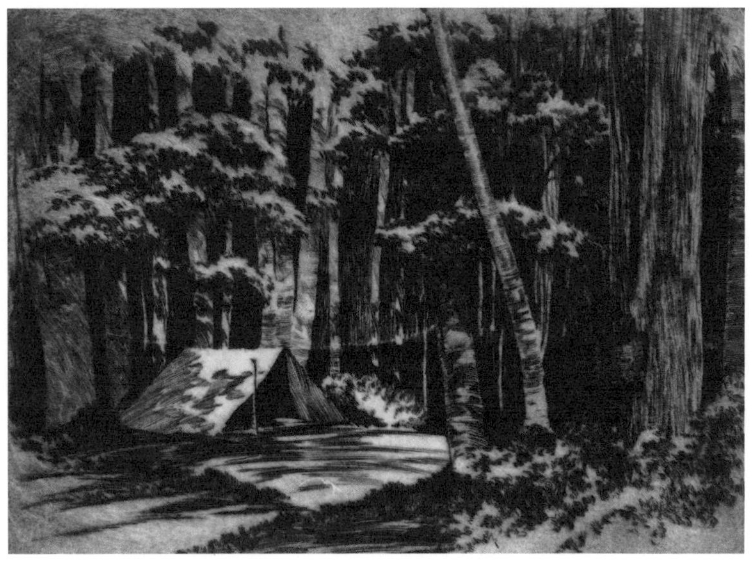

mers with his family in the Adirondacks, first at Raquette Lake, then at Long Lake. His etchings of Adirondack scenes, made in the 1890s, are charming and technically competent. His camp at Raquette Lake, Oteetiwi, is featured in several of these etchings (117, 120). Other subjects were done during his many canoe trips, such as *The End of the Carry* (105) of 1893. The portrait of Alvah Dunning (110) was the only print sold by Gerster. He did so to raise funds to replace a watch lost by Dunning while fishing. When presented with the new watch, Dunning fainted from surprise, or so the story goes.[79]

Herbert S. Kates (1894-1947) was a New York artist and illustrator who grew to love the Adirondacks as a counselor at a girls' summer camp in the Adirondacks in the early 1920s. He later was commissioned to provide illustrations for Russell M. Carson's history of the region, *Peaks and People of the Adirondacks* published by the Adirondack Mountain Club in 1927. He and his brother climbed the forty-six high peaks in the 1920s, so he was well acquainted with the trails and campsites that he depicted in his etchings. Typical of this genre is *Adirondack Campsite* (136). His sweeping topographic views of the High Peaks, such as *Marcy from Haystack* (134) and *Mt. Whiteface - Adirondacks* (133), and his depictions of campsites (136, 137) recall the work of the artists of the mid-nineteenth century.[80]

The printed images of the Adirondacks of the nineteenth century capture not just the pristine wilderness sought by landscape artists, but evidence of battles, early settlements, exploration, economic development, activities of sportsmen, tourists, and year-round residents. Such depictions describe the region and its people with a degree of specificity that make these prints useful documents. When combined with information about the circumstances of publication, the motivation of the publishers is revealed, and the role of prints to document the exploration, promotion, and celebration of the Adirondacks can be delineated.

FOOTNOTES

1 *The Voyages and Explorations of Samuel de Champlain, 1604-1616,* translated by Annie Nettleton Bourne, Edward Gaylord Bourne, ed. (New York: Allerton Book Co., 1922), 1: 205-207.

2 "Hudson's Voyage in 1609," translated by J. Romeyn Brodhead, *Collections of the New-York Historical Society,* 2nd series, vol. 2, part 1 (New York: New-York Historical Society, 1848), pp. 367-370. Unfortunately, Hudson did not write an extensive commentary on his explorations as Champlain did.

3 Lewis Evans compiled the *General Map of the Middle British Colonies,* which was issued in Evans's *Geographical, Historical, Political, Philosophical, and Mechanical Essays* published by Benjamin Franklin and David Hall in Philadelphia in 1755.

4 Horatio Gates Spafford, *A Gazetteer of the State of New York* (Albany: H. C. Southwick, 1813), pp. 75-76.

5 Information on Anburey is to be found in Sydney Jackman's introduction to his *With Burgoyne from Quebec* (Toronto: Macmillan, 1963), pp. 1-15. This book is volume one of Anburey's *Travels through the Interior Parts of North America* (London: William Lane, 1789).

6 Anburey, *Travels through the Interior Parts of North America,* p. 350.

7 Edward Comstock, Jr., lists these prints in "A Catalogue Raisonné of Prints of the Adirondack Region of Northern New York," available at the Adirondack Museum. Comstock prepared this list as a student at Syracuse University in 1973.

8 Lesueur's sketches of North America are described in Robert W. G. Vail's article, "The American Sketchbooks of a French Naturalist, 1816-1837," *Proceedings of the American Antiquarian Society* 48 (April 1938): 49-155. The drawings are in the collection of the Musée de l'histoire naturelle in LeHavre, France.

9 *Diary of William Dunlap (1766-1839) The Memoirs of a Dramatist, Theatrical Manager, Painter, Critic, Novelist, and Historian* (New York: New-York Historical Society, 1931), I: xxii-xxv. The watercolors of Lake George and Ticonderoga are in the collection of the Addison Gallery.

10 John F. Sear's *Sacred Places. American Tourist Attractions in the Nineteenth Century* (New York: Oxford University Press, 1989) fully explores this theme. Unfortunately, the Adirondacks do not play a role in the treatment of the subject.

11 Betty Ahearn Buckell, *Old Lake George Hotels* (Lake George, N.Y.: Buckle Press, 1986), p. 25.

12 *Meyer's Universarum* (New York: Hermann J. Meyer, 1852), p. 269.

13 Edward J. Nygren and Bruce Robertson, *Views and Visions. American Landscape before 1830* (Washington: The Corcoran Gallery of Art, 1986), pp. 264-5. The painting, in the collection of the Detroit Institute of Arts, is reproduced in color on page 215. Additional information on Guy is found in the article "Francis Guy, Painter of Gentlemen's Seats" by J. Hall Pleasants in *Antiques* 65 (1954): 288-90.

14 Timothy Dwight, *Travels in New England and New York,* Barbara Miller Solomon, ed. (Cambridge: The Belknap Press of Harvard University Press, 1969), 3: 293.

15 Dwight, *Travels,* vol. 3, p. 238.

16 Ibid., pp. 247-252.

17 Benjamin Silliman, *Remarks, made on a short tour, between Hartford and Quebec, in the Autumn of 1819* (New Haven: S. Converse, 1820), p. 73.

18 *The Analectic Magazine* 11, no. 4 (April 1818): 325.

19 Karol Ann Peard Lawson, "An Inexhaustible Abundance: The National Landscape Depicted in American Magazines, 1780-1820," *Journal of the Early Republic* 12 (Fall 1992): 330.

20 *Itinéraire pittoresque du fleuve Hudson et des parties latérales de l'Amérique du Nord, d'après les dessins originaux pris sur les lieux* (Paris: Gaugain et Cie., 1828-29).

21 An excellent account about Milbert is Constance D. Sherman's "A French

Explorer in the Hudson River Valley," *New-York Historical Society Quarterly* 45 (July 1961): 255-280.

22 The publication of *The Hudson River Portfolio* is described in *A Checklist of The American Engravings of John Hill (1770-1850)* by Richard J. Koke (New York: New-York Historical Society, 1961).

23 Chapter four of Ann Shelby Blum's *Picturing Nature. American Nineteenth-Century Zoological Illustration* (Princeton: Princeton University Press, 1993) discusses both state and federal surveys and their importance. Twenty-two states initiated surveys between 1820 and 1850.

24 Ebenezer Emmons, *Geology of New-York. Part II* (Albany: Printed by W. & A. White & J. Visscher, 1842), p. 218.

25 For more information on this painting, see Patricia C. F. Mandel, *Fair Wilderness* (Blue Mountain Lake, N.Y.: The Adirondack Museum, 1990), p. 73.

26 Bufford was a commercial lithographer in New York. His firm turned out various kinds of prints including billheads, advertisements, views, and sheet music. Trained in Boston, he had his own firm in New York from 1835 to 1839 before returning to Boston where he eventually directed his own firm from 1845 until his death in 1870. His career is well documented by David Tatham in "John Henry Bufford, American Lithographer," *Proceedings of the American Antiquarian Society* 86 (April 1976): 47-73.

27 See Koke, *A Checklist of The American Engravings of John Hill (1770-1850)*, pp. 29-41.

28 *The New-York Geological and Mineralogical Reports for 1837* (Albany: Published by Oliver Steele, 1840), p. 220.

29 About 300 impressions of each of the plates in *The Hudson River Portfolio* were produced. See Koke, pp. 29-41.

30 This information is drawn from the biographical sketch by Warder Cadbury in *A. F. Tait: Artist in the Adirondacks* (Blue Mountain Lake, N. Y.: The Adirondack Museum, 1974), pp. 9-12.

31 Cadbury, *Arthur Ftizwilliam Tait: Artist in the Adirondacks* (Newark: University of Delaware Press; London and Toronto: Associated University Presses, 1986), pp. 327-8. Louis Prang reproduced ten paintings by Tait; other publishers issued nine others.

32 The *Second Supplement to Catalogue of Goupil & Co.* (New York: Goupil & Co., December 1856) lists *The Halt in the Woods* together with a variety of religious and genre prints. *The County Election and The Stump Speech* after paintings by Bingham were also for sale. These three prints each cost $5.00 uncolored and $10.00 colored. Only one other print, *Mass in Kabylie* engraved by Martinet after Vernet, cost more.

33 *A. F. Tait, Artist in the Adirondacks,* p. 11.

34 Allan Nevins and Frank Weitenkampf, *A Century of Political Cartoons. Caricature in the United States from 1800 to 1900* (New York: Charles Scribner's Sons, 1944; reprint, New York: Octagon Books, 1975), p. 72.

35 *Ballou's Pictorial* 14 (April 3, 1858): 209.

36 *Ballou's Pictorial* 15 (July 17, 1858): 33.

37 Edward Comstock, Jr., in his article "Satire in the Sticks: Humorous Wood Engravings of the Adirondacks" (*Prints and Printmakers of New York State, 1825-1940,* David Tatham, ed., Syracuse: Syracuse University Press, 1986) provides additional information on Thorpe, Fenn, William L. Sheppard, Seneca Ray Stoddard, Augustus Hoppin, and other pictorial satirists.

38 *Harper's New Monthly Magazine* 19 (July 1859): 160.

39 Typescript of Raquette Lake Hotel Register, Adirondack Museum Library, MS 65-26, Box 8, Folder 4. Among other visitors was A. F. Tait in 1861, 1863, 1869, and 1873. James D. Smillie, the painter and etcher, stayed there in 1872.

40 Warder H. Cadbury's introduction to William K. Verner's edition of Murray's classic published by The Adirondack Museum and Syracuse University Press in 1989 is extremely informative. This account of Murray is derived from that excellent introduction.

41 *Appleton's Journal of Popular Literature, Science, and Art* 1, no. 17 (1869): 538.

42 Philip C. Beam, *Winslow Homer's Magazine Engravings* (New York: Harper & Row, Publishers, 1979), pp. 260-1.

43 See *Winslow Homer in the Adirondacks. An Exhibition of Paintings* (Blue Mountain Lake, N.Y.: The Adirondack Museum, 1959), and David Tatham's essays, "The Two Guides: Winslow Homer at Keene Valley, Adirondacks," *American Art Journal* 20, no. 2 (1988) and "Winslow Homer at the North Woods Club" in Nicolai Cikovsky, Jr., ed. *Winslow Homer: A Symposium* (Hanover, N.H.: University Press of New England, 1990).

44 *Harper's Weekly* 20 (October 14, 1876): 843.

45 *Harper's Weekly* 29 (January 24, 1885): 58.

46 Quoted in Francis Murphy's introductory essay to *The Book of Nature: American Painters and the Natural Sublime* (Yonkers, N.Y.: The Hudson River Museum, 1983), p. 6.

47 Cole's work in the Catskills is thoroughly described in Kenneth Myers's *The Catskills. Painters, Writers, and Tourists in the Mountains, 1820-1895* (Yonkers, N.Y.:

The Hudson River Museum of Westchester, 1987). *Thomas Cole: Landscape into History,* William H. Truettner and Alan Wallach, eds. (New Haven and London: Yale University Press and Washington, D.C.: National Museum of Art, 1994) also incorporates Cole's work in the Adirondack region.

48 Painting is in the collection of the Fort Ticonderoga Museum. Pell had purchased Fort Ticonderoga from Union and Columbia Colleges in 1820.

49 *The Correspondence of Thomas Cole and Daniel Wadsworth,* J. Bard McNulty, ed. (Hartford: Connecticut Historical Society, 1983), p. 57. There are a total of eleven engravings in the work after landscapes by Cole.

50 This painting is thoroughly discussed in Mandel's *Fair Wilderness,* pp. 44-45.

51 *A Landscape Book by American Artists* (New York: George P. Putnam, 1868), p. 45.

52 Eugene C. Worman, Jr., "A Geographical Catalog of Bartlett prints in *American Scenery,*" *Imprint* 19 (Autumn, 1994): 2.

53 Nathaniel P. Willis, *American Scenery* (London: George Virtue, 1840), p. iii.

54 Dale Roylance, *American Graphic Arts. A Chronology to 1900 in Books, Prints, and Drawings* (Princeton: Princeton University Library, 1990), p. 125.

55 Some information on Willis and *American Scenery* is found in Henry A. Beers, *Nathaniel Park Willis* (Boston: Houghton, Mifflin and Company, 1885), pp. 247-8. Eugene C. Worman, Jr., has written widely on Bartlett's American and European views. His most useful articles are "Bartlett's Travels in the United States (1836-1837)," *Antiquarian Bookman* 84 (October 30, 1989): 1643-1657 and "*American Scenery* and the Dating of Its Bartlett Prints" in *Imprint* 12 (Autumn 1987): 2-11.

56 William H. Bartlett, *History of the United States* (London: George Virtue, 1853).

57 Joel T. Headley, *The Adirondack; or, Life in the Woods* (New York: Baker and Scribner, 1849), p. iv. This title was reprinted by Harbor Hill Books of Harrison, New York, in 1982.

58 *The Opening of the Adirondacks* (New York: Hurd and Houghton, 1865).

59 Thomas P. Bruhn, *The American Print: Originality and Experimentation 1790-1890* (Storrs, Conn.: The William Benton Museum of Art, 1993), p. 76.

60 One set of lithographs published in Boston in 1859 by Phillips & Sampson was titled *Pictures Painted & Lithographed by Wm. M. Hunt.* Often prints from this set are found separately. *Western Romantic Scenery* containing four lithographs was published in Cincinnati by Otto Onken about 1850; *New England Scenery from Nature* was published in Boston by M. J. Whipple in 1852.

61 Cover, part nineteen, Bryant's *Picturesque America* (New York: D. Appleton, 1873).

62 *Picturesque America* is the subject of a monograph by Sue Rainey scheduled for publication in 1995 by Vanderbilt University Press.

63 *The Ladies' Repository* 25 (September 1865): 576.

64 *The Ladies' Repository* 1 (January 1844): 1.

65 This account of David Henderson's death and the history of the Adirondack Iron Works is taken from Alfred L. Donaldson's *A History of the Adirondacks* (New York: Century, 1921; reprint, Fleischmanns, N.Y.: Purple Mountain Press, 1992), 1: 136-148.

66 *The Ladies' Repository* 33 (September 1873): 238.

67 William J. Linton, *The History of Wood-Engraving in America* (Boston: Estes and Lauriat, 1882; reprint, Watkins Glen, N.Y.: The American Life Foundation & Study Institute, 1976), pp. 32-3.

68 *Forest Scenes* was published in New York by Hurd & Houghton in 1860.

69 Linton, *The History of Wood-Engraving in America,* p. 33.

70 *The Aldine* 7 (October 1874): 196.

71 *The Aldine* 5 (February 1872): 41.

72 *The Aldine* 5 (October 1872): 195-6.

73 *The Aldine* 6 (August 1873): 155.

74 See Thomas Bruhn, *The American Print: Originality and Experimentation 1790-1890* (Storrs, Conn.: The William Benton Museum of Art, 1993), pp.67-8. Bruhn refers to Hill's 1859 etching, *The Chestnut Tree,* as "brilliant." The Boston Museum of Fine Arts and the New York Public Library both have excellent collections of Hill's etchings. The latter collection includes at least six done at Lake George from 1870 to 1874. An excellent selection of Hill's work is discussed in *The New Path: Ruskin and the American Pre-Raphaelites* (Brooklyn: The Brooklyn Museum, 1985), an exhibition catalogue by Linda S. Ferber and William H. Gerdts.

75 Ms 61-166, Adirondack Museum Library.

76 *Nelson's Guide to Lake George and Lake Champlain* (London: T. Nelson and Sons, 1868), p. 15.

77 A useful description of Parrish's career as an etcher is found in Thomas Bruhn's *American Etchings: The 1880s* (Storrs, Conn.: The William Benton Museum of Art, 1985), pp. 112-134.

78 Mandel, *Fair Wilderness,* p. 93.

79 Information on Dr. Gerster can be found in the curatorial files at the Adirondack Museum.

80 Kates's work was shown in an exhibition at the Adirondack Museum in 1983. An article by his brother, Jerome S. Kates, and Peggy O'Brien appeared in the January 1984 issue of *Adirondac.*

Checklist of Prints

Compiled by Georgia B. Barnhill

The checklist of the Adirondack Museum print collection is divided into four sections based on medium: Metal Engravings, Artists' Etchings, Lithographs, and Wood Engravings. In each section the arrangement of entries varies slightly, according to what is best for the prints within each medium. Multiple impressions of some of the prints are in the collection because of variants in states or the presence of hand coloring. These prints do not receive separate listings; multiple museum accession numbers at the end of an entry indicate more than one impression of that entry in the collection. The final checklist number of 571 indicates the number of discrete images in the collection at this time, though there are more than that many prints.

Many of the prints in the collection are illustrations detached from the books and periodicals in which they were originally published. A great deal of effort has been expended to provide the publishing context for these images. All information about these prints is presented as known. Additions to this knowledge would be gratefully received by the museum. Supplemental descriptions of the images are available on the cataloguing worksheets maintained by the museum registrar.

Acorn symbols indicate prints illustrated in the text or checklist, where they precede entries. Print titles appear two different ways, depending on a print's original use: Quotation marks denote that the image originally appeared as a published illustration; italics denote the image was produced separately.

All dimensions given represent height by width, in inches. Artists' dates are given when known. Titles or other information that is supplied by the museum or the checklist compiler are enclosed in square brackets.

Metal Engravings

Entries are arranged alphabetically by artist. Where entries can be grouped according to their original publication, this has been done, arranged alphabetically by title. Earlier publications precede later ones within the same artist listing. In these cases, publication data appears once, after the last print in a group. Prints by the same artist but with separate publication information appear alphabetically by title.

After titles, engravers' names are included where known, followed by dimensions, publication data and accession number(s). Prints derived from photographs form separate groups (under photographers' names), followed by prints by anonymous artists.

Thomas Anburey

1. "The Section and Plan of a Blockhouse." 1789. 8 3/8 x 5 13/16. 76.137.1.

2. "A View of a Saw Mill and Block House Upon Fort Anne Creek the Property of Gen. 'Skene, which on Gen Burgoyne's Army Advancing was set Fire to by the Americans." 1789. 6 15/16 x 9. 76.137.2.

Numbers 1 and 2 published in Thomas Anburey, *Travels Through the Interior Parts of America* (London: William Lane, 1789).

William Henry Bartlett (1809-54)

3. "Ballston Springs." J. Sands, engraver. 4 3/4 x 6 15/16. 73.124.12.

4. "Barhydt's Lake, Near Saratoga." Edward Radclyffe (1810-63), engraver. 4 11/16 x 7. 61.53.7; 61.53.13; 71.35.6.

5. "Black Mountain, (Lake George)." Robert Wallis (1794-1878) and Thomas Creswick (1811-69), engravers. 4 13/16 x 7 1/16. 61.53.4; 62.37.1, 66.53.2.

6. "Bridge at Glens Fall [*sic*]. (On the Hudson)." Francis W. Topham (1808-77), engraver. 4 3/4 x 7 1/4. 66.57.1; 66.64.4.

7. "Caldwell. (Lake George)." John Cousen (1804-80), engraver. 4 3/4 x 7 1/16. 61.53.15; 66.64.2.

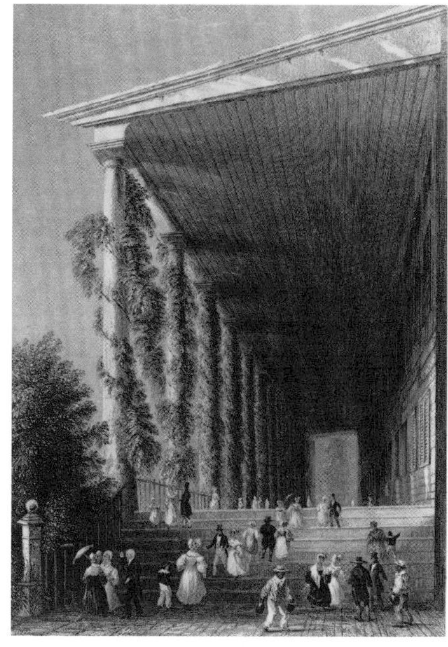

8. "Colonnade of Congress-Hall. (Saratoga Springs)." H. Griffiths, engraver. 6 15/16 x 4 3/4. 82.11.8.

9. "Little Falls. (On the Mohawk)." Thomas Creswick (1811-69) and Robert Brandard (1803-62), engravers. 4 11/16 x 7 1/8. 82.11.9.

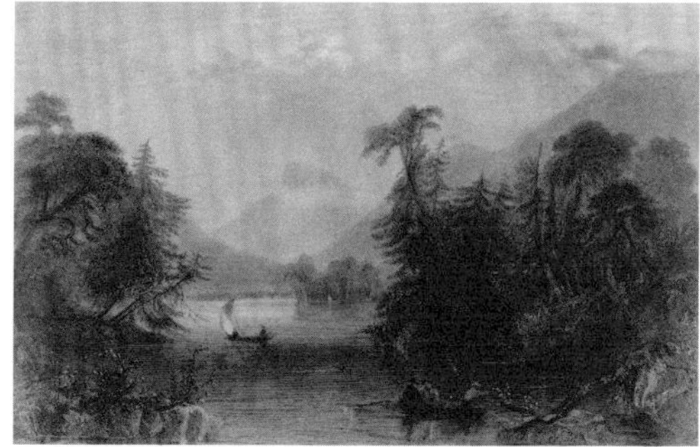

10. "The Narrows, (Lake George)." Francis W. Topham (1808-77), engraver. 4 3/4 x 7 3/16. 62.37.2.

11. "Rail-Road Scene, Little Falls. (Valley of the Mohawk)." R. Sands, engraver. 78.124.2.

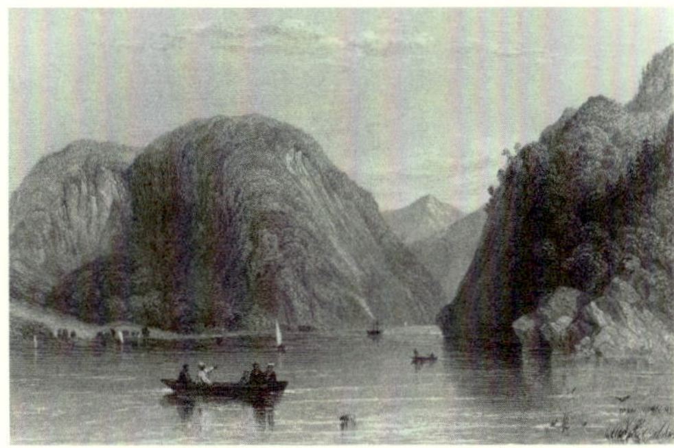

12. "Rogers' Slide, Lake George." John Cousen (1804-80) and Thomas Creswick (1811-69), engravers. 4 5/8 x 7. 61.53.3; 62.37.3.

13. "Sabbath Day Point. (Lake George.)" H. Adlard, engraver. 4 3/8 x 7 1/4. 61.53.6; 62.37.5.

14. "Saratoga Lake." Robert Wallis (1794-1878), engraver. 4 11/16 x 7. 61.53.5; 62.37.6.

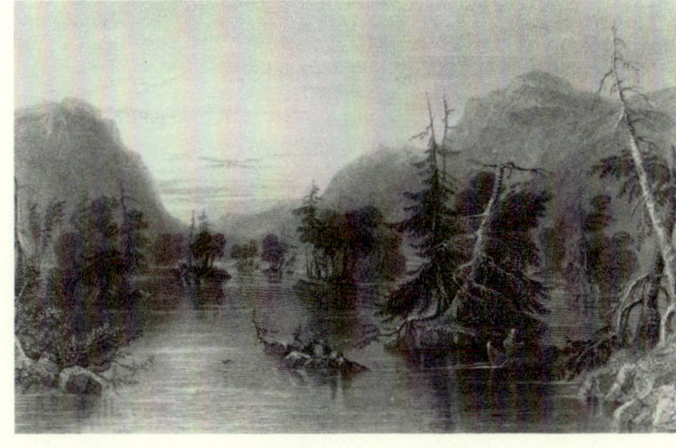

15. "Scene Among the Highlands on Lake George." James T. Willmore (1800-63), engraver. 4 7/8 x 7 3/16. 61.53.14; 66.64.1.

16. "Trenton Falls, View Down the Ravine." James T. Willmore (1800-63), engraver. 4 3/4 x 7 1/8. 61.53.111.

17. "Utica." Robert Brandard (1803-62), engraver. 4 7/8 x 7 1/4. 66.124.16.

18. "View of the Ruins of Fort Ticonderoga." T. A. Prior (1809-54), engraver. 4 11/16 x 7 3/8. 66.54.1; 66.64.5.

19. "View on the Erie Canal Near Little Falls." James T. Willmore (1800-63), engraver. 82.11.10.

20. "Village of Little Falls. (Mohawk River)." S. Bradshaw, engraver. 4 15/16 x 7 1/8. 82.11.11.

Numbers 3-20 published in Nathaniel P. Willis, *American Scenery*, 2 vols. (London: George Virtue, 1840-42).

21. "St. Regis, Indian Village. (St. Lawrence)." W. L. Ormsby, engraver. 4 9/16 x 6 7/8. 67.163.1.

22. "A Shanty on Lake Chaudière." Robert Brandard (1803-62), engraver. 4 5/8 x 7. 69.59.1.

Numbers 21 and 22 published in Nathaniel P. Willis, *Canadian Scenery* (London: George Virtue, 1842).

23. "Barhydt's Lake (Near Saratoga)." 4 1/16 x 6 1/16. Published in Charles A. Dana, *The United States Illustrated* (New York: Herrmann J. Meyer, ca. 1850). 74.328.2.

24. "On Lake George." 4 x 6 1/16. Published in *Meyer's Universarum*, vol. 1 (New York: Herrmann J. Meyer, 1852). 77.14.6.

25. "Scene Among the Highlands on Lake George." (New York: Herrmann J. Meyer, ca. 1850). 4 7/16 x 6 9/16. 74.328.1.

26. [Rogers' Slide, Lake George]. 4 11/16 x 7 1/16. 70.73.1.

27. [Winter night]. J. Rogers, engraver. 4 9/16 x 7 3/8. 92.41.1.

Henry Beckwith

28. "Trout Fishing in the Hamilton County Lakes, N. Y." Alexander L. Dick, engraver. 4 x 5 1/4. Published in an unidentified book or periodical, New York, ca. 1840. 78.48.1.

William James Bennett (1787-1844)

29. *View of the High Falls of Trenton, West Canada Creek, N. Y.* 15 3/16 x 21 1/2. New York: Currier & Ives, ca. 1860. 67.56.1.

T. R. Brown

30. "Lake Henderson at the Adirondacks." 4 9/16 x 7 9/16. Published in *The Ladies Repository* 25 (Cincinnati: Poe & Hitchcock, Sept. 1865). 77.109.1.

Charles Burton (fl. 1819-42)

31. "Piazza of Congress Hall, Saratoga Springs." Thomas Illman (d. ca. 1859), engraver. 5 1/4 x 7 7/16. Published in John H. Hinton, *History and Topography of the United States*, vol. 2 (Boston: Walker & White, 1856). Attribution to the artist is based on an engraving in the 1834 edition of this title. 82.11.13.

John William Casilear (1811-93)

32. "Lake George." Robert Hinshelwood (b. 1812), engraver. $4^{13}/_{16}$ x $8^{7}/_{8}$. Published in *Appleton's Journal* 2 (New York: D. Appleton & Co., October 23, 1869). 66.53.1.

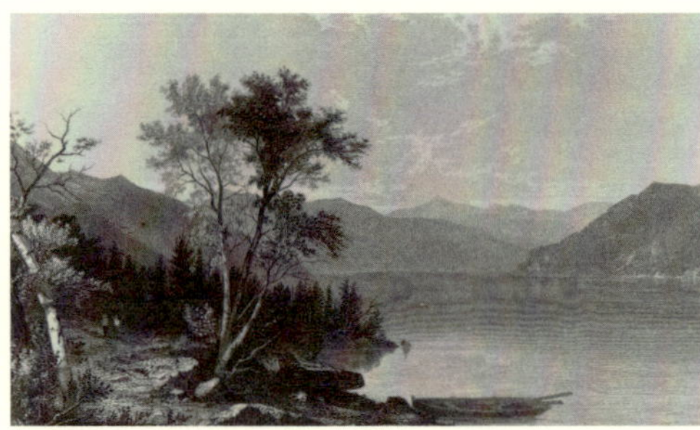

33. "Lake George." Robert Hinshelwood (b. 1812), engraver. $5^{5}/_{16}$ x $8^{7}/_{8}$. Published in William Cullen Bryant, ed., *Picturesque America*, vol. 2 (New York: D. Appleton & Co., 1874). 67.101.2; 87.13.1.

34. "The Slide—Lake George New York." Robert Hinshelwood (b. 1812), engraver. $4^{5}/_{8}$ x $7^{15}/_{16}$. Published in *The Ladies Repository* 22 (Cincinnati: Poe & Hitchcock, Sept. 1862). 79.6.3.

Alonzo Chappel (1828-87)

35. "Battle of Plattsburg [*sic*]." $5^{11}/_{16}$ x $7^{3}/_{8}$. Published in Henry B. Dawson, *Battles of the United States by Sea and Land* (New York: Johnson, Fry & Co., 1858-59). 76.136.2.

36. "Capture of Fort Ticonderoga. 'By What Authority?' 'In the Name of the Great Jehovah and the Continental Congress.'" Thomas Phillibrowne, engraver. $5^{1}/_{16}$ x $6^{15}/_{16}$. Published in Jesse A. Spencer, *History of the United States*, vol. 1 (New York: Johnson, Fry and Company, 1858). 76.136.1.

37. "John J. Audubon." $7^{1}/_{4}$ x $5^{3}/_{8}$. Published in Evert A. Duyckinck, *National Portrait Gallery of Eminent Americans*, vol. 2 (New York: Johnson, Fry & Company, 1862). 69.179.17.

William F. Cogswell (1819-1903)

38. *General Grant and His Family.* John Sartain (1808-97), engraver. $24^{1}/_{2}$ x $18^{5}/_{8}$. Published in Rochester, N. Y., and Philadelphia by Bradley & Co. and R. H. Curren, 1868. 60.22.8.

Thomas Cole (1801-48)

39. "Lake George." Fenner, Sears & Co., engraver. $3^{11}/_{16}$ x $5^{1}/_{2}$. 67.101.1.

40. "Timber Raft on Lake Champlain." Fenner, Sears & Co., engraver. $3^{7}/_{8}$ x $5^{1}/_{2}$. 66.57.2.

Numbers 39 and 40 published in John Howard Hinton, *The History and Topography of the United States of America*, vol. 2 (London: Hinton, Simpkin & Marshall, 1831).

41. "Lake George, N. Y." William Chapin (1802-88), engraver. $4^{7}/_{8}$ x $7^{3}/_{8}$. Published in John Howard Hinton, *The History and Topography of the United States*, vol. 2 (Boston: Samuel Walker, 1836). 61.53.8; 70.76.2.

42. "Lake George." $3^{3}/_{4}$ x $5^{7}/_{16}$. 68.29.5.

43. "Ruins of Fort Ticonderoga, New York." $6^{3}/_{4}$ x $8^{11}/_{16}$. 68.29.2.

44. "Timber Raft on Lake Champlain." Fenner, Sears & Co., engraver. $6^{1}/_{2}$ x $8^{1}/_{2}$. Central image printed from the same plate as 66.57.2 (checklist 40). 68.29.4; 69.9.2.

Numbers 42-44 published in John Howard Hinton, *The History and Topography of the United States* (London: John Tallis & Co., 1850).

45. "Lake George, N. Y." William Chapin (1802-88), engraver. $4^{7}/_{8}$ x $7^{3}/_{8}$. Artist's and engraver's names effaced on this state. Published in John Howard Hinton, *The History and Topography of the United States*, vol. 2 (Boston: Walker & White, 1856). 69.98.1.

Jasper Francis Cropsey (1823-1900)

46. "Lake George (In the Olden Times)." William Wellstood (1819-1900), engraver. $4^{3}/_{4}$ x $6^{1}/_{2}$. Published in *The Ladies Repository* 23 (Cincinnati: Poe & Hitchcock, Jan. 1863). 79.6.2.

Thomas Seir Cummings (1804-94)

47. "White-Hall, Victorious May 20th 1825." Samuel Maverick (1790-1845) and John F. Morin (fl. 1825-40), engravers. $3^{5}/_{16}$ x $4^{7}/_{8}$. Published in Cadwallader Colden, *Memoir Prepared...at...the Completion of the New York Canals* (New York, 1825). 81.25.6.

Archibald Dick (ca. 1805-ca. 1855)

48. "Lunatic Asylum Bloomingdale, N. Y." H. Fossette, engraver. $3^{5}/_{16}$ x $5^{11}/_{16}$. Published in an unidentified book, ca. 1835. 73.74.1.

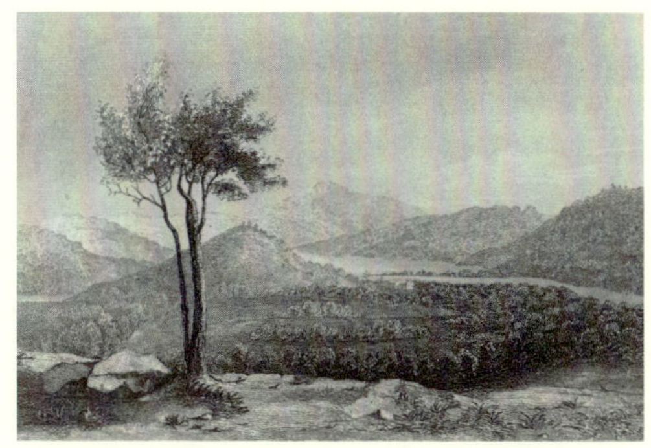

Asher Brown Durand (1796-1886)

49. "Lake Schroon." Charles Kennedy Burt (1823-92), engraver. $3^{3}/_{16}$ x $4^{5}/_{8}$. Published in Joel T. Headley, *The Adirondack; or, Life in the Woods* (New York: Baker & Scribner, 1849). 70.147.2.

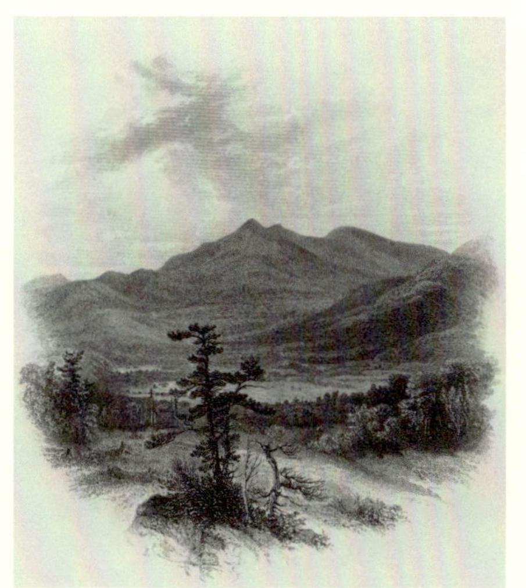

50. "A Scene in the Adirondack Mountains From a Painting by A. B. Durand." John Kirk (ca. 1823-ca. 1862), engraver. This image appeared without the title in *The Poet and the Painter* (New York: D. Appleton and Company, 1869). 6 x $5^{1}/_{4}$. 80.24.2.

Regis François Gignoux (1816-82)

51. "Lake Henderson." Charles Kennedy Burt (1823-92), engraver. $3^{1}/_{4}$ x $4^{5}/_{8}$. Published in Joel T. Headley, *The Adirondack; or, Life in the Woods* (New York: Baker & Scribner, 1849). 70.147.5.

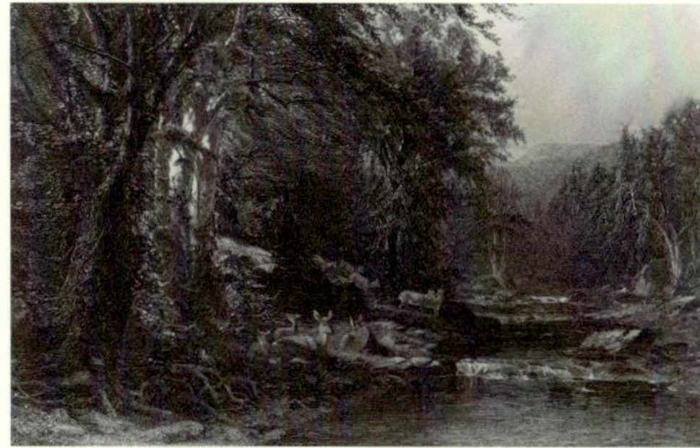

James McDougal Hart (1828-1901)

52. "The Adirondack Woods From a Painting by J. M. Hart." Robert Hinshelwood (b. 1812), engraver. $5^{11}/_{16}$ x $8^{7}/_{8}$. Published in William Cullen Bryant, ed., *Picturesque America* (New York: D. Appleton & Co., 1874). Based on Hart's painting [*A Bit of Lake Placid*], 1890, in the Adirondack Museum collection (67.220.4). 66.45.4; 67.99.5; 68.99.1; 87.13.2.

William M. Hart (1823-94)

53. "The Au-Sable at Keen [*sic*] Flats Adirondacs [*sic*]." $5^{11}/_{16}$ x $4^{7}/_{16}$. Published in *The Ladies Repository*. 90.32.1.

John William Hill (1812-79)

54. "View on Raquette Lake." Charles Kennedy Burt (1823-92), engraver. $3^{1}/_{4}$ x $4^{5}/_{8}$. Published in Joel T. Headley, *The Adirondack; or, Life in the Woods* (New York: Baker & Scribner, 1849). 70.147.4.

Robert Hinshelwood (b. 1812)

55. "Heart of the Adirondack. (Morning at Calamity Pond)." $7^{1}/_{4}$ x $4^{7}/_{8}$. Published in *The Ladies Repository* (Cincinnati: Hitchcock & Walker, 1874). 78.8.1.

Richard William Hubbard (1816-88)

56. "Lake Champlain, from St. Albans." William Wellstood (1819-1900), engraver. $8^{1}/_{4}$ x 13. Published in *Gallery of Landscape Painters* (New York: G. P. Putnam & Sons; and London: Low, Son, Marston & Searle, 1872). Also published in *National Gallery of American Landscape* (New York: William Pate & Co.; and Boston: L. A. Elliot, n.d.). 72.41.2.

Charles Cromwell Ingham (1796-1863)

57. "Adirondack Pass." Charles Kennedy Burt (1823-92), engraver. $3^{3}/_{16}$ x $4^{5}/_{8}$. Based on Ingham's painting *The Great Adirondack Pass, Painted on the Spot*, 1837, in the Adirondack Museum collection (66.114.1). 70.147.6.

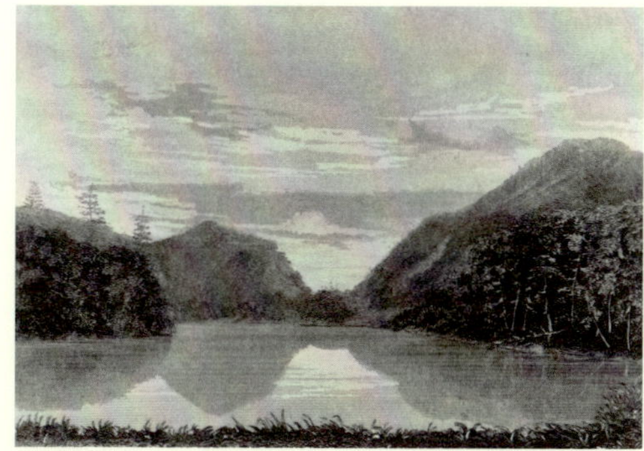

58. "Lake Colden." Charles Kennedy Burt (1823-92), engraver. $3^{1}/_{4}$ x $4^{5}/_{8}$. 70.147.1.

Numbers 57 and 58 published in Joel T. Headley, *The Adirondack; or, Life in the Woods* (New York: Baker & Scribner, 1849).

Henry Inman (1801-46)

59. "Trout Fishing." William G. Jackman, engraver. $4\frac{5}{8} \times 5\frac{3}{4}$. Published in an unidentified book, ca. 1845. 77.34.1.

David Johnson (1827-1908)

60. "Cat Mountain. Lake George (From a Point Opposite Bolton)." William Wellstood (1819-1900), engraver. $4\frac{1}{2} \times 6\frac{3}{4}$. Published in *The Ladies Repository* 33 (Cincinnati: Hitchcock & Walder, Sept. 1873). 69.226.4.

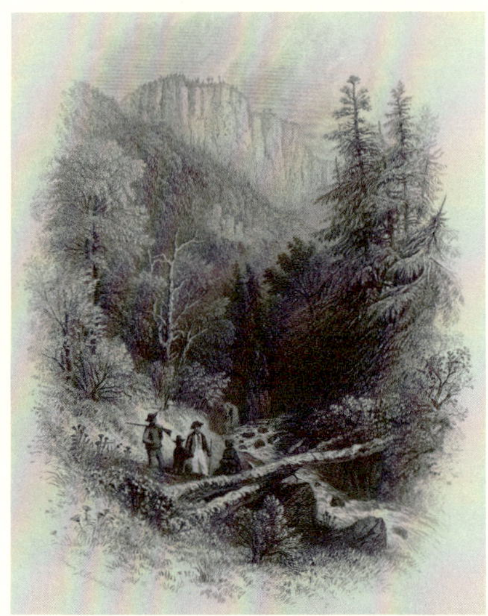

Benson John Lossing (1813-91)

61. "Source of the Hudson in the Indian Pass." $6\frac{3}{8} \times 4\frac{3}{4}$. Published in Benson John Lossing, *The Hudson, From the Wilderness to the Sea* (New York: Virtue and Yorston, 1866). 67.86.1.

Jacques Gérard Milbert (1766-1840)

62. "Lake George." S. Cholet, engraver. $3\frac{5}{8} \times 5\frac{3}{16}$. 75.143.2.

63. "Ruines du Fort Ticonderoga." $3\frac{3}{8} \times 5\frac{3}{16}$. 77.93.1.

Numbers 62 and 63 possibly published in Milbert, *Picturesque Views of North America* (Paris, 1825).

William Rickarby Miller (1818-93)

64. "Lake George. The Narrows with Black Mountain and Bolton." Samuel Valentine Hunt (1803-93), engraver. $4\frac{11}{16} \times 6\frac{15}{16}$. Possibly first published in New York by George P. Putnam & Co., 1856. Reprinted in *A Landscape Book by American Artists and Authors* (New York: George P. Putnam & Son, 1868) and B. F. De Costa, *Lake George; Its Scenes and Characteristics* (New York: Anson D. F. Randolph & Co., 1869). 80.24.3.

65. "Ruins of Fort Ticonderoga—Lake Champlain." Samuel Valentine Hunt (1803-93), engraver. $4\frac{3}{4} \times 7\frac{1}{8}$. Possibly published in New York by George P. Putnam & Co., 1856. Reprinted in B. F. De Costa, *Lake George; Its Scenes and Characteristics* (New York: Anson D. F. Randolph & Co., 1869). 81.25.5.

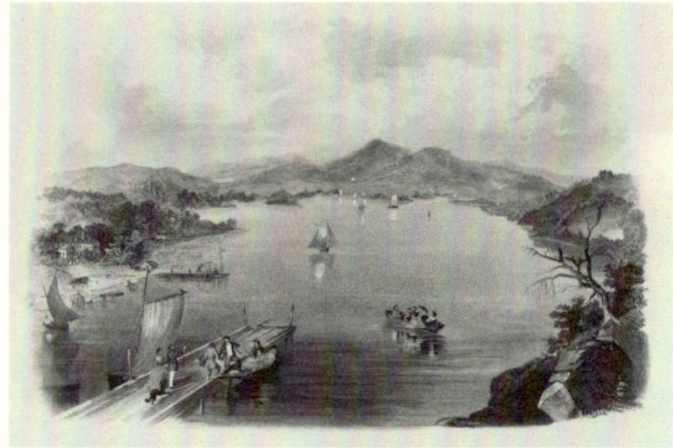

William Momberger (b. 1829)

66. "Lake George." Robert Hinshelwood (b. 1812), engraver. $9\frac{1}{2} \times 14\frac{1}{8}$. Published in *Gallery of Landscape Painters* (New York: G. P. Putnam & Sons; and London: Low, Son, Marston & Searle, 1872). Also issued in *National Gallery of American Landscape* (New York: William Pate & Co.; and Boston: L. A. Elliot, n.d.). 72.41.1; 72.152.1.

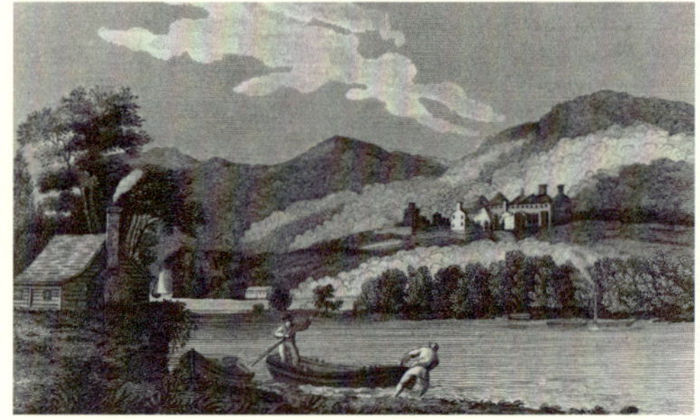

Hugh Reinagle (ca. 1788-1834)

67. "View of the Ruins of Ticonderoga Forts [*sic*] on Lake Champlain." Gideon Fairman (1774-1827), engraver. $3\frac{1}{2} \times 5\frac{13}{16}$. Published in *Analectic Magazine* 11 (Philadelphia, April 1818). 69.178.1.

Thomas Addison Richards (1820-1900)

68. [Lake in Adirondacks]. $4\frac{3}{4}$ x $6\frac{5}{8}$. Published in Thomas Addison Richards, *American Scenery Illustrated* (New York: Leavitt & Allen Bros., 1854). 94.27.5.

Henry Room (ca. 1802-50)

69. "W. H. Bartlett." H. B. Holl, engraver. $4\frac{15}{16}$ x 4. Published in Nathaniel P. Willis, *American Scenery* (London: George Virtue, 1840). 61.54.1.

Fred. B. Schell

70. *General Grant & His Family.* Samuel Sartain (1830-1906), engraver. $13\frac{1}{4}$ x $9\frac{15}{16}$. Published in Philadelphia by Daughaday & Becker, 1868. 59.24.4.

James David Smillie (1833-1909)

71. [Upper Ausable Lake]. Engraved by the artist. $9\frac{3}{8}$ x $12\frac{1}{4}$. Published in *Gallery of Landscape Painters* (New York: G. P. Putnam & Co.; and London: Low, Son, Marston & Searle, 1872). 64.188.1.

Arthur Fitzwilliam Tait (1819-1905)

72. *Halt in the Woods.* Cottin, engraver. 22 x 31. Engraved in Paris. New York: Goupil & Co., 1856. 67.59.1.

Hendrick-Dirk Kruseman Van Elten (1829-1904)

73. "Mountain Mists. A Glimpse of Colden from the Lake." Robert Hinshelwood (b. 1812), engraver. $4\frac{7}{8}$ x $7\frac{5}{16}$. Published in *The Ladies Repository* (Cincinnati: Hitchcock & Walker, 1874). 92.41.2.

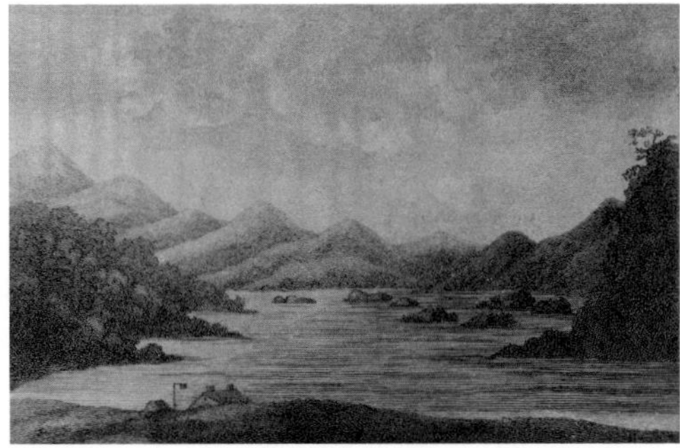

Daniel Wadsworth (1771-1848)

74. "Lake George, from Fort George." Simeon Smith Jocelyn (1799-1879), engraver. $2\frac{15}{16}$ x $4\frac{7}{16}$. Published in Benjamin Silliman, *Remarks Made, on a Short Tour Between Hartford and Quebec* (New Haven: S. Converse, 1820). 71.122.1.

William Guy Wall (1792-after 1863)

75. "The Junction of the Sacandaga and Hudson Rivers. No. 2 of the Hudson River Port Folio." John Rubens Smith (1775-1849) and John Hill (1770-1850), engravers. Aquatint, 14 x $21\frac{1}{8}$. Koke 76. 75.169.1.

76. "Hadley Falls. No. 5 of the Hudson River Port Folio." John Rubens Smith (1775-1849) and John Hill (1770-1850), engravers. Aquatint, $13\frac{3}{4}$ x $21\frac{1}{8}$. Koke 78, second state. 75.169.2.

Numbers 75 and 76 published in *The Hudson River Portfolio* (New York: H. I. Megarey & W. B. Gilley; and Charleston, S.C.: John Mill, 1821-2).

77. "Baker's Falls. No. 8 of the Hudson River Port Folio." John Hill (1770-1852), engraver. Aquatint, 14 x $21\frac{3}{16}$. Published in *The Hudson River Portfolio* (New York: G. & C. H. Carvill, 1828). Koke 87, second state. 75.169.3.

78. "The Erie Canal. And the Little Falls on the River Mohawk." Fenner Sears & Co., engraver. 7 x $8\frac{5}{8}$. Published in John Howard Hinton, *The History and Topography of the United States* (London: J. & F. Tallis, 1850). Attributed to Wall on the basis of 78.124.3 (checklist 79). 65.73.590.

79. "View of the Canal. At the Little Falls Mohawk River." Fenner Sears & Co., engraver. $3\frac{15}{16}$ x $6\frac{1}{16}$. Published in John Howard Hinton, *The History and Topography of the United States* (London: Simpkin, Marshall, and Wardle, 1830-32). 78.124.3.

Jacob C. Ward (1809-91)

80. "Outlet of Lake George: Rogers' Rock in the Distance." Thomas Hastings Cushman (1815-41), engraver. $4\frac{3}{4}$ x 7. Published on title page of *The New Yorker: A Weekly Journal* (New York: Horace Greeley & Co., 1840). 67.64.5.

Metal Engravings Based on Photographs

Silas A. Holmes

81. "Caldwell—Lake George. From the grounds of Fort William Henry Hotel." $2\frac{7}{8}$ x $4\frac{3}{4}$. 77.210.1.

82. "Head Waters of Lake George. From the grounds of Fort William Henry Hotel." $2\frac{13}{16}$ x $4\frac{13}{16}$. 77.210.2.

Numbers 81 and 82 published in *Nelson's Guide to Lake George and Lake Champlain* (New York and London: Thomas Nelson, 1859). The illustrations also appeared in later editions of this book. Holmes' studio was in New York City.

Anonymous Artists, Known Engravers

83. "The Adirondack." Charles Kennedy Burt (1823-92), engraver. 3 1/4 x 4 9/16. 67.96.44.

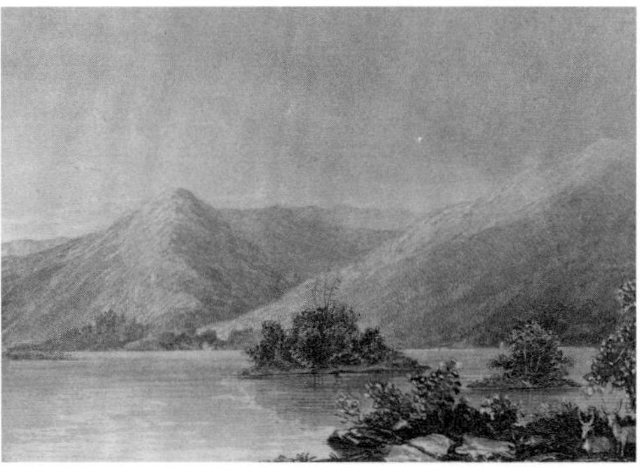

84. "A Scene on Forked Lake." Charles Kennedy Burt (1823-92), engraver. 3 1/4 x 4 9/16. 70.147.3.

Numbers 83 and 84 published in Joel T. Headley, *The Adirondack; or, Life in the Woods* (New York: Baker & Scribner, 1849).

85. "Lewis Lawrence." H. B. Hall's Sons, engraver. 7 5/16 x 5 1/16. Published in Thomas J. Brown, *Lewis Lawrence* (Utica: L. C. Childs & Son, 1887). 71.94.6.

86. "Lyman R. Lyon." Henry B. Hall & Sons, engraver. 4 3/8 x 4 1/2. Published in New York by H. B. Hall & Sons in an unidentified book. 66.101.1008.

87. "A North View of Fort Frederic or Crown Point." Proud, engraver. 6 7/8 x 9 1/8. Published in *The Royal Magazine* (London, January 1760). 77.93.2.

Anonymous Artists, Unknown Engravers

88. "Bear Fight." Vignette for bank note published by the National Bank Note Company, New York. 1 1/2 x 3. 61.34.2.

89. "Canoe." Vignette for bank note published by the National Bank Note Company, New York. 1 1/4 x 2 5/8. 61.34.1.

90. "Barclay's Iron Works, Ulston." 6 11/16 x 9 1/4. 68.29.1.

91. "The Palisade Rocks on the Hudson River, West Bank, New York." 6 11/16 x 9. 68.29.3.

Numbers 90 and 91 published in John Howard Hinton, *The History and Topography of the United States* (London: J. & F. Tallis, 1850).

92. "The Wild Lakes." 2 13/16 x 5 3/16. Published in John Todd, *Summer Gleanings: Or, Sketches and Incidents of a Pastor's Vacation* (Northampton: Hopkins, Bridgman and Co., 1852). 77.71.1.

93. "Erie Canal bei Little Falls." 4 1/16 x 6 1/16. Published in Germany, ca. 1859. Possibly copied from 82.11.10 (checklist 19). 82.11.7.

94. "Saratoga Lake." 4 x 6. Published in *Meyer's Universarum*, vol. 1 (New York: Herrmann J. Meyer, 1852). Possibly copied from 61.53.5 (checklist 14). 74.328.3.

95. "Trenton Falls (New-York)." 4 x 6. Published in Charles A. Dana, *The United States Illustrated*, vol. 1 (New York: Herrmann J. Meyer, ca. 1855). Possibly copied from 61.53.111 (checklist 16). 61.53.11.

96. "A Perspective View of Lake George." 10 1/16 x 6 1/8. Published in *The Universal Magazine of Knowledge and Pleasure* 25 (London: John Hinton, Nov. 1759). 76.78.1.

Artists' Etchings

Entries are arranged by artist, followed in alphabetical order by title, date, dimensions and accession number. On the rare occasion when an etching appeared in a publication, the publishing data (including dates) follow dimensions.

ALLEN BLAGDEN (b. 1938)

97. *Saranac.* 1988. $4^{15}/_{16}$ x $7^{5}/_{16}$. 88.41.1; 88.41.2.

98. *Saginaw.* 1988. $7^{1}/_{4}$ x $4^{15}/_{16}$. 88.41.3; 88.41.4.

PAUL BRANSOM (1885-1979)

99. [Buck]. ca. 1945. 7 x 5. 87.1.26.

WILLIAM DE LA MONTAGNE CARY (1840-1922)

100. [Fishing]. $7^{3}/_{8}$ x $21^{7}/_{8}$. (New York: Max Jacoby, 1892). 73.72.1.

101. [Trout fishing triptych]. $6^{7}/_{8}$ x $20^{15}/_{16}$. (New York: C. Klackner, ca. 1890). 77.178.1.

FOSTER DISINGER (fl. 1948-59)

102. *Great Pine. 8th Lake.* ca. 1950. $5^{15}/_{16}$ x $3^{3}/_{8}$. 66.56.1.

CHURCHILL ETTINGER

103. [Pair of geese landing]. ca. 1950. $5^{7}/_{8}$ x $7^{3}/_{4}$. 67.106.1.

104. *The Right Fly.* ca. 1950. $8^{15}/_{16}$ x $11^{7}/_{8}$. 67.106.2.

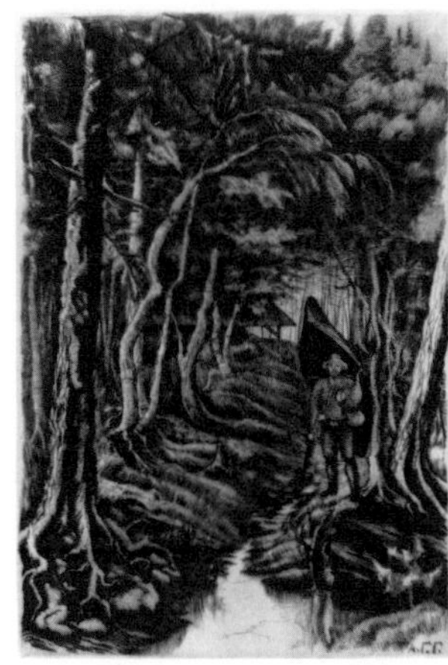

ARPAD GEYZA GERSTER (1848-1923)

105. *The End of the Carry.* 1893. $8^{11}/_{16}$ x $5^{3}/_{4}$. 58.273.1.

106. *Dandy.* n.d. 4 x 6. 58.273.2.

107. *Hank Bradley.* 1895. $4^{13}/_{16}$ x $4^{15}/_{16}$. 58.273.3.

108. [Big birch on Sumner Lake]. n.d. $2^{15}/_{16}$ x $4^{7}/_{8}$. 58.273.4.

109. *A Northwoods Island.* 1894. $4^{3}/_{8}$ x $5^{1}/_{2}$. 58.273.5.

110. *Alvah Dunning.* 1892. $5^{1}/_{2}$ x $5^{11}/_{16}$. 58.273.7.

111. [An old tramp]. 1892. $5^{5}/_{8}$ x $5^{1}/_{2}$. 58.273.8.

112. *Carry Pond. Sep. 10. 92. Dawn in the Adirondacks.* 1892. 4 x $5^{1}/_{4}$. 58.273.9.

113. *My Camp at Carry Point. Sept. 1892.* 1892. $3^{7}/_{16}$ x $5^{5}/_{8}$. 58.273.10.

114. *Ruins of Herreshoff Manor, Adirondacks.* 1893. $5^{3}/_{8}$ x $8^{5}/_{8}$. Gerster's drawing of the same subject is in the Adirondack Museum collection (81.26.47). 58.273.11.

115. *Bill Dart.* 1893. $3^{3}/_{4}$ x $3^{15}/_{16}$. 58.273.12.

116. *Bill Dart.* 1893. $3^{3}/_{4}$ x $3^{15}/_{16}$. 58.273.13.

117. *Cozy Corner in Camp Oteetiwi Raquette Lake Adirondacks.* 1893. $5^{3}/_{8}$ x $8^{3}/_{4}$. Gerster's drawing of the same subject is in the Adirondack Museum collection (81.26.34). 58.273.14.

118. *Old Jeff. Oct. 21, '84. Shedd Lake.* 1884. $2^{7}/_{8}$ x $4^{15}/_{16}$. 58.273.15.

119. *Pig Feast* [Menu]. 1899. $7^{7}/_{8}$ x $5^{15}/_{16}$. 58.273.16.

120. *Oteetiwi and Dandy Sept. 19, 1890.* 1890. $4^{7}/_{8}$ x $5^{15}/_{16}$. 58.273.17.

121. *Sumner Lake [1]890.* 1890. $3^{3}/_{8}$ x $5^{7}/_{8}$. 58.273.18.

122. [Camp]. n.d. $5^{5}/_{8}$ x $9^{3}/_{8}$. 58.273.19.

123. [Marsh with ducks]. n.d. $3^{1}/_{4}$ x $5^{15}/_{16}$. Gerster's drawings of the same subject are in the Adirondack Museum collection (81.26.17 and .22). 58.273.20.

124. [Marsh with boat]. n.d. $3^{1}/_{4}$ x $5^{7}/_{8}$. 58.273.21.

125. [Lake and mountains]. n.d. $5^{1}/_{2}$ x $8^{1}/_{2}$. 58.273.22.

126. [North Creek]. 1890. $3^{1}/_{4}$ x $5^{7}/_{8}$. Gerster's drawing of the same subject is in the Adirondack Museum collection (81.26.13). 58.273.23.

127. [Self portrait]. 1894. $4^{7}/_{8}$ x 3. 62.67.6.

JOHN HENRY HILL (1839-1922)

128. [Portrait of John William Hill]. $8^{7}/_{8}$ x $7^{7}/_{8}$. Published in John Henry Hill, *John William Hill: An Artist's Memorial* (New York: 1888). 57.132.5.

129. *The Narrows Lake George.* George W. Hill, surveyor. 1871. $7^{7}/_{8}$ x $11^{3}/_{8}$. 57.132.6.

130. *Upper Cascades of Shelving Rock.* October 1871. $7^{15}/_{16}$ x $11^{3}/_{8}$. 57.132.7.

131. [Lake George from Bolton]. 1872. $6^{7}/_{16}$ x $9^{3}/_{8}$. 92.4.1.

WINSLOW HOMER (1836-1910)

132. *Fly Fishing, Saranac Lake 1889.* 1889. $14^{1}/_{8}$ x $20^{7}/_{8}$. 76.217.1.

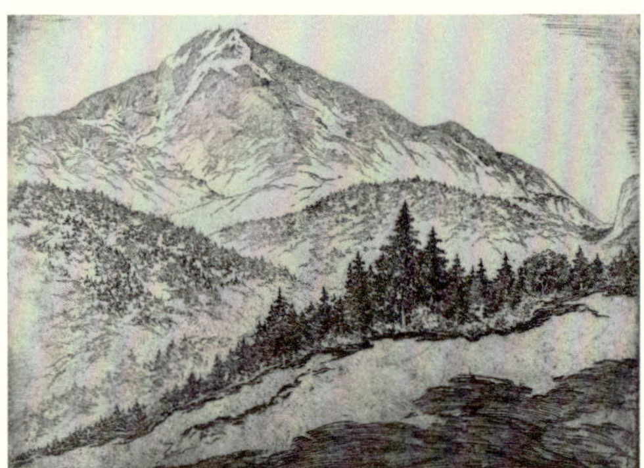

HERBERT S. KATES (1894-1947)

133. *Mt. Whiteface—Adirondacks.* n.d. 8 3/4 x 11 3/4. 66.112.8.

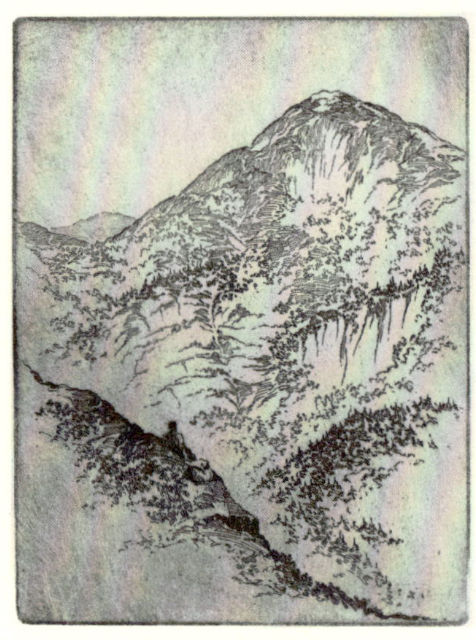

134. *Marcy from Haystack.* n.d. 7 15/16 x 5 15/16. Later state of 68.168.10 (checklist 144). 66.112.9.

135. *Cold River Country—Adirondacks.* n.d. 11 3/4 x 8 3/4. 68.168.1.

136. *Adirondack Campsite.* n.d. 9 x 11 7/8. 68.168.2.

137. *Wanika Falls Lean-to.* n.d. 8 3/4 x 11 5/8. 68.168.3.

138. *Lake Placid Valley from Cobble Hill.* n.d. 11 13/16 x 7 3/8. 68.168.4.

139. *Indian Falls Camp on Mt. Marcy—Adirondack Mountain.* n.d. 7 13/16 x 12. 68.168.5.

140. *The Range—Adirondack Mountains.* n.d. 5 x 11. 68.168.6.

141. *Flowed Lands—Adirondacks.* n.d. 5 3/4 x 7 3/4. 68.168.7.

142. *Adirondack Lean-to.* n.d. 2 7/8 x 4 1/4. 68.168.8.

143. *Indian Pass Lean-to.* n.d. 9 7/8 x 6 5/8. 68.168.9.

144. *Marcy from Haystack.* n.d. 7 3/4 x 5 7/8. Earlier state of 66.112.9 (checklist 134). Kates' drawing of the same subject is in the Adirondack Museum collection (77.103.1). 68.168.10.

145. *Giant Mountain from St. Hubert's.* n.d. 4 7/8 x 6 7/8. 68.168.11.

146. *Adirondack Mountain Club Lodge.* 1926. 4 7/8 x 6 5/8. 77.102.1.

147. *Hills Rock.* [Home of Rev. Walter Lowrie, Keene Valley]. n.d. 3 1/4 x 4 3/8. 77.102.2.

148. *The MacDonald Hospice on Marcy.* n.d. 3 x 2 3/8. 77.102.3.

STEPHEN PARRISH (1846-1938)

149. [Flooded Lands—Adirondacks]. 1880. 4 1/4 x 7 3/8. Parrish's oil sketch of the same subject is in the Adirondack Museum collection (82.131.1). 82.131.2.

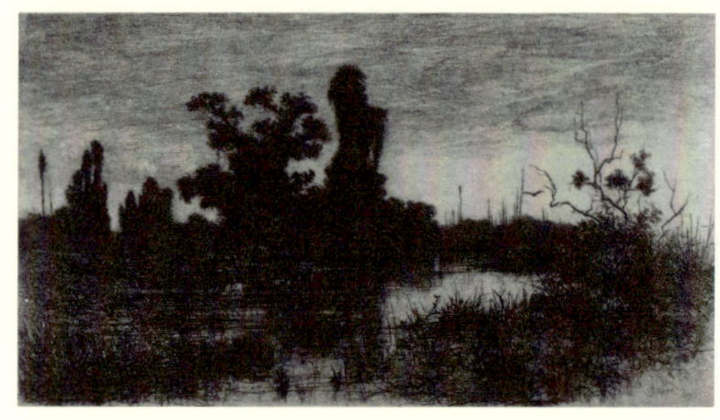

150. [On the Schroon—Evening]. 1880. 8 3/4 x 15 1/4 . 82.131.3.

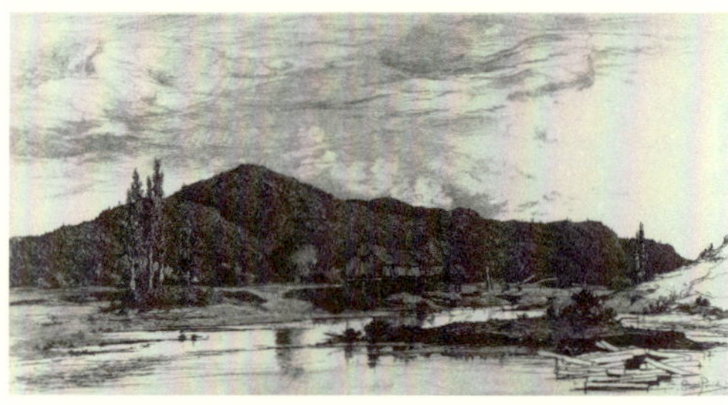

151. [The Upper Hudson]. ca. 1880. 10 x 18 7/8. 82.131.4.

152. *On the Schroon—Drought.* ca. 1880. 3 7/8 x 7 1/8. 82.131.5.

153. *Lewisburg on the Scroon* [*sic*]. ca. 1880. 4 13/16 x 8 1/4. 82.131.6.

154. *Deserted Mill—Adirondacks.* ca. 1880. 4 1/2 x 7 1/8. 82.131.7.

155. *Mills on the Schroon.* ca. 1880. 5 5/8 x 10 1/2. 82.131.8.

GEORGE H. SHORER

156. *The Wilderness.* n.d. 9 7/8 x 7 7/8. 66.45.12.

JAMES DAVID SMILLIE (1833-1909)

157. *A Glass with the Squire.* 1886. 8 3/8 x 6 3/4. After Eastman Johnson (1824-1906). 62.67.8.

158. *A Voice from the Cliff. After Winslow Homer.* 1886. 6 13/16 x 10 1/8. 62.67.

Lithographs

Generally, entries are arranged alphabetically by lithographer. Where possible, prints appear grouped according to their original publication or publisher, listed alphabetically by title. Names of artists and draftsmen follow titles, then dimensions, date or publishing data (unless grouped), and accession number(s).

Exceptions to this order include prints associated with Colvin (artist, not lithographer). Since the museum's collection of his prints originally appeared in reports to the state of New York, they are arranged by date of report, then by order of appearance, i.e. original plate number, within a report.

Lithographs after the artist Milbert present a second exception. Under his name they are listed alphabetically by title, grouped within their original publication.

A. T. Anthony & Co.

159. [Ausable Chasm]. W. G. Waters, artist. Chromolithograph, 20 x 14. Published ca. 1890. 61.2.2.

John T. Bowen (ca. 1801-ca. 1856)

160. "Gulo Luscus, Lin. The Wolverine." John James Audubon (1785-1851), artist. $16\frac{3}{8}$ x $23\frac{1}{2}$. Published in John James Audubon and John Bachman, *The Viviparous Quadrupeds of North America* (Philadelphia, 1845-48). 78.43.1.

John H. Bufford (1810-70)

161. "Distant View of Mt. Marcy." Ebenezer Emmons (1799-1863), artist. 58.321.4; 61.38.5.

162. "Falls of the Genesee." $6\frac{3}{8}$ x $8\frac{1}{8}$. 61.38.1.

163. "Rossie Lead Vein." 8 x $5\frac{15}{16}$. 61.38.3; 58.321.5.

❦ 164. "Trap Dyke at Avalanche Lake." Charles Cromwell Ingham (1796-1863), artist. $9\frac{1}{4}$ x $11\frac{1}{4}$. 58.321.2; 68.155.1.

165. "Trap Dyke at Avalanche Lake." Charles Cromwell Ingham (1796-1863), artist. $9\frac{1}{4}$ x $11\frac{1}{4}$. Same subject as above, redrawn for the second edition of the text. 61.38.9.

166. "View at Lake Colden." Charles Cromwell Ingham (1796-1863), artist. 7 x $10\frac{1}{2}$. Attributed to Ingham on the basis of 70.147.1 (checklist 58), the engraving in Headley's *The Adirondack; or, Life in the Woods*. 58.321.6; 61.38.7.

167. "View of Mt. McMartin." $6\frac{1}{4}$ x $8\frac{7}{8}$. 58.321.3; 61.38.4.

168. "View of the Adirondack Mountains." Ebenezer Emmons (1799-1863), artist. $7\frac{7}{16}$ x $12\frac{3}{8}$. 58.321.7; 61.38.8; 67.84.1.

169. "View of the Dial Mountain." $5\frac{7}{8}$ x 8. 58.31.8; 61.38.10.

❦ 170. "View of the Indian Pass." Charles Cromwell Ingham (1796-1863), artist. $9\frac{1}{8}$ x $9\frac{13}{16}$. Based on Ingham's painting *The Great Adirondack Pass, Painted on the Spot*, 1837, in the Adirondack Museum collection (66.114.1). 61.38.6; 65.35.1.

171. "View of the Indian Pass, from Lake Henderson." $6\frac{3}{16}$ x $8\frac{5}{16}$. 58.321.1; 61.38.2.

Numbers 161-171 published in Ebenezer Emmons, *New York State Geological Report for 1837* (Albany 1838 and 1840), except for numbers 164 and 165, published only in the first and second editions, respectively.

172. [Three children]. $14\frac{1}{8}$ x 11. Published in Boston by John H. Bufford's Sons, 1876. 74.288.1.

173. *Deer Shooting in the Adirondacks*. $5\frac{1}{2}$ x $7\frac{1}{8}$. Published in Boston by J. H. Bufford's Sons, 1880. 66.51.1.

Lucien R. Burleigh (1853-1923)

174. *Port Henry, N. Y.* $15\frac{1}{2}$ x $28\frac{3}{4}$. Published in Troy, N. Y., by L. R. Burleigh, 1889. 82.25.1.

175. *Warrensburgh* [*sic*], *N. Y.* $10\frac{3}{8}$ x $29\frac{1}{2}$. Published in Troy, N. Y., by L. R. Burleigh, 1891. 74.93.1.

Verplanck Colvin (1847-1920)

176. "Mount Seward, from Lake Incapahcho or Long Lake." $4\frac{3}{4}$ x 8. Published in "Ascent and Barometrical Measurement of Mount Seward" in *The 24th Annual Report on the New York State Museum of Natural History for the Year 1870* (Albany: The Argus Company, 1872). 67.96.43.

177. "Station, Crown Point Light House." $5\frac{1}{4}$ x $4\frac{15}{16}$. [Plate 1]. 70.147.48.

178. "Automatic Signal. Stan-Helio." $4\frac{1}{4}$ x $3\frac{3}{4}$. [Plate 2]. 70.147.49.

179. "Adirondack Survey 1873 Primary Triangle of Mount Hurricane." 9¾ x 16½. [Plate 4]. 85.26.2; 94.27.4.
180. "The Heart of the Adirondacks. View from Nippletop." E. H. Ricke, lithographic draftsman. 13 x 34. [Plate 5]. 70.147.42.
181. "Blue Mountain. Middle chopping—rendering visible the Mountain Peaks necessary for measurement." 4 3/16 x 3 13/16. [Plate 8]. 70.147.44.
182. "On Blue Mountain. Timber cutting for view of Snowy Mtn. and triangular measurement." 4 1/16 x 3 9/16. [Plate 9]. 70.147.45; 94.27.1.
183. "On Ampersand Mountain. Adirondack Survey Clearing." 4⅜ x 6. [Plate 10]. 70.147.73.
184. "Mud Lake. Winter march, westward into the unexplored." 4 1/16 x 6⅞. [Plate 12]. 70.147.46; 94.27.2.
185. "St. Lawrence Co. Line. Decaying condition of marked trees." 5½ x 4 3/16. [Plate 13]. 70.147.51.
186. "Oven Lake. Accident to the second boat—the Guides [*sic*] baggage and instruments in danger." 5⅜ x 4⅞. [Plate 14]. 70.147.47.
187. "Rocket Signal. New method of approximately determining the location of new lakes in the woods." 5⅞ x 4¾. [Plate 15]. 70.147.50.
188. "Plan Showing Method of Mountain Measurement with barometer and spirit-level Distances by Triangulation." E. H. Ricke, lithographic draftsman. 7⅛ x 4 1/16. [Plate 16]. 70.147.62; 94.27.3.

Numbers 177-188 published in *Report on the Topographical Survey of the Adirondack Wilderness of New York*. (Albany: Printed by Weed, Parsons and Company for the State of New York, 1874). Plates lithographed by Weed, Parsons and Company.

189. "Lake Tear of the Clouds. The Source of the Hudson River." Chromolithograph. 4¼ x 7. [Plate 1]. 70.147.70.
190. "Triangulation. Signals at Base-line, New Form devised by the Superintendent." [Five illustrations]. 6¼ x 4. [Plate 2]. 70.147.63.
191. "Triangulation. New Method of centering Signal over Monument used on the Adirondack Survey." 6½ x 4 1/16. [Plate 3]. 70.147.60.
192. "Triangulation. Portable Revolving Signal, Devised by the Superintendent." 4 x 5⅝. [Plate 4]. 70.147.57.
193. "Self Recording Deep-Water Thermometer, Used on hydrographic work of Survey." 6 7/16 x 4. [Plate 5, instrument descending]. 70.147.55.
194. "Self Recording Deep-Water Thermometer, Used on hydrographic work of Survey." 6⅜ x 4. [Plate 6, instrument ascending]. 70.147.56.
195. "Improved Signaling Instrument. The Adirondack Survey paralell [*sic*]-movement Heliotrope." 4 1/16 x 6⅜. [Plate 7]. 70.147.67.
196. "Rod-Level and Tripod. Devised by the Superintendent, and used on Division of Levels of Adirondack Survey." 6⅜ x 4 1/16. [Plate 8]. 70.147.61.
197. "The Crest of the Gothics. View Southward." 9¼ x 26¾. [Plate 9]. 70.147.41.
198. "Lower Au Sable Lake. Survey Party on the return from Mount Marcy. March on the Ice Nov. 1875." 4⅛ x 6⅜. [Plate 10]. 70.147.79.
199. "Meteorology. Remarkable Triple Rainbow, June 1876." Chromolithograph, 4⅛ x 6½. [Plate 11]. 70.147.72.
200. "Triangulation. Survey Party leaving Summit of Mt. Hurricane. The Guides carrying the grand Theodolite and Telescope &c." 4⅛ x 6 15/16. [Plate 12]. 70.147.66.
201. "Time Signal. Nine o'clock Powder-Flash on Mt. Emmons. 1876." 4⅛ x 6 15/16. [Plate 13]. 70.147.74.
202. "Fulton Chain of Lakes. View E. - S. E. From Mt. Louis or Bald Mountain of the Fulton Chain." 9¼ x 24⅞. [Plate 14]. 70.147.40.
203. "Triangulation. Mount St. Louis. The Bald Mountain of The Fulton Chain." 6 7/16 x 4¼. [Plate 15]. 70.147.53.
204. "Tertiary Triangulation. Sub-Base-Line. Measured on the Ice of Raquette Lake Feb. 1877." 4¼ x 6¼. [Plate 16]. 70.147.77.
205. "Above the Clouds. Signal on the Summit of Mt. Marcy. The highest Land in New York. July 1877." 6 5/16 x 4 3/16. [Plate 17]. 70.147.54.
206. "Mount Haystack From Upper Ausable Inlet." 4⅛ x 7. [Plate 18]. 70.147.68.
207. "Exploration. Middle Western Division. Hawk Lake from the South Shore.—July 1878." 4¼ x 6⅜. [Plate 19]. 70.147.76.
208. "Exploration. Camp of the Mid. Western Division on Hawk Lake." Chromolithograph, 4⅛ x 6½. [Plate 20]. 70.147.78.
209. "The Great Corner. From which the Lines of the Patents of Totten and Crossfield and Macomb part, dividing Millions of Acres of Land." 4⅛ x 6⅜. [Plate 21]. 70.147.69; 94.28.2.
210. "North Eastern Division. River Survey Party, Showing Camp Transitmen, Flagmen and Chainmen, and Triangulation Signal on Mountain." 4 1/16 x 6⅜. [Plate 22]. 70.147.75.

211. "Primary Triangulation. Guides and Packmen carrying Instruments and Supplies to the Summit of Lyon Mountain." 6 3/8 x 4 1/8. [Plate 23]. 92.41.13.
212. "Triangulation. Lyon Mountain Station, Head-Quarters of Survey 1878. Sketch showing the Signal, Grand Theodolite, Buildings and Clearings made to afford a View of the Signals on other Mountain Peaks. View Southward, Whiteface Mountain in the Distance." 13 3/8 x 20 3/8. [Plate 24]. 70.147.43.
213. "Sextant Reconnaissance. Lyon Mountain 1878." 4 1/8 x 6 5/16. [Plate 25]. 70.147.71.
214. "River Survey. High Falls of the Saranac River, Showing difficulties encountered in Chain-Measurement." 6 15/16 x 4 1/16. [Plate 26]. 92.41.12.
215. "Division of Levels. Measurement of Whiteface Mountain with Spirit-Level and graduated Rod." 5 3/4 x 4 1/4. [Plate 27]. 70.147.58.
216. "Meteorology. Ulloa's Rings. Observed from Summit of Whiteface Mt. Oct. 1878." Chromolithograph, 6 1/2 x 4 1/4. [Plate 28]. 70.147.64.
217. "S. N. Y. Adirondack Survey Verplanck Colvin, Superintendent. Sketch Showing Plan of Station on Lyon Mountain 1878." 9 5/8 x 11 1/2. 70.147.38.

Numbers 188-217 published in *Seventh Annual Report of the Topographical Survey of the Adirondack Region of New York* (New York: Printed by Weed, Parsons and Company for the State of New York, 1880). Plates lithographed by Weed, Parsons and Company.

218. "Chateaugay Lake. From Near the Outlet. Showing Character of Lands in Township 5 of Old Military Tract" 5 5/8 x 17 7/8. [Plate 15]. 70.147.39.
219. "High Adirondack Peaks and Wild Forest. Westward From Basin Mountain." 5 15/16 x 39 1/2. 74.133.1.

Numbers 218 and 219 published in *Report on the Adirondack and State Land Surveys to the Year 1884* (Albany: Printed by Weed, Parsons and Company for the State of New York, 1884). Plates lithographed by Weed, Parsons and Company.

220. [Surveyors on mountain top in winter]. H. W. Whicks, lithographic draftsman. 11 7/8 x 18 3/8. Probably printed in one of the survey reports. 67.11.1.

Nathaniel Currier (1813-88)

221. *American Forest Scene. Maple Sugaring.* Arthur Fitzwilliam Tait (1819-1905), artist. 18 3/8 x 26 5/8. 1856. 72.137.1.
222. *American Winter Sports. Trout Fishing "on Chateaugay Lake." (Franklin Co. N. Y.)* A. F. Tait, artist. Drawn on stone by Charles Parsons (1821-1910). 18 x 25 13/16. Printed in New York by Endicott & Co., 1856. 65.42.7.
223. *Arguing the Point.* A. F. Tait, artist. Drawn on stone by Louis Maurer (1832-1932). 18 3/8 x 24. 1855. 65.42.14.
224. *Catching a Trout. "We hab you now, sar."* A. F. Tait, artist. Drawn on stone by Otto Knirsch. 18 3/16 x 25 3/4. 1854. 64.152.1.
225. [American Winter Sports. Deer Shooting "On the Shattagee [*sic*]"]. A. F. Tait, artist. Drawn on stone by Louis Maurer (1832-1932). 17 13/16 x 25 7/8. Title supplied. 1855. Based on Tait's painting *Still Hunting on the First Snow: A Second Shot*, 1855, in the Adirondack Museum collection (65.36.1). 64.152.4.
226. *Surrender of General Burgoyne at Saratoga, N. Y., Oct. 17th, 1777.* John Trumbull (1756-1843), artist. Drawn on stone by Otto Knirsch. 15 9/16 x 24 5/8. 1852. 81.50.1.

Numbers 221-226 published in New York by N. Currier.

Nathaniel Currier (1813-88) and James Merritt Ives (1824-95)

227. *Saratoga Lake.* William Henry Bartlett (1809-54), artist. 8 1/2 x 12 1/2. n.d. 73.124.10.
228. *Indian Lake—Sunset.* B. Hess, artist. 14 3/8 x 22 5/8. 1866. 58.322.1.
229. *Indian Lake—Sunset.* B. Hess, artist. Drawn on stone by Frederick Blumner. 14 3/4 x 22 3/4. 1860. 65.42.12.
230. *Camping Out. "Some of the Right Sort."* Louis Maurer (1832-1932), artist. 18 3/4 x 27 1/4. 1856. 64.152.9.
231. *Life in the Woods. "Starting Out."* Louis Maurer (1832-1932), artist. 18 3/4 x 27 3/8. 1860. 72.59.1.
232. *American Hunting Scenes. "A Good Chance."* Arthur Fitzwilliam Tait (1819-1905), artist. 18 1/2 x 27 1/2. 1863. 64.152.8.
233. *American Hunting Scenes. "An Early Start."* A. F. Tait, artist. 18 3/4 x 27 1/2. 1863. 64.152.7.
234. *American Speckled Brook Trout.* A. F. Tait, artist. Chromolithograph, 16 x 22. Printed by Charles Parsons (1821-1910). 1864. 73.140.1.
235. *Camping in the Woods. "A Good Time Coming."* A. F. Tait, artist. 18 1/2 x 27 1/2. 1863. 63.203.1.

236. *Camping in the Woods. "Laying Off."* A. F. Tait, artist. 18 3/4 x 27 5/8. 1863. 64.152.5.

237. *The Infant Brood.* A. F. Tait, artist. 8 3/4 x 12 7/16. n.d. 73.124.13.

238. *Life of a Hunter. "Catching a Tartar."* A. F. Tait, artist. 18 1/2 x 27 3/16. 1861. 64.152.6.

239. *Among the Pines. A First Settlement.* 8 7/16 x 12 1/2. n.d. 73.124.16.

240. *An Anxious Moment. "A Three Pounder Sure."* 14 x 18 1/2. 1874. 65.42.11.

241. *Autumn on Lake George.* 8 1/2 x 12 3/8. n.d. 67.90.1.

242. *Autumn on Lake George.* 7 15/16 x 12 7/16. n.d. 91.16.1.

243. *Autumn in the Adirondacks. Lake Harrison.* 7 15/16 x 12 1/4. n.d. 66.240.1.

244. *Brook Trout,—Just Caught.* 11 x 16 3/4. n.d. 68.189.3.

245. *Deer Shooting. In the Northern Woods.* 8 1/2 x 12 3/8. n.d. 65.42.6.

246. *Flushing a Woodcock.* 7 7/16 x 12 1/2. n.d. 73.124.20.

247. *Home from the Brook. The Lucky Fishermen.* 16 3/4 x 27 7/8. 1867. 65.42.9.

248. *A Home in the Wilderness.* 7 15/16 x 12 1/2. 1870. 65.42.1.

249. *The Home of the Deer.* 9 7/8 x 15 3/8. n.d. 67.34.1.

250. *The Hunter's Shanty. In the Adirondacks.* 14 15/16 x 20 7/16. 1861. 62.10.1.

251. *Hunting Fishing and Forest Scenes. Shanty-ing on the Lake Shore.* 17 x 25. 1867. 65.42.8.

252. *Hunting in the Northern Woods.* 8 7/16 x 12 7/16. n.d. 65.42.5.

253. *In the Northern Wilds. Trapping Beaver.* 7 7/8 x 12 7/16. n.d. 65.42.3.

254. *Lake George. Black Mountain.* 8 x 12 1/2. n.d. 68.53.2.

255. *Life in the Woods. "Returning to Camp."* 18 3/4 x 27 1/2. 1860. 64.152.10.

256. *The Life of a Sportsman. Camping in the Woods.* 8 7/16 x 12 1/2. 1872. 73.124.5.

257. *The Life of a Sportsman. Coming into Camp.* 8 7/16 x 12 1/2. 1872. 67.90.2.

258. *The Life of a Sportsman. Going Out.* 8 7/16 x 12 3/8. 1872. 73.124.8.

259. *The Lincoln Family.* 8 1/16 x 12 1/2. 1867. 66.3.67.

260. *Maple Sugaring. Early Spring in the Northern Woods.* 8 1/2 x 12 7/16. 1872. 73.124.9.

261. *A Mountain Ramble.* 8 3/8 x 12 7/16. n.d. 65.42.13.

262. *Patridge [sic] Shooting.* 8 3/16 x 12 1/2. 1870. 73.124.17.

263. *Placid Lake. Adirondacks.* 8 x 12 7/16. n.d. 65.42.10.

264. *Racquet [sic] River. "Adirondacks."* 8 1/2 x 12 1/2. n.d. 91.16.2.

265. [Quails]. 8 3/8 x 12 7/16. 1871. 73.124.2.

266. *Sacandaga Creek.* 5 3/8 x 7 3/8. n.d. 71.153.1.

267. *Saratoga Springs, N. Y.* 7 15/16 x 12 3/8. n.d. 73.124.19.

268. *The Source of the Hudson, in the Indian Pass, Adirondacks.* 8 3/8 x 12 7/16. n.d. 65.42.2.

269. *Sunrise on Lake Saranac.* 18 11/16 x 27 1/4. 1860. 64.152.2.

270. *View on the St. Lawrence. Indian Encampment.* 7 7/8 x 12 7/16. n.d. 68.189.1.

271. *The Washington Family.* 8 1/16 x 12 3/8. 1867. 66.3.66.

272. *A Well-bred Setter.* 7 7/8 x 12 3/8. 1871. 73.124.18.

273. *Wild Duck Shooting. On the Wing.* 8 x 12 3/8. n.d. 73.124.14.

274. *Woodcock Shooting.* 8 x 12 7/16. 1870. 73.124.6.

Numbers 227-274 published in New York by Currier & Ives.

George Endicott (1802-48)

275. "Lake Catharine." John William Hill (1812-79), artist. 6 7/8 x 9 1/2. 85.26.1.

276. "Lake Catharine, Hamilton Co." John William Hill (1812-79), artist. Drawn on stone by Eliphalet M. Brown, Jr. (1816-86). 81.75.1; 66.95.2.

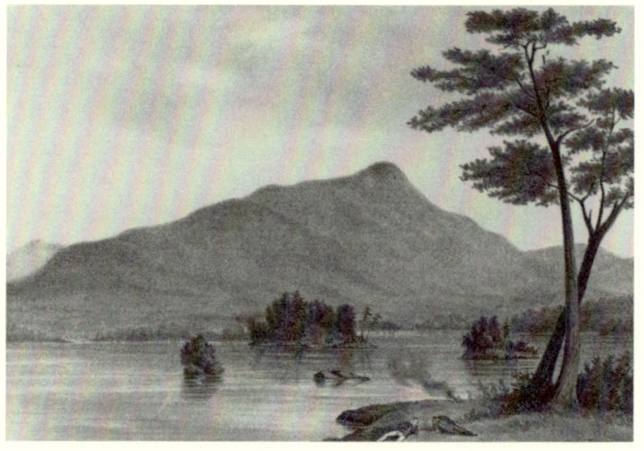

277. "Lake Janet, Hamilton Co. New York." John William Hill (1812-79), artist. 6 3/4 x 9 1/2. 66.95.1.

278. "Lake Janet, Hamilton Co." John William Hill (1812-79), artist. Drawn on stone by Hill. 6 13/16 x 9 7/16. 70.147.11.

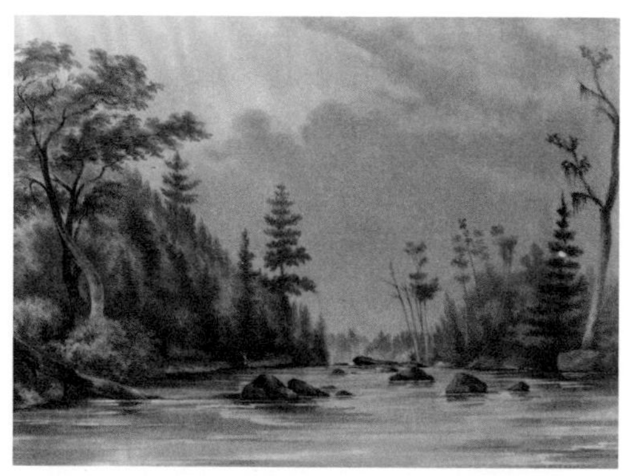

279. "View on Cedar River, Hamilton County." John William Hill (1812-79), artist. 7¼ x 9½. 70.147.10.

Numbers 275-279 printed in New York by George Endicott. Published in Ebenezer Emmons, *Geology of New-York, Part IV, No. 2* (Albany, 1842).

280. *View from Prospect Hill. Near Lake George.* John William Hill (1812-79), artist. 8¼ x 12⅝. Published in New York by George Endicott, 1834. 79.29.1.

Gray Lithograph Company

281. *Peoples Evening Line. New Jersey Steamboat Company.* Chromolithograph, 18¾ x 37¾. Advertisement published in New York in 1896. 66.124.9; 66.124.12.

W. L. Greene & Company

282. *Lake George.* Chromolithograph, 9 11/16 x 11⅝. Published in Boston, probably as a supplement for *The Congregationalist.* 70.95.1.

Hallen & Weiner

283. *Mill on Indian Lake, N. Y.* Chandler, artist. Chromolithograph, 16 x 20. 77.221.1.

Laurence S. Harris

284. *Good Bye, Dad, I'm Off To Fight For Old Glory, You Buy U. S. Gov't Bonds.* World War I poster. 88.2.3.

Haskell & Allen

285. *Autumn on Lake George.* 8½ x 12¾. Published in Boston by Haskell & Allen. 67.85.1.

286. *Placid Lake. Adirondacks.* 7 15/16 x 12⅜. Published in Boston by Haskell & Allen. Copied from Currier & Ives print with same title, 65.42.10 (checklist 263). 64.93.2.

J. Hoover

287. [Landscape]. W. S. Hunt, artist. Chromolithograph, 16⅛ x 21 15/16. Published in Philadelphia by J. Hoover, 1893. 77.100.1.

288. [Landscape with deer]. Chandler, artist. Chromolithograph, 16 x 22. Published in Philadelphia by J. Hoover, 1893. 77.100.2.

289. [Mill at Night]. Chromolithograph, 15¼ x 18⅞. Published in Philadelphia by J. Hoover & Son, 1897. 55.1.112.

Thomas Hunter

290. *Autumn Scene in the Adirondacks.* A. H. Bosch, artist. Chromolithograph, 11⅜ x 16⅞. Published in Philadelphia by Hunter & Duval, 1872. 58.355.1.

291. *Autumn Scene in the Adirondacks.* A. H. Bosch, artist. Chromolithograph, 11⅜ x 16⅞. Published in Philadelphia by Thomas Hunter for the National Chromo Co., 1872. 75.49.1.

E. B. & E. C. Kellogg

292. "Alexander Macomb." William Henry Brown (1808-83), artist. 13⅜ x 9 15/16. Published in *Portrait Gallery of Distinguished Americans* (Hartford: E. B. & E. C. Kellogg, 1846). 66.58.1.

Rockwell Kent (1882-1970)

293. *Adirondack Cabin.* 9½ x 12 7/16. Signed by the artist in pencil, 1946. 90.11.1.

William Lees & Co.

294. *Blue Mountain Lake. Adirondacks.* Levi Wells Prentice (1851-1935), artist. 10 3/16 x 15½. Published in Syracuse, N. Y., by William Lees & Co., n.d. 57.272.1.

Lyon & Company

295. *Life in the Woods. The Hunter's Camp.* Drawn on stone by Jacob Rau. 16½ x 23¾. Published in New York by Lyon & Co., 1867. 78.30.1.

Ferdinand Mayer

296. "Spaulding House, Main Street Crown Point, N. Y." 7½ x 12. Possibly published in an atlas, ca. 1876. 94.28.6.

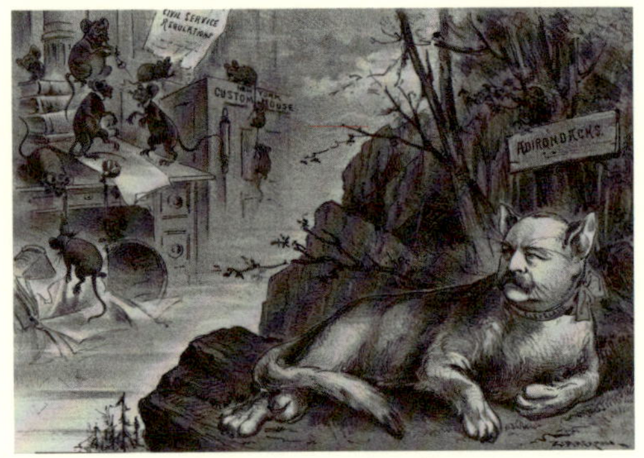

Mayer, Merkel & Ottmann

297. *When the Cat's Away, the Mice Will Play.* Zimmerman, artist. Chromolithograph, $7^{1}/_{2}$ x $11^{7}/_{8}$. Published in *Puck* (New York, 1885). 84.3.6.

Andrew Melrose

298. *Lake George.* Andrew Melrose, artist. Chromolithograph, 22 x 36. n.p., n.d. 78.128.1.

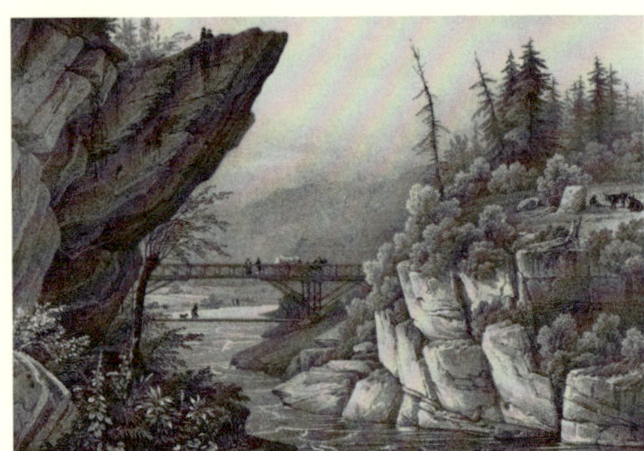

Jacques Gérard Milbert (1766-1840)

299. "Bridge on the Hudson River near Luzerne." $7^{3}/_{4}$ x $11^{1}/_{4}$. 93.12.4.

300. "Canada Creek Falls." $7^{7}/_{16}$ x $11^{3}/_{16}$. 68.231.1.

301. "Commencement of the Falls of Canada Creek." $7^{1}/_{2}$ x 11. 68.231.2.

302. [Cours de l'Hudson et Moulins Près Sandy-Hill]. $7^{3}/_{4}$ x $11^{1}/_{4}$. Proof before letters, title inscribed in pencil. 78.49.3.

303. "Deer Creek Falls." $11^{1}/_{4}$ x $7^{1}/_{2}$. 69.88.2.

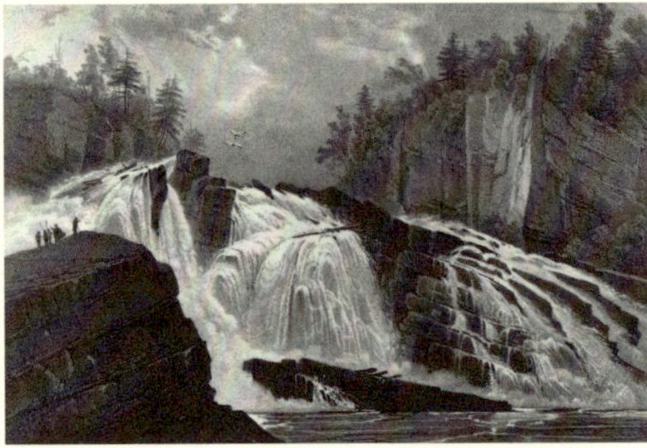

304. [Extrémité de la Chute d'Adley's]. $7^{3}/_{4}$ x $11^{1}/_{4}$. Proof before letters, title inscribed in pencil. 78.49.2.

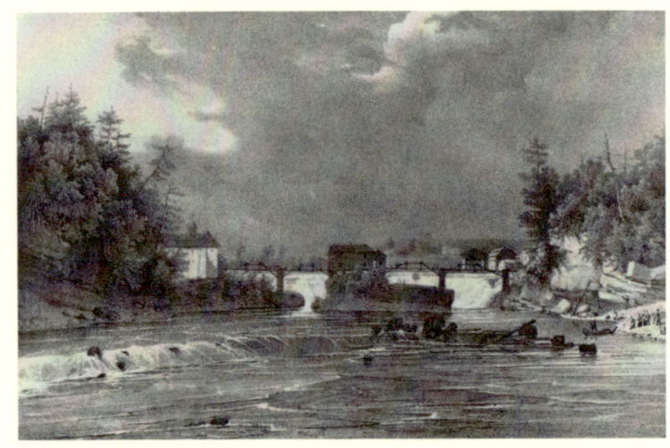

305. "Hudson Fall [*sic*] at the village of Gleens [*sic*]." $7^{7}/_{8}$ x $11^{1}/_{4}$. 93.12.1.

306. "Jessups Landing." $7^{11}/_{16}$ x $11^{3}/_{16}$. 68.231.3.

307. "Lake George and the Village of Caldwell." $7^{3}/_{4}$ x $11^{1}/_{8}$. 72.150.1; 93.12.3.

308. "Mills on the Black River." $7^{9}/_{16}$ x $11^{1}/_{8}$. 93.12.5.

309. [Rapides de l'Hudson à Adeley's]. $7^{5}/_{8}$ x $11^{3}/_{16}$. Proof before letters, title inscribed in pencil. 78.49.1.

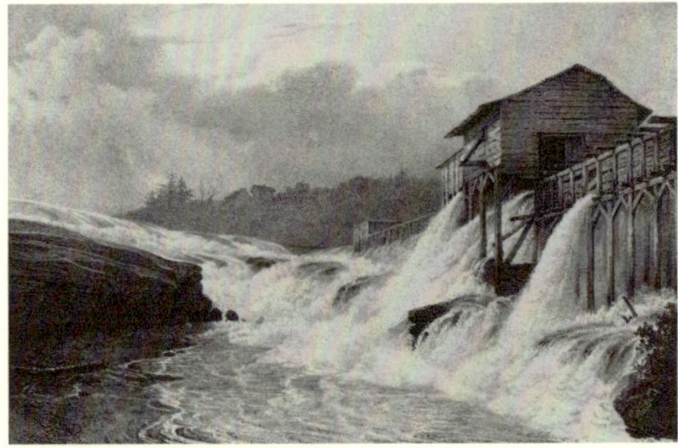

310. "Saw-mill at the village of Glenns [*sic*]." $7^{5}/_{8}$ x $11^{5}/_{8}$. 93.12.2.

311. "Sawmill near Luzerne Source of the Hudson." $7^{3}/_{34}$ x $11^{1}/_{8}$. 69.88.1.

312. "White-Hall, Lake Champlain." $7^{5}/_{8}$ x $11^{3}/_{16}$. 72.150.2.

Numbers 299-312 published in Jacques Gérard Milbert, *Itinéraire pittoresque du fleuve Hudson et des parties latérales de l'Amérique du Nord* (Paris: Gaugain et Cie., 1828-29).

Muller, Luchsinger & Co.

313. *Skating by Moonlight.* Chandler, artist. Chromolithograph, $13^{3}/_{4}$ x $18^{3}/_{8}$. Published in New York by Muller, Luchsinger & Co., 1895. 55.1.113.

Frank F. Oakley

314. *View on the Raquette River, N. Y.* Frederic Rondel (1826-92), artist. $7^{7}/_{8}$ x $10^{3}/_{8}$. Published in Boston by Frank F. Oakley, ca. 1861. 87.9.1.

J. Ottmann Lith. Co.

315. *In the Adirondacks.* Arthur Fitzwilliam Tait (1819-1905), artist. Chromolithograph, 16 x 11. Published by J. Ottmann Lith. Co. as a supplement to *The Art Amateur*, no. 230. 85.63.1.

Richard H. Pease

316. *A Prospective View of the Battle Fought near Lake George on the 8th of Sept. 1755, between 2000 English, with 250 Mohawks.* 9 15/16 x 19 3/4. Lithographed by R. H. Pease of Albany in 1852 from a survey by Samuel Blodget engraved by Thomas Jeffreys of London in 1756. 83.83.2.

Louis Prang & Company

317. *Blacksmith Shop.* Chromolithograph, 12 x 19 7/8. Published in Boston by L. Prang & Co., 1874. 68.90.1.

318. *Quails.* Arthur Fitzwilliam Tait (1819-1905), artist. C. W. Harring, drawn on stone. Chromolithograph, 10 1/4 x 14. Published in Boston by L. Prang & Co., 1867. 66.12.1.

319. [Quails]. Proof book for *Quails*, 16 sheets, 10 1/4 x 14. 67.50.1.

Sackett & Wilhelms Litho. & Printing Company

320. "Midsummer Medley. Roughing it in the Adirondack Mountains." Color halftone. 11 x 17. Published in New York by the Judge Publishing Company in a magazine dated 1897. 88.34.1.

F. Sala

321. *American Hunting Scenes.* 17 1/4 x 22 3/4. Published in Berlin by F. Sala, n.d. 65.63.1; 65.63.2.

Gretchen Dow Simpson

322. *Franny's Chairs.* Lithograph and silkscreen, printed in color. 11 7/8 x 8 5/8. 1986. Title, artist's signature, date, and edition statement (32/100) in pencil below image. 87.7.1.

Edward Sintzenich

323. *Lake George.* Richard William Hubbard (1816-88), artist. Chromolithograph, 15 x 26. Printed by Thomas S. Sinclair (ca. 1805-81) of Philadelphia for Edward Sintzenich of New York, 1865. 66.184.1.

F. M. Spiegle

324. *Care and Carelessness.* 17 3/4 x 28 1/2. Poster issued by New York State Conservation Commission, 1915. 74.196.2.

Thomas W. Strong

325. "Hadley Falls, Hudson River." 4 5/8 x 7 5/8. 75.23.1.

326. "View of Lake George." 4 1/2 x 7 7/8. 75.23.2.

Numbers 325 and 326 possibly issued in a drawing book published in New York by Thomas W. Strong, ca. 1844.

Arthur Fitzwilliam Tait (1819-1905)

327. *Eruption of Vesuvius by Danan.* 14 1/4 x 10 1/4. Probably done in Manchester, England, ca. 1845. 63.64.12.

328. *Hyde Unitarian Chapel, Cheshire.* 3 x 9 3/4. Printed by M. Donkhouse, York. Published in Manchester, England, ca. 1845. 63.65.3.

329. *Piper-Heidsieck. 1785.* Chromolithograph, 21 3/4 x 29 1/4. Advertisement printed in Paris by George Blott in 1906; after painting by Tait dated 1877. 63.65.175.

330. *W. W. Tait.* 3 13/16 x 3 1/2. Portrait lithographed by A. F. Tait, 1830. 74.74.1.

H. P. Whinnery

331. *Paul Smith's, of the Adirondacks.* 10 x 14 3/16. Sketched in 1877. 66.112.4.

Gustav Adolf Wiegand (1869-1957)

332. [Summer scene]. Chromolithograph, 12 x 16. Reproduction of painting. 79.71.2.

H. Wood, Jr.

333. *Lake Henderson, N. Y. Sunrise in the Adirondacks.* Grisi, artist. Chromolithograph, 8 x 12. Published in New York by H. Wood, Jr., n.d. 65.46.1.

334. *Lake Henderson, N. Y. Sunrise in the Adirondacks.* Grisi, artist. Chromolithograph, 8 x 11 7/8. Published in New York by H. Wood, Jr., n.d. 65.46.2.

Unidentified Lithographers

335. "Adirondack or Indian Pass. Essex County." 3 1/16 x 4 1/16. Published in an unidentified book. 67.64.4.

336. "Lake George." 8 x 5 3/4. Published in an unidentified book. 75.143.1.

337. "Merry Christmas. Happy New Year." Chromolithograph, 7 5/8 x 6. Christmas card, n.d. 76.39.1.

338. "Yours Truly, F. N. Benedict." 4 1/2 x 3 1/4. Portrait of Farrand Northrup Benedict. Published in an unidentified book. 66.99.1.

Wood Engravings

Entries are arranged alphabetically by artist. Where entries can be grouped according to their original publication, this has been done, arranged alphabetically by title. In these cases, publication data appears once, after the last print in a group. Prints by the same artist but with separate publication information appear alphabetically by title.

Prints after Fenn published in *Picturesque America* are grouped by publication, then listed in order of appearance within each volume, rather than alphabetically by title. This order is reflected in the prints' accession numbers.

After titles, engravers' names are included where known, followed by dimensions, publication data and accession number(s). Prints derived from photographs form separate groups (under photographers' names), followed by prints by anonymous artists.

John Warner Barber (1798-1885)

339. "Northern View of Whitehall, N. Y." $2\frac{1}{8}$ x $3\frac{13}{16}$. Published in *The Rural Repository* 20 (Hudson, N. Y.: William B. Stoddard, Sept. 9, 1843). 76.13.1.

340. "View of Plattsburg [*sic*], N. Y." $2\frac{1}{8}$ x 4. Published in *The Rural Repository* 20 (Hudson, N. Y.: William B. Stoddard, July 27, 1844). 76.13.3.

Numbers 339 and 340 appeared earlier in John Warner Barber, *Historical Collections of the State of New York* (New York: Tuttle, 1841).

William Henry Bartlett (1809-54)

341. "View of Caldwell, on Lake George, N. Y." $2\frac{1}{8}$ x 4. Published in *The Rural Repository* 20 (Hudson, N. Y.: William B. Stoddard, Feb. 24, 1844). Illustration appeared earlier in John Warner Barber, *Historical Collections of the State of New York* (New York: Tuttle, 1841). 76.13.2.

342. "Bluff on the Erie Canal, Near Little Falls." George Wyand, engraver. $6\frac{1}{4}$ x $9\frac{3}{8}$. Attributed to Bartlett on the basis of 82.11.10 (checklist 19). 61.55.3.

343. "Roger's [*sic*] Slide, Lake George." George Wyand, engraver. $6\frac{3}{16}$ x $9\frac{1}{4}$. Attributed to Bartlett on the basis of 61.53.3 (checklist 12). 61.55.2.

344. "Sabbath-Day Point, Lake George." H. D. Turner, engraver. $6\frac{3}{16}$ x $9\frac{1}{8}$. Attributed to Bartlett on the basis of 61.53.6 (checklist 13). 61.55.5.

Numbers 342-344 published in John David Williams, *America Illustrated* (New York: The Arundel Print, 1874).

Daniel Carter Beard (1850-1941)

345. "A Double Surprise—A Sporting Incident in the Adirondack." $13\frac{1}{2}$ x 9. Published in *Frank Leslie's Illustrated Newspaper* (New York: Judge Publishing Company, August 22, 1891). 71.54.2.

346. "'Evicted Tenants' of The Adirondacks." $13\frac{3}{8}$ x 9. Published in *Harper's Weekly* 29 (New York: Harper & Brothers, Feb. 28, 1885). 71.54.1; 77.196.5; 78.8.4.

347. "New York. Fishing in the Adirondacks." $13\frac{3}{4}$ x $8\frac{3}{16}$. Published in *Frank Leslie's Weekly* (New York: Judge Publishing Company, 1889). 66.112.5.

348. "Trout Fishing in the Adirondacks.—A Double Strike." $13\frac{1}{4}$ x $9\frac{5}{8}$. Published in *Frank Leslie's Weekly* (New York: Judge Publishing Company, April 28, 1892). 71.54.3.

George Bowditch

349. *The 'Coop'—Putnam Camp.* $3\frac{5}{8}$ x $3\frac{3}{8}$. n.d. 67.23.1.

Paul Cannon

350. "New York. The Forest Fires in Clinton County. The Inhabitants of the Burned Districts Seeking Refuge." $9\frac{1}{8}$ x $13\frac{7}{8}$. Published in *Harper's Weekly* 21 (New York: Harper & Brothers, July 2, 1877). 88.34.3.

William de la Montagne Cary (1840-1922)

351. "Holiday Excursions—in the Mountains." A. Garde, engraver. 13 x $9\frac{1}{4}$. Published in *Harper's Weekly* 22 (New York: Harper & Brothers, Sept. 28, 1878). 69.98.2.

352. "'Vot Doesh You Peddles?'" J. Augustus Bogert, engraver. $10\frac{7}{8} \times 8\frac{1}{2}$. Published in *The Aldine* 6 (New York: James Sutton & Co., Aug. 1873). 72.77.4.

FREDERICK SCHILLER COZZENS (1846-1928)

353. "The Annual Meet of the American Canoe Association." Six vignettes: "The Upset Sailing Race"; "S. R. Stoddard's Cruising Canoe 'Atlantis'"; "R. W. Gibson of Albany, Winner of the Trophy in the Canoe, 'Notus'"; "The 'Pecowsic,' A Winner of Two Races"; "The Veteran Cook's Canoe, the 'Carrier Pigeon'"; "The 'Blanch,' owned by Paul Butler of Lowell." $13\frac{7}{8} \times 9\frac{3}{8}$. Published in *Harper's Weekly* 31 (New York: Harper & Brothers, Sept. 10, 1887). 81.25.2.

RUDOLF CRONAU

354. "Die Lederstrumpfhohle auf der Hudsoninsel bei Glens Falls." $9\frac{3}{8} \times 6\frac{3}{4}$. 82.11.5.

FELIX OCTAVIUS CARR DARLEY (1822-88)

355. "'And finally approach and stand happy in her reward,—my caress.'" $3 \times 4\frac{7}{8}$. Published in William H. H. Murray, *Adventures in the Wilderness; or, Camp-Life in the Adirondacks* (Boston: Fields, Osgood, & Co., 1869). 70.147.12.

JOHN S. DAVIS

356. "In the Adirondack Wilderness." $4\frac{5}{8} \times 7\frac{15}{16}$. ca. 1882. Published in an unidentified almanac; cut down from 77.196.3 (checklist 357). 78.69.3.

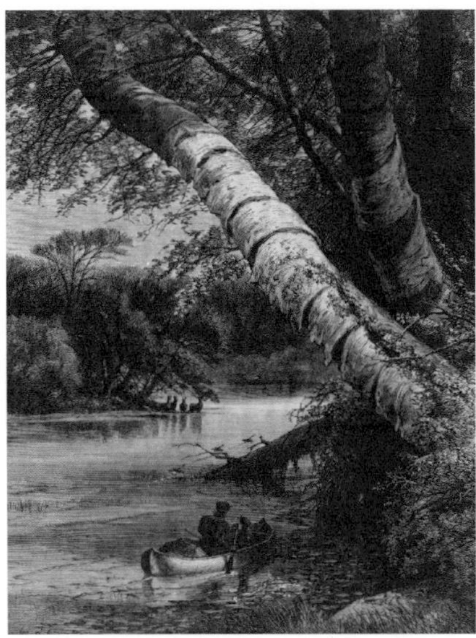

357. "Morning in the Adirondacks." R. Schelling, engraver. $12\frac{5}{8} \times 9\frac{7}{16}$. 77.196.3.

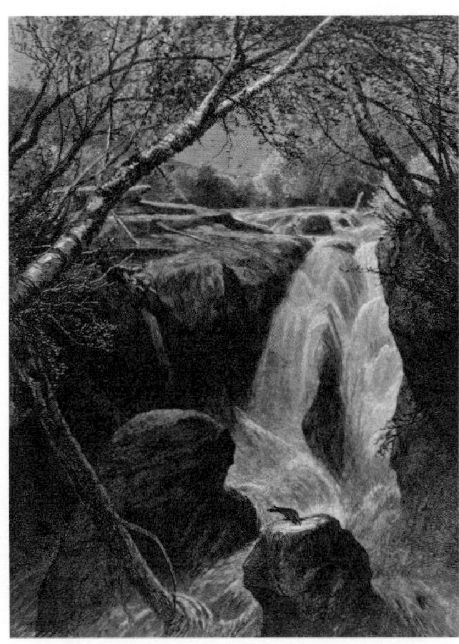

358. "Wilmington Falls, Adirondacks." X. Mexiom, engraver. $13 \times 9\frac{1}{8}$. 77.196.4.

THEODORE RUSSELL DAVIS (1840-94)

359. "Bee Hunting in the Adirondacks." Two vignettes: "Smudging for Bees"; "Working Down the Bee Tree." $6\frac{7}{8} \times 9\frac{3}{16}$. Published in *Harper's Weekly* 12 (New York: Harper & Brothers, Sept. 26, 1868). 78.8.5.

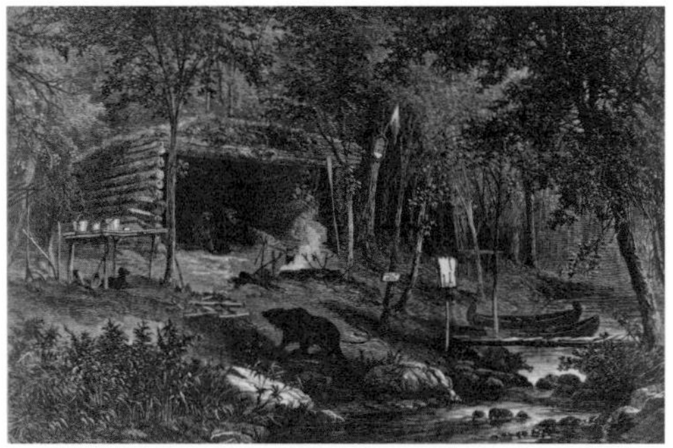

360. "The Centennial—The Hunters' Camp." X. Mexiom, engraver. $9\frac{1}{8} \times 13\frac{3}{4}$. Published in *Harper's Weekly* 20 (New York: Harper & Brothers, Oct. 14, 1876). 67.199.4; 78.123.1A.

361. "Floating for Deer in the Adirondacks." C. P., engraver. $6\frac{7}{8} \times 9\frac{1}{8}$. Published in *Harper's Weekly* 12 (New York: Harper & Brothers, Oct. 24, 1868). 66.112.6; 94.27.11.

362. "Sketches in the Adirondack Region." Six vignettes: "The Corduroy"; "Ballanced [*sic*] Boulder"; "The Deserted Village of Adirondack"; "The Indian Pass from Lake Henderson"; "Fly Fishing"; "The Shanty." $13\frac{3}{4} \times 9\frac{1}{8}$. Published in *Harper's Weekly* 12 (New York: Harper & Brothers, Nov. 21. 1868). 62.16.22; 67.37.1.

DREKA

363. "Prospect House." $3\frac{1}{16} \times 5\frac{3}{8}$. On cover of brochure for Propsect House, Blue Mountain Lake, N. Y., 1891. 75.160.2.

Harry Fenn (1845-1911)

364. "'I looked at John; his eyes were fastened on the rod.'" $2\frac{15}{16}$ x $4\frac{13}{16}$. 70.147.13.

365. "'It is pleasant for a man, in the position that I was in, to feel that he has something under him.'" $2\frac{15}{16}$ x $4\frac{15}{16}$. 70.147.18.

366. "'Martin,' shouted I, 'Hang on; that's your deer.'" $2\frac{15}{16}$ x $4\frac{15}{16}$. 70.147.16.

367. "'Never was I signalled before to look at such an object.'" John Parker Davis (1832-1910), engraver. $2\frac{15}{16}$ x 5. 70.147.17.

368. "'O, royal sight it was to see them come one after another over the verge!'" 3 x $4\frac{15}{16}$. 70.147.15.

369. "'Steady there!'" $2\frac{15}{16}$ x $4\frac{15}{16}$. 70.147.19.

370. "'When, high in mid air he shook himself, the crystal drops were flung into my very face.'" Samuel Smith Kilburn, engraver. $2\frac{15}{16}$ x 5. 70.147.14.

Numbers 364-370 published in William H. H. Murray, *Adventures in the Wilderness; or, Camp-Life in the Adirondacks* (Boston: Fields, Osgood, & Co., 1869).

371. "Sherman Fall." John Karst (1836-1922), engraver. $6\frac{1}{4}$ x 6. 67.99.1A.

372. "General View of Trenton Falls, from East Bank." Langridge, engraver. $9\frac{1}{8}$ x $6\frac{1}{4}$. 67.99.1B.

373. "High Falls." Andrew Varick Stout Anthony (1835-1906), engraver. $6\frac{1}{8}$ x $9\frac{1}{8}$. 67.99.1C.

374. "Part of High Fall." J. G. Smithwick, engraver. 8 x $6\frac{1}{4}$. 67.99.1D.

375. "Alhambra Fall." $6\frac{1}{8}$ x $5\frac{3}{8}$. 67.99.1E.

376. "Head of the Ravine." $6\frac{1}{4}$ x $5\frac{3}{8}$. 67.99.1F.

377. "Lovers' Walk." Joseph S. Harley, engraver. $6\frac{1}{4}$ x $8\frac{7}{8}$. 67.99.1G.

Numbers 371-377 published in William Cullen Bryant, ed., *Picturesque America: Trenton Falls*, Part 19 (New York: D. Appleton & Co., 1873).

378. "Lake George from Prospect Mt." $2\frac{5}{8}$ x $9\frac{1}{4}$. 67.99.3A.

379. "Lake George from Glen's-Falls [*sic*] Road." $3\frac{1}{2}$ x $9\frac{1}{8}$. 67.99.3B.

380. "Fort George." W. J. Palmer, engraver. $4\frac{3}{8}$ x $6\frac{1}{8}$. 67.99.3C.

381. "Scenes on Lake George." W. J. Palmer, engraver. $9\frac{1}{4}$ x $6\frac{3}{8}$. 67.99.3D.

382. "Lake George, South from Tea Island." $4\frac{1}{2}$ x $6\frac{1}{4}$. 67.99.3E.

383. "Sloop Island." $2\frac{1}{2}$ x $6\frac{1}{4}$. 67.99.3F.

384. "Lake George, North from Tea Island. J. Sachs, engraver. $4\frac{1}{2}$ x $6\frac{1}{4}$. 67.99.3G.

385. "The Hermitage." J. Sachs, engraver. 2 x $6\frac{1}{4}$. 67.99.3H.

386. "Black Mountain, from the Narrows." $3\frac{1}{4}$ x $9\frac{1}{4}$. 67.99.3I.

387. "Shelving-Rock Falls." $7\frac{1}{4}$ x $6\frac{1}{4}$. 67.99.3J.

388. "Davis's [*sic*] Hollow, Sabbath-Day Point." $4\frac{1}{2}$ x $6\frac{1}{4}$. 67.99.3K.

389. "Black Mountain, from Sabbath-Day Point." $2\frac{3}{8}$ x $6\frac{1}{4}$. 67.99.3L.

390. "Rogers's [*sic*] Slide." $3\frac{1}{2}$ x $7\frac{7}{8}$. 67.99.3M.

391. "Falls, Ticonderoga Village." $7\frac{1}{2}$ x $6\frac{1}{4}$. 67.99.3N.

392. "Fort Ticonderoga." $3\frac{1}{8}$ x $9\frac{1}{4}$. 67.99.3O.

393. "Fort Ticonderoga, from Eastern Shore." 3 x $9\frac{1}{4}$. 677.99.3P.

394. "Looking south from Fort Ticonderoga, Lake Champlain." $7\frac{3}{8}$ x $6\frac{1}{4}$. 67.99.3Q.

395. "Ticonderoga Landing." $5\frac{7}{8}$ x $6\frac{1}{8}$. 67.99.3R.

396. "Lake Champlain, near Whitehall." 2 x $6\frac{1}{8}$. 67.99.3S.

397. "Lake Champlain, near Ticonderoga." $2\frac{1}{8}$ x $6\frac{1}{8}$. 67.99.3T.

398. "Crown Point and Port Henry, Lake Champlain." J. Sachs, engraver. 4 x $6\frac{1}{8}$. 67.99.3U.

399. "Split Rock, Lake Champlain." $3\frac{1}{2}$ x $9\frac{1}{8}$. 67.99.3V.

400. "Burlington Bay." $2\frac{3}{4}$ x $9\frac{1}{8}$. 67.99.3W.

401. "Lake Champlain, from Plattsburg [*sic*] to St. Albans." W. J. Palmer, engraver. $9\frac{1}{4}$ x $6\frac{1}{4}$. 67.99.3X.

Numbers 378-401 published in William Cullen Bryant, ed., *Picturesque America: Lake George and Lake Champlain*, Part 35 (New York: D. Appleton & Co., 1873).

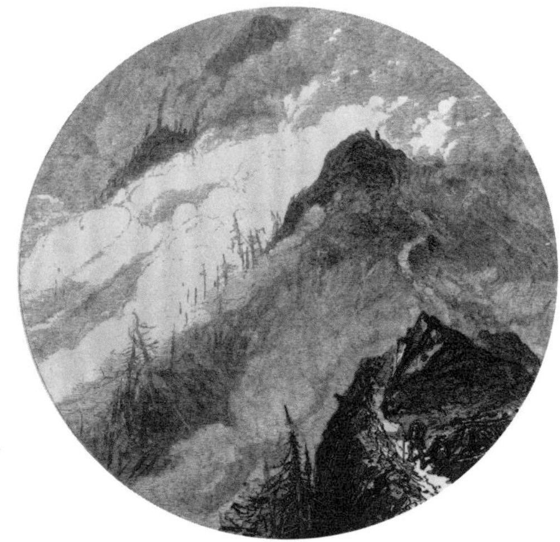

402. "Ascent of Whiteface." Samuel M. Slader, engraver. (Attribution by William J. Linton). $6\frac{3}{8}$ x $6\frac{1}{4}$. 67.99.4A; 70.147.23; 92.41.4.

403. "The Ausable Chasm." W. J. Palmer, engraver. $9\frac{1}{8}$ x $3\frac{5}{8}$. 67.9.4B; 70.147.25; 92.41.5B.

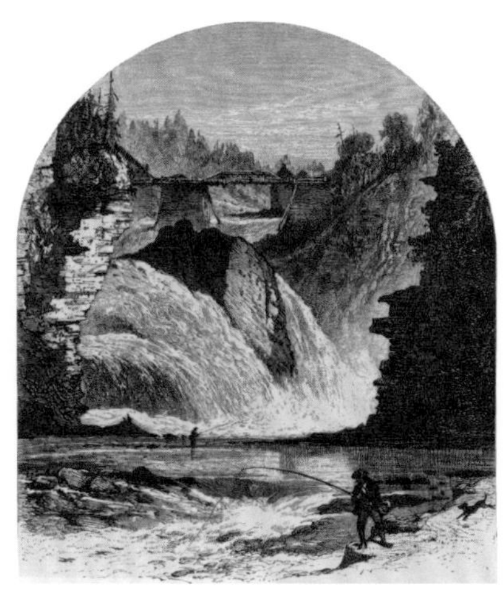

404. "Birmingham Falls, Ausable Chasm." 7 1/2 x 6 1/4. 67.99.4C; 92.41.5A.
405. "The Stairway, Ausable Chasm." 9 1/8 x 3 5/8. 67.99.4D; 70.147.28; 92.41.6B.
406. "Clearing a Jam, Great Falls of the Ausable." William J. Linton (1812-97), engraver. 9 1/8 x 6 1/4. 67.9.4E; 92.41.6A.
407. "Climbing Tahawus." W. A. Cranston, engraver. 8 7/8 x 6 1/8. 67.9.4F.
408. "Whiteface, from Lake Placid." 6 1/4 x 5. 67.99.4G; 70.147.31.
409. "Lower Saranac Lake." 3 3/8 x 9 1/8. 67.99.4H; 70.147.80.
410. "Round Lake, from Bartlett's." F. W. Quartley, engraver. 4 7/8 x 6 1/8. 67.99.4I.
411. ""Indian Carry, Upper Saranac." John Karst, engraver. 3 1/2 x 6 1/4. 67.99.4J.
412. "St. Regis Lake." Henry Duff Linton (1815-99), engraver. 3 7/8 x 9 1/8. 67.99.4K; 70.147.24.
413. "Tupper Lake by Moonlight." Greenaway, engraver. 2 5/8 x 9 1/4. 67.99.4L; 70.147.30.
414. "On Tupper Lake." Henry Duff Linton (1815-99), engraver. 1 1/2 x 6 1/8. 67.99.4M
415. "Bog River Falls, Tupper Lake." Henry Duff Linton (1815-99), engraver. 1 3/4 x 6 1/4. 67.99.4N
416. "Sand Point, Little Tupper Lake." W. A. Cranston, engraver. 2 7/8 x 9 1/4. 67.99.4O; 70.147.29.
417. "A Carry Near Little Tupper Lake." 7 1/2 x 6 1/4. 67.99.4P.
418. "Long Lake, from the Lower Island." 2 7/8 x 6 3/8. 67.99.4Q.
419. "Mount Seward, from Long Lake." 1 1/2 x 6 3/8. 67.99.4R; 70.147.27.
420. "Round Island, Long Lake." 1 1/2 x 6 3/8. 67.99.4S; 70.147.26.
421. "Watching for Deer, on Long Lake." 9 1/4 x 4. 67.99.4T.
422. "The Indian Pass." W. J. Palmer, engraver. 9 x 3 7/8. 67.99.4U; 67.5.1; 74.306.1.

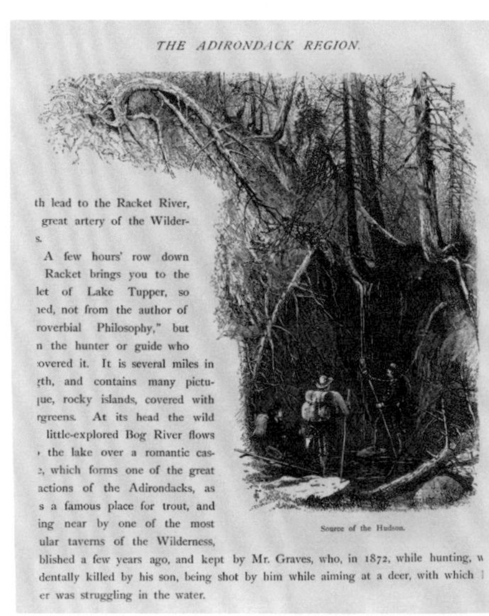

THE ADIRONDACK REGION.

th lead to the Racket River, great artery of the Wilders.

A few hours' row down Racket brings you to the let of Lake Tupper, so ned, not from the author of roverbial Philosophy," but n the hunter or guide who overed it. It is several miles in gth, and contains many pictuque, rocky islands, covered with rgreens. At its head the wild little-explored Bog River flows the lake over a romantic case, which forms one of the great actions of the Adirondacks, as s a famous place for trout, and ing near by one of the most ular taverns of the Wilderness, blished a few years ago, and kept by Mr. Graves, who, in 1872, while hunting, w dentally killed by his son, being shot by him while aiming at a deer, with which er was struggling in the water.

Source of the Hudson.

423. "Source of the Hudson." Joseph S. Harley, engraver. 6 1/8 x 6. 67.99.4V; 78.76.2.
424. "Opalescent Falls." W. J. Palmer, engraver. 9 1/8 x 3 5/8. 67.99.4W; 78.76.1.
425. "The Hudson, Twenty Miles from its Source." Joseph S. Harley, engraver. 6 1/8 x 6 1/8. 67.99.4X; 78.76.3.

Numbers 402-425 published in William Cullen Bryant, ed., *Picturesque America: The Adirondack Region*, Part 41 (New York: D. Appleton & Co., 1874).

426. "Summer Resorts—Mount McGregor." Six vignettes: "Floating Islands Lake Bonita"; "Glimpse of Saratoga Lake from the Summit"; "The Eastern Lookout"; "The Western Lookout"; "On the Mt. McGregor R.R."; "The Art Gallery." 13 3/8 x 9 1/8. Published in *Harper's Weekly* 27 (New York: Harper & Brothers, July 14, 1883). 94.27.13.

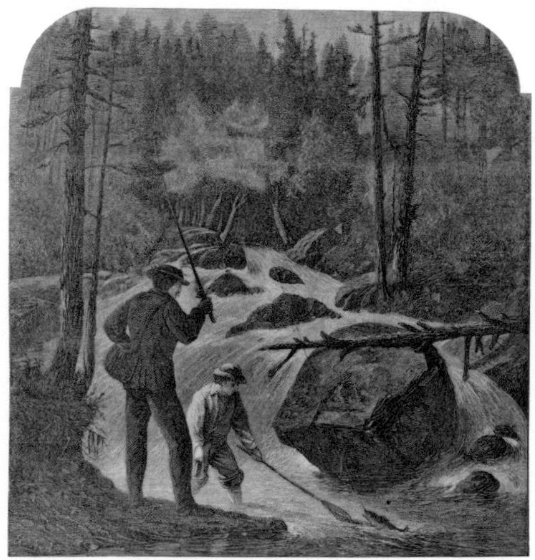

EDWIN FORBES (1839-95)
427. "Trout-Fishing in the Adirondacks." 9 1/4 x 3 3/16. Issued in a periodical, New York, May 15, 1869. 79.85.1.

Arthur Burdett Frost (1851-1928)

428. "A Carry—The Start." 3 x $4^{3}/_{4}$. Published in *Harper's New Monthly Magazine* 63 (New York: Harper & Brothers, Oct. 1881). 69.179.10.

429. "A Carry—The End." $2^{5}/_{8}$ x $4^{3}/_{4}$. Published in *Harper's New Monthly Magazine* 63 (New York: Harper & Brothers, Oct. 1881). Based on Frost's drawing in the Adirondack Museum collection (83.77.17). 69.179.11.

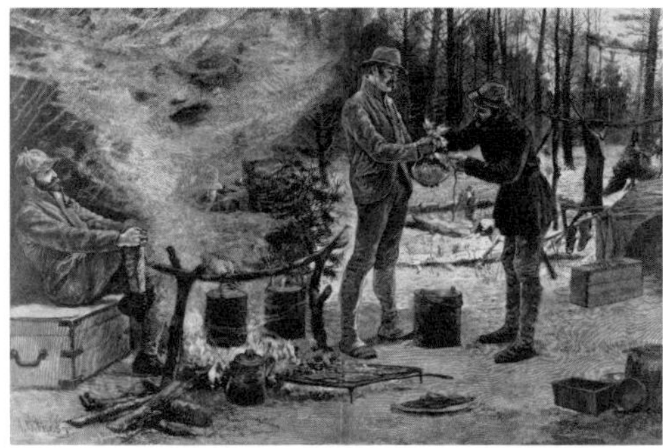

430. "Christmas in Camp—Tying up the Pudding." $13^{5}/_{16}$ x $19^{3}/_{4}$. Published in *Harper's Weekly* 29 (New York: Harper & Brothers, Dec. 12, 1885). 92.41.11.

431. "Deer Shooting on an American Lake." H. Claudius, engraver. $9^{1}/_{16}$ x $12^{7}/_{8}$. Published in *Illustrated London News* (London, August 20, 1887). 62.67.5.

432. "In Camp." G. J. B., engraver. $2^{7}/_{8}$ x $4^{3}/_{4}$. Published in *Harper's New Monthly Magazine* (New York: Harper & Brothers, 1888). 69.179.13.

433. "On the Watch Ground." $5^{5}/_{8}$ x $4^{3}/_{4}$. Published in *Harper's New Monthly Magazine* (New York: Harper & Brothers, 1888). 69.179.15.

William Hamilton Gibson (1850-96)

434. "Saratoga: Langenanficht des Broadway." Robert Hoskins, engraver. $5^{3}/_{4}$ x $4^{3}/_{8}$. 82.11.4.

Sanford Robinson Gifford (1823-80)

435. "Sunset in the Adirondacks." W. H. M. (W. H. Morse?), engraver. $6^{3}/_{4}$ x $5^{7}/_{16}$. Published in *The Art Journal* 2 (New York: D. Appleton & Co., 1876). 66.45.3.

David Henderson (d. 1845)

436. [Adirondack Group as seen from Newcomb]. $3^{1}/_{4}$ x $4^{13}/_{16}$. Published in Ebenezer Emmons, *Geology of New-York, Part IV, Vol. 2* (Albany, 1842). Illustration attributed to Henderson in the list of plates. 70.147.81.

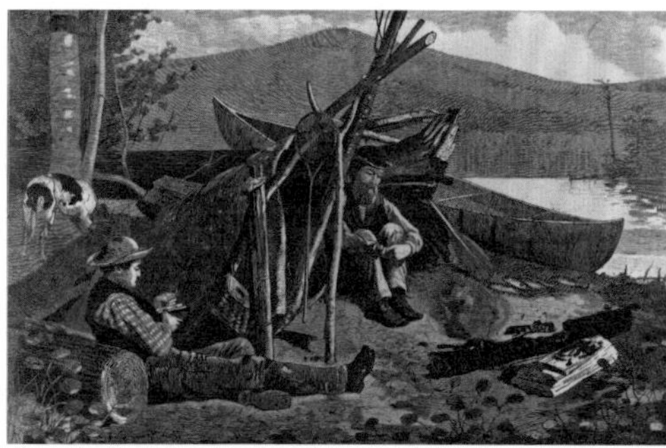

Winslow Homer (1836-1910)

437. "Camping out in the Adirondack Mountains." Ed. Lagarde, engraver. $9^{1}/_{8}$ x $13^{3}/_{4}$. Published in *Harper's Weekly* 18 (New York: Harper & Brothers, Nov. 7, 1874). 77.7.1; 83.62.1.

438. "Deer-Stalking in the Adirondacks In Winter." J. S., engraver. $7^{1}/_{4}$ x $9^{3}/_{4}$. Published in *Every Saturday* 2 (Boston: Fields, Osgood & Co., Jan. 21, 1871). 66.112.3; 67.64.3.

439. "Lumbering in Winter." John Parker Davis (1832-1910), engraver. $11^{3}/_{4}$ x $8^{3}/_{4}$. Published in *Every Saturday* 2 (Boston: Fields, Osgood & Co., Jan. 28, 1871). 66.112.2.

440. "On the Road to Lake George." $6^{1}/_{8}$ x $6^{11}/_{16}$. Published in *Appleton's Journal of Literature, Science and Art* 1 (New York: D. Appleton & Co., July 24, 1869). 63.60.1.

441. "Trapping in the Adirondacks." John Parker Davis (1832-1910), engraver. $8^{7}/_{8}$ x $11^{5}/_{8}$. Published in *Every Saturday* 1 (Boston: Fields, Osgood & Co., Dec. 24, 1870). 70.147.8; 94.28.9.

442. "Waiting for a Bite." Ed. Lagarde, engraver. $9^{1}/_{8}$ x $13^{3}/_{4}$. Published in *Harper's Weekly* 18 (New York: Harper & Brothers, Aug. 22, 1874). 67.6.3; 77.23.1; 94.28.11.

Augustus Hoppin (1828-96)

443. "Professor Tigwissel in the Adirondacks." $14^{3}/_{4}$ x $12^{1}/_{2}$. Published in *The Daily Graphic* (New York: The Graphic Company, Aug. 21, 1880). Illustration signed "Hop"; attribution provided by Adirondack Museum. 63.78.167.

John Augustus Hows (1832-74)

444. "The Pines of the Racquette [*sic*]." William J. Linton (1812-97), engraver. $12^{7}/_{8}$ x $8^{7}/_{8}$. Published in *The Aldine* 5 (New York: James Sutton & Co., June 1872). 66.45.27; 66.63.2.

445. "White Birches of the Saranac." William J. Linton (1812-97), engraver. 14 x 9. Published in *The Aldine* 6 (New York: James Sutton & Co., March 1873). 66.45.11.

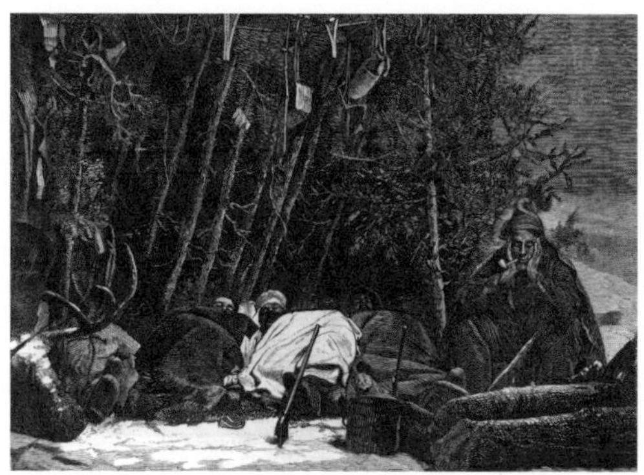

J. S. JAMESON

446. "New York. Sportsmen in Camp Among the Adirondacks. A Winter-night scene." $6\frac{7}{8}$ x $9\frac{3}{16}$. Published in *Frank Leslie's Illustrated Newspaper* 33 (New York: Frank Leslie, Feb. 17, 1872). 74.248.414.

447. "New York. Sportsmen in Camp Among the Adirondacks. Preparing for a tramp over the Snow-Drifts." $6\frac{13}{16}$ x $9\frac{3}{16}$. Published in *Frank Leslie's Illustrated Newspaper* 33 (New York: Frank Leslie, Feb. 24, 1872). 74.248.415.

SAMUEL SMITH KILBURN

448. "Bridge Over the Ausable River, at Keeseville, New York." $5\frac{1}{2}$ x $9\frac{3}{8}$. Published in *Ballou's Pictorial* 14 (Boston: M. M. Ballou, July 17, 1858). 68.215.1.

449. "Chazy Lake and Lion [*sic*] Mountain." $2\frac{1}{4}$ x $3\frac{9}{16}$. 69.226.3A.

450. "Meacham Pond." $2\frac{5}{8}$ x $3\frac{7}{16}$. 69.226.3B.

Numbers 449 and 450 published in H. Perry Smith, *The Modern Babes in the Wood* (Hartford: Columbian Book Company, 1872).

ALEXANDER LAWRIE (1828-1917)

451. "Elizabeth Valley, Essex County, New York." Charles Maurand, engraver. 9 x 13. Published in *The Aldine* 6 (New York: James Sutton & Co., Oct. 1873). 66.45.9.

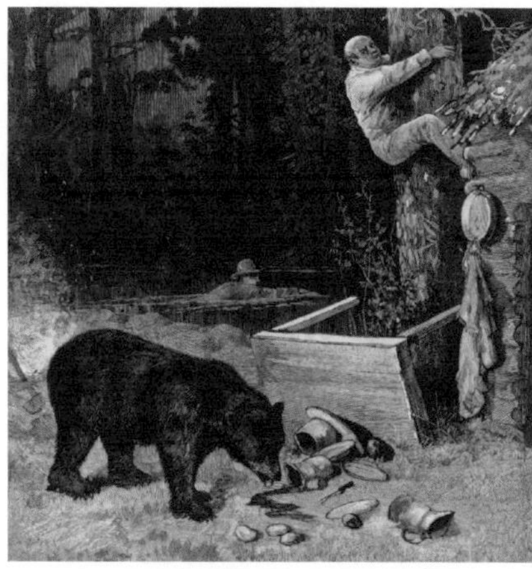

CULVER H. LEWIS

452. "An Adirondack Episode. Taking Possession of the Camp." $9\frac{7}{8}$ x $9\frac{1}{4}$. Published in *Frank Leslie's Illustrated Newspaper* 56 (New York: Mrs. Frank Leslie, July 14, 1883). 75.155.1.

WILL HICOCK LOW (1853-1932)

453. "Postoffice [*sic*] in the Adirondacks." J. G. Smithwick, engraver. $10\frac{3}{8}$ x $8\frac{7}{8}$. Published in *The Illustrated Christian Weekly* 4 (New York: American Tract Society, July 25, 1874). 67.64.7.

BENSON JOHN LOSSING (1813-91)

454. "The Loon." $2\frac{1}{16}$ x $2\frac{1}{2}$. Published in Benson John Lossing, *The Hudson. From the Wilderness to the Sea* (New York: Virtue and Yorston, 1866). 94.27.6B.

J. MACDONALD

455. "Hunting on Snow Shoes." $9\frac{3}{16}$ x $13\frac{5}{8}$. 1884. 66.45.16.

W. S. MACY

456. "Indian Pass." Held, engraver. $2\frac{5}{8}$ x $4\frac{3}{4}$. Published in *Harper's New Monthly Magazine* (New York: Harper & Brothers, 1888). 69.179.9.

457. "Mist Rising Off Mount Whiteface." G. J. B., engraver. $2\frac{7}{8}$ x $4\frac{3}{4}$. Published in *Harper's New Monthly Magazine* (New York: Harper & Brothers, 1888). 69.179.8.

458. "Swan Lake." H. Woolf, engraver. Published in *Harper's New Monthly Magazine* (New York: Harper & Brothers, 1888). 69.179.16.

RICHARD P. MALLORY

459. "St. Jermain's Hotel, Chazy Lake, Northern New York." Samuel Smith Kilburn, Jr., engraver. $5\frac{3}{8}$ x $9\frac{3}{8}$. Published in *Ballou's Pictorial* 14 (Boston: M. M. Ballou, April 3, 1858). 66.112.11.

HOMER DODGE MARTIN (1836-97)

460. "An Adirondack Stream." Charles Maurand, engraver. $5\frac{15}{16}$ x $4\frac{1}{2}$. Published in an unidentified almanac dated 1882. 78.69.2.

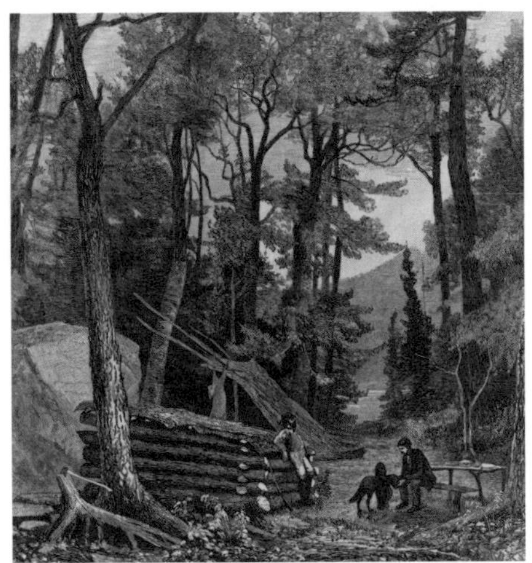

461. "In the Adirondacks.—Camping in the Upper Ausable." John Parker Davis (1832-1910), engraver. $9^{15}/_{16}$ x $8^{7}/_{8}$. 77.68.3.

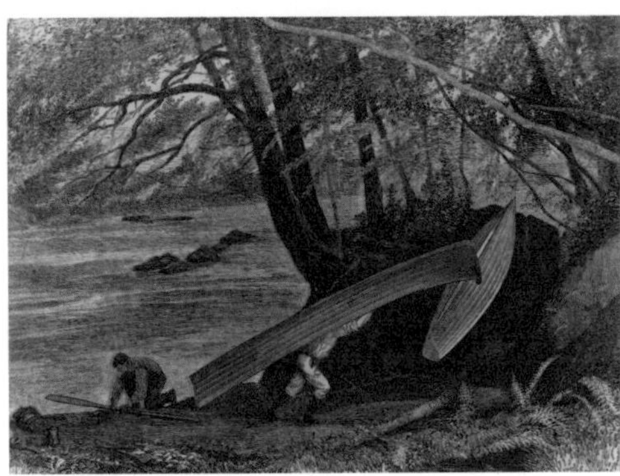

462. "In the Adirondacks.—A Carry on Racquette [*sic*] River." John Parker Davis (1832-1910), engraver. $8^{7}/_{8}$ x $11^{7}/_{8}$. 78.85.1.
463. "In the Adirondacks.—Mountain View on the Saranac." Stewart, engraver. $8^{13}/_{16}$ x $11^{7}/_{8}$. Based on Martin's painting *Mountain View on the Saranac*, 1868, in the Adirondack Museum collection (71.46.1). 66.52.3; 77.68.1; 83.83.1; 94.28.8.

Numbers 461-463 published in *Every Saturday* 1 (Boston: Fields, Osgood & Co., Sept. 3, 1870).

William Rickarby Miller (1818-93)
464. "Steamboat Landing, Foot of Lake George." Henry Bricher, engraver. $4^{3}/_{4}$ x 6. Published in *Gleason's Pictorial Drawing Room Companion* 5 (Boston: F. Gleason, Oct. 1, 1853). 76.27.1.
465. "Ticonderoga, From the Foot of Mount Defiance." Major, engraver. $6^{1}/_{4}$ x $9^{3}/_{8}$. Published in *Gleason's Pictorial Drawing-Room Companion* (Boston: F. Gleason, n.d.). 94.28.5.

Thomas Moran (1837-1926)
466. "Cat Mountain, Lake George." Charles Maurand, engraver. $5^{7}/_{16}$ x $8^{7}/_{16}$. Published in *The Aldine* 7 (New York: James Sutton & Co., April 1874). 94.28.6.
467. "A Difficult Passage." $3^{3}/_{4}$ x $4^{7}/_{8}$. Published in *Harper's New Monthly Magazine* (New York: Harper & Brothers, 1888). 69.179.12.
468. "Edmonds's [*sic*] Pond." J. A. Bogert, engraver. $4^{13}/_{16}$ x $4^{1}/_{4}$. Published in *Harper's New Monthly Magazine* (New York: Harper & Brothers, 1888). 69.179.7.
469. "Der Georgsee im Statte New-York." $5^{3}/_{8}$ x $8^{3}/_{8}$. 82.11.1.
470. "Fourteen-Mile Island, Lake George." Charles Maurand and J. A. Bogert, engravers. $5^{3}/_{8}$ x $8^{3}/_{8}$. Published in *Illustrated Christian Weekly* (New York: American Tract Society, Aug. 9, 1879). 78.15.6.
471. "Lake Champlain." $4^{3}/_{8}$ x $7^{1}/_{8}$. Published in *Scribner's Popular History of the United States* (New York: Charles Scribner's Sons, 1898). 82.11.3.

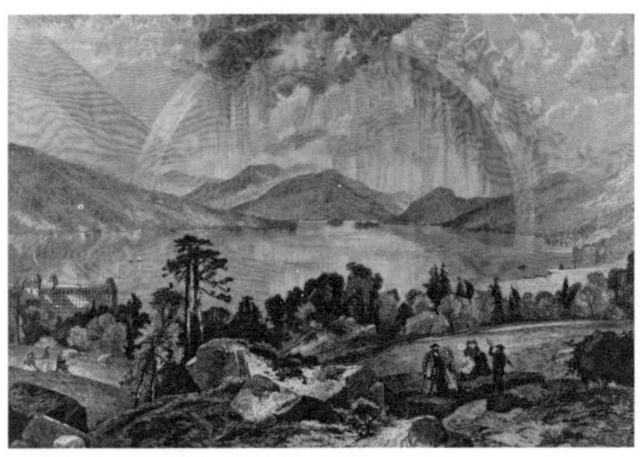

472. "Lake George." Charles Maurand, engraver. $8^{7}/_{8}$ x $12^{3}/_{4}$. Published in *The Aldine* 7 (New York: James Sutton & Co., April 1874). 73.37.1.
473. "A Swim for Life." Dakey, engraver. $3^{3}/_{8}$ x $4^{13}/_{16}$. Published in *Harper's New Monthly Magazine* 63 (New York: Harper & Brothers, 1888). 69.179.14.
474. "View of Lake George." Charles Maurand, engraver. $5^{1}/_{2}$ x $7^{15}/_{16}$. Printed from the same, but trimmed, block as 73.37.1 (checklist 472). 82.11.2.

Matthew Somerville Morgan (1839-90)
475. "Duck-Shooting on Saratoga Lake." $6^{7}/_{8}$ x $9^{1}/_{8}$. Published in John David Williams, *America Illustrated* (New York: The Arundel Print, 1874). 61.55.6.

Nealy
476. "The Mountaineer." 14 x $11^{5}/_{16}$. Published in *The Weekly Graphic* (New York: Weekly Graphic, June 6, 1874). 66.45.13.

Henry Alexander Ogden (1856-1936)
477. "A Summer Pastime. New York. Drill of the 'Sunflower Brigade,' at Hulett's Landing, on Lake George." $10^{5}/_{8}$ x $9^{3}/_{16}$. Published in

Frank Leslie's Illustrated Newspaper (New York: Mrs. Frank Leslie, 1883). 85.8.1.

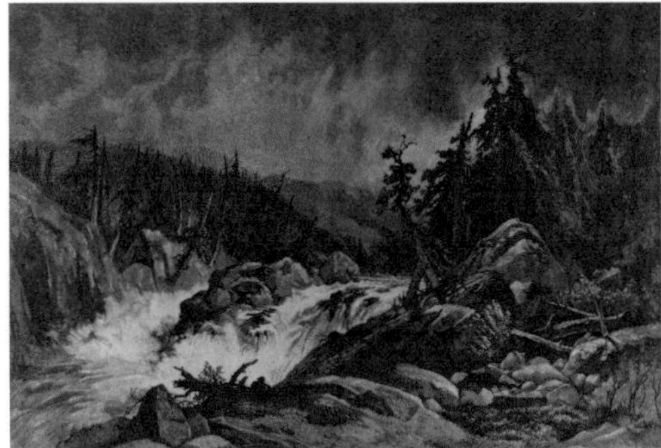

ARTHUR PARTON (1842-1914)

478. "Rapids of the Au Sable." Charles Maurand, engraver. 9 x 13. Published in *The Aldine* 7 (New York: The Aldine Company, Oct. 1874). 66.45.33; 79.6.1A.

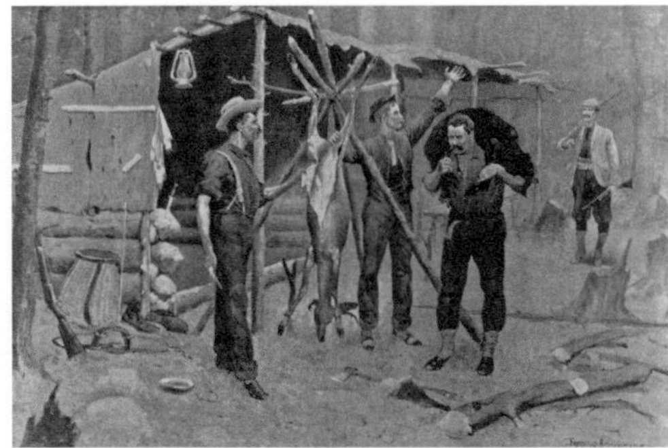

FREDERIC SACKRIDER REMINGTON (1861-1909)

479. "A Good Day's Hunting in the Adirondacks." Half-tone, Henry [?] Kurtz, engraver. $13^{7}/_{8}$ x 20. Published in *Harper's Weekly* 36 (New York: Harper & Brothers, Jan. 16, 1892). 61.52.1; 77.196.8; 78.8.7; 78.85.2.

480. "His Bag." Half-tone. $7^{7}/_{8}$ x $7^{7}/_{8}$. Published in unidentified issue of *Harper's Weekly*. 84.4.4.

481. "Spring Trout-Fishing in the Adirondacks—An Odious Comparison of Weights." Half-tone, Henry [?] Kurtz, engraver. $13^{3}/_{4}$ x $18^{3}/_{4}$. Published in *Harper's Weekly* 34 (New York: Harper & Brothers, May 24, 1890). Based on Remington's painting *Spring Trout-Fishing in the Adirondacks—An Odious Comparison of Weights*, 1890, in the Adirondack Museum collection (70.196.1). 61.52.2; 77.196.7; 78.8.6.

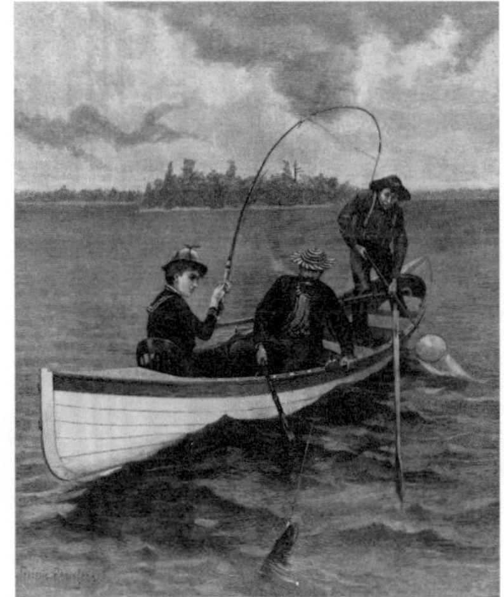

482. "Her First Muskallonge [*sic*]." $11^{3}/_{8}$ x $9^{1}/_{4}$. Published in *Harper's Weekly* 32 (New York: Harper & Brothers, Oct. 6, 1888). 73.37.2.

THOMAS ADDISON RICHARDS (1820-1900)

483. "The Great Indian Pass." $6^{1}/_{4}$ x $4^{1}/_{8}$. 78.59.2.

484. "The Storm in the Forest." $5^{1}/_{4}$ x $4^{1}/_{4}$. 78.59.3.

485. "Lake Sanford." $4^{1}/_{8}$ x $4^{3}/_{8}$. 78.59.4.

486. "Echo Mountain, from Lake Sanford." $3^{1}/_{8}$ x 4. 78.59.5.

487. "Mount Colden, From Lake Henderson." $3^{3}/_{8}$ x 4. 78.59.6.

488. "The Indian Pass, from Lake Henderson." $5^{1}/_{4}$ x $4^{1}/_{8}$. 78.59.7.

489. "Mount M'Intyre—Outlet of Lake Henderson." $4^{1}/_{2}$ x $4^{1}/_{2}$. 78.59.8.

490. "Deer Hunt at the Preston Woods." $4^{3}/_{8}$ x $4^{1}/_{4}$. 78.59.9.

491. "The Ascent of Mount Marcy." $5^{3}/_{8}$ x $4^{1}/_{8}$. 78.59.11.

492. "Santanoni Mountains, from the Great Indian Pass." $4^{1}/_{4}$ x $3^{1}/_{8}$. 78.59.12.

Numbers 483-492 published in Richards' article, "The Adirondack Woods and Water," *Harper's New Monthy Magazine* 19 (New York: Harper & Brothers, Sept. 1859).

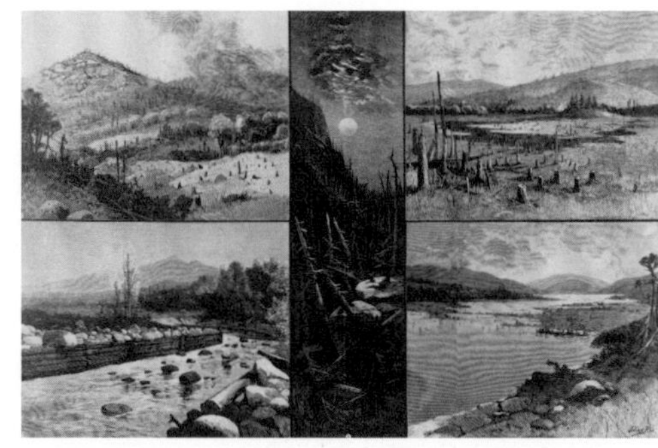

JULIAN WALBRIDGE RIX (1850-1903)

493. "Destruction of Forests in the Adirondacks." Five vignettes: "Dead Timber, Mount Maxon"; "Mount Maxon"; "Dead Water, Schroon River"; "Coffer-Dam, Lower Works, at Tahawus, Hudson River"; "Indian Lake, Overflowed Lands." $13^{1}/_{4}$ x 20. 77.196.9; 94.27.14.

494. "Destruction of Forests in the Adirondacks. Great Burned Tract on the Road to Indian Lake." A. H. and G. S. B., engravers. $11^{1}/_{8}$ x 9. 77.196.1.

Numbers 493 and 494 published in *Harper's Weekly* 28 (New York: Harper & Brothers, Dec. 6, 1884).

495. "Forest Destruction in the Adirondacks. The Effects of Logging and Burning Timber. A Feeder of the Hudson—As It Was. A Feeder of the Hudson—As It Is." Lawson, engraver. 2 rectangles, each $8^{7}/_{8}$ x 6. Published in *Harper's Weekly* 29 (New York: Harper & Brothers, Jan. 24, 1885). 77.196.2; 69.179.5A and B; 92.41.9A and B; 94.27.12A and B.

496. "Greenwood Lake." Five vignettes: "From the Club-House Window, Looking South"; "Ruins of a Blast Furnace"; "The Club-House"; "A Likely Nook for Bass"; "Looking up the Lake, North." $12^{3}/_{8}$ x $9^{3}/_{16}$. Published in *Harper's Weekly* 29 (New York: Harper & Brothers, July 25, 1885). 78.8.3.

William Allen Rogers (1854-1931)

497. "The Annual Meet of the American Canoe Association at Lake Champlain." Three vignettes: "The Sea-Serpent Makes his Appearance"; "The Camp Fire at Squaw Point"; "The Main Camp." 14 x $9^{1}/_{4}$. Published in *Harper's Weekly* 25 (New York: Harper & Brothers, Aug. 29, 1881). 76.4.3.

498. "Camping Out as a Fine Art"; "Exterior of a 'Camp'"; and "The Dining Room." $6^{1}/_{2}$ x $9^{1}/_{16}$. Published in *Harper's Weekly* 27 (New York: Harper & Brothers, Nov. 17, 1883). 78.139.1.

499. "Canoeing in the North Woods—A 'Carry.'" 9 x $13^{7}/_{16}$. Published in *Harper's Weekly* 32 (New York: Harper & Brothers, Sept. 22, 1888). 66.240.2; 74.191.1.

500. "Miss Diana in the Adirondacks—A Shot Across the Lake." $11^{1}/_{16}$ x $9^{1}/_{8}$. Published in *Harper's Weekly* 27 (New York: Harper & Brothers, Aug. 25, 1883). 69.177.3; 94.27.10.

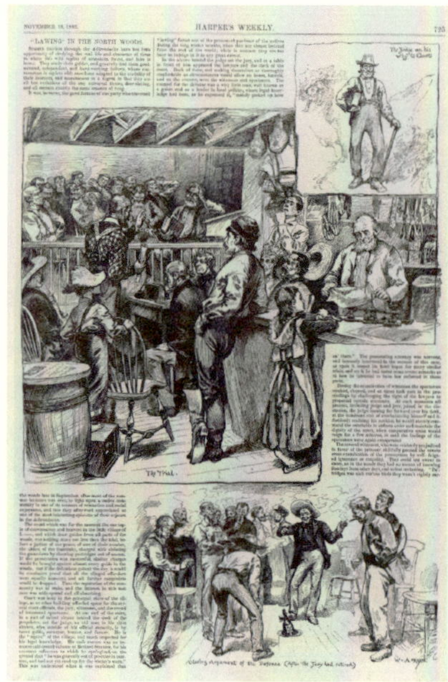

501. "'Lawing' in the North Woods." Three vignettes: "The Judge on his way to Court"; "The Trial"; "Closing Argument of the Defense (After the Jury had retired)." 14 x $9^{1}/_{4}$. Published in *Harper's Weekly* 26 (New York: Harper & Brothers, Nov. 18, 1882). 74.156.1.

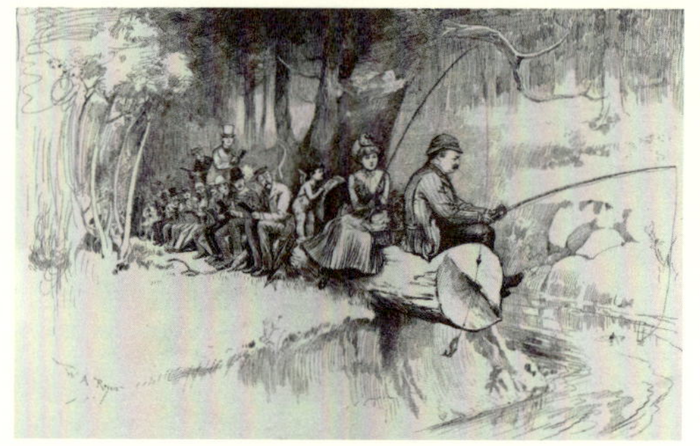

502. "The President's Vacation. How Sweet is Solitude." $8^{3}/_{4}$ x 13. Published in *Life* 7 (New York: Life, Aug. 26, 1886). 77.216.1.

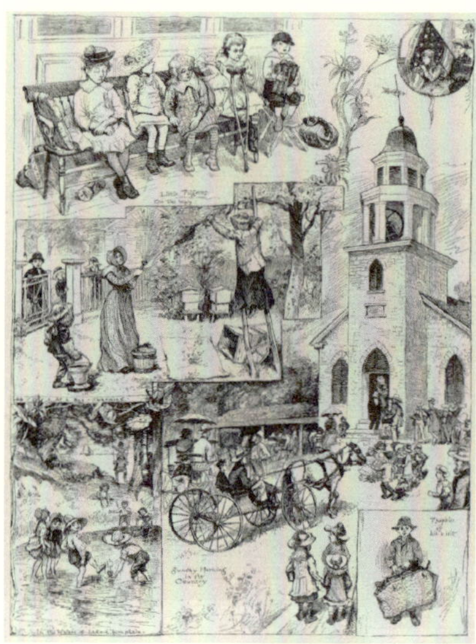

503. "The 'Tribune' Fresh-Air Fund.—Children's Excursion to Lake Champlain." Five vignettes: "Little Pilgrim's on the way"; "At a Bee Swarming"; "In the waters of Lake Champlain"; "Sunday Morning in the Country"; "Trophies of his visit." $12^{1}/_{2}$ x $9^{1}/_{4}$. Published in *Harper's Weekly* 26 (New York: Harper & Brothers, July 29, 1882). 74.70.5.

Francis H. Schell (1834-1909) and Thomas Hogan

504. "Adirondacks Prospect House, Blue Mountain Lake, Hamilton Co., N. Y. Geo. W. Tunnicliff, Manager." R. M. Smart, engraver. $3\frac{3}{4}$ x $5\frac{13}{16}$. Published in *Harper's Weekly* 26 (New York: Harper & Brothers, June 27, 1882). 74.70.2.

George Henry Smillie (1840-1921)

505. "Adirondack Scenery." Philip Meeder and Frederick Y. Chubb, engravers. $11\frac{1}{16}$ x $8\frac{7}{8}$. 66.45.30.

506. "Adirondack Scenery—Morning on the Ausable." John Filmer, engraver. $9\frac{1}{2}$ x $14\frac{3}{8}$. 66.45.14.

Numbers 505 and 506 published in *The Aldine* 5 (New York: James Sutton & Co., Feb. 1872).

507. "Adirondack Woods." Frederick William Quartley (1808-74), engraver. $6\frac{7}{16}$ x $6\frac{1}{8}$. Published in *Appleton's Journal* 4 (New York: D. Appleton & Co., Sept. 24, 1870). 84.16.3A.

508. "A Characteristic Bit of Adirondack Scenery." Philip Meeder and Frederick Y. Chubb, engravers. 11 x $8\frac{7}{8}$. Published in *Illustrated Christian Weekly* 9 (New York: American Tract Society, July 12, 1879). 78.15.5.

509. "Gothic Mountains from Au Sable Lake." Robert S. Bross, engraver. $3\frac{7}{8}$ x $6\frac{3}{8}$. Published in *Appleton's Journal* 4 (New York: D. Appleton & Co., Sept. 24, 1870). 69.179.2.

510. "Headwaters of the Hudson in the Adirondacks." Philip Meeder and Frederick Y. Chubb, engravers. $8\frac{5}{16}$ x $6\frac{1}{16}$. Printed from the same, but trimmed, block as 66.45.30 (checklist 505). 92.41.3.

511. "In the Adirondack Wilderness—Morning on the Ausable." John Filmer, engraver. $9\frac{1}{2}$ x $14\frac{3}{8}$. Published in *Illustrated Christian Weekly* 9 (New York: American Tract Society, Oct. 18, 1879). Same image as 66.45.14 (checklist 506). 78.15.7A.

James David Smillie (1883-1909)

512. "Chapel Pond, Adirondack." James H. Richardson, engraver. $5\frac{3}{4}$ x 4. Published in *Appleton's Journal* 4 (New York: D. Appleton & Co., Sept. 24, 1870). Reprinted in J. Perry Smith, *The Modern Babes in the Wood* (Hartford: Columbian Book Company, 1872). 69.179.4; 84.16.3B.

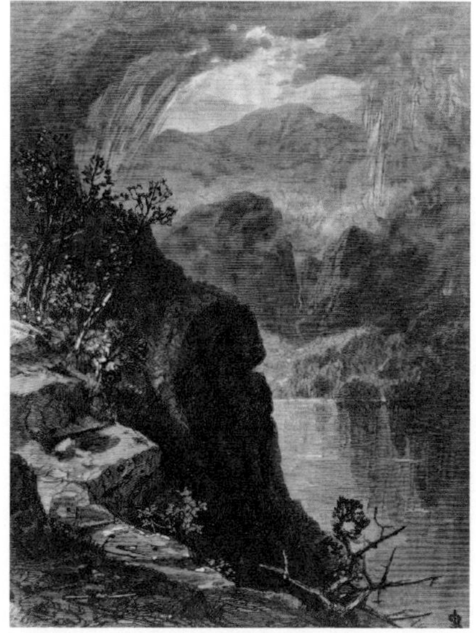

513. "In the Adirondacks." X. Mexiom, engraver. $9\frac{1}{8}$ x $6\frac{5}{8}$. Published in *Harper's Weekly* 23 (New York: Harper & Brothers, May 17, 1879). 77.14.8.

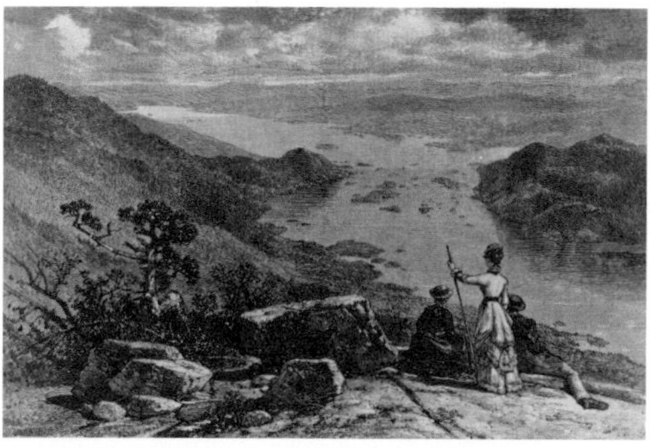

514. "Lake George, Looking Southwest from Black Mountain." Halliwell, engraver. $9\frac{1}{4}$ x $13\frac{5}{8}$. Published in *Harper's Weekly* 23 (New York: Harper & Brothers, Aug. 1, 1879). 77.14.7.

515. "Placid Lake from Whiteface Mountain." Frederick William Quartley (1808-74), engraver. $3\frac{15}{16}$ x $6\frac{7}{16}$. Published in *Appleton's Journal* 4 (New York: D. Appleton & Co., Sept. 24, 1870). 69.179.1.

J. Smith

516. "An Adirondack Surprise." $4\frac{1}{4}$ x $7\frac{5}{8}$. Published in *Judge*, 1889. 88.34.2.

William Poinsette Snyder (b. 1853)

517. "A Day on Lake George." $11\frac{1}{4}$ x $8\frac{3}{4}$. Published in *Harper's Weekly* 35 (New York: Harper & Brothers, July 25, 1891). 94.28.10.

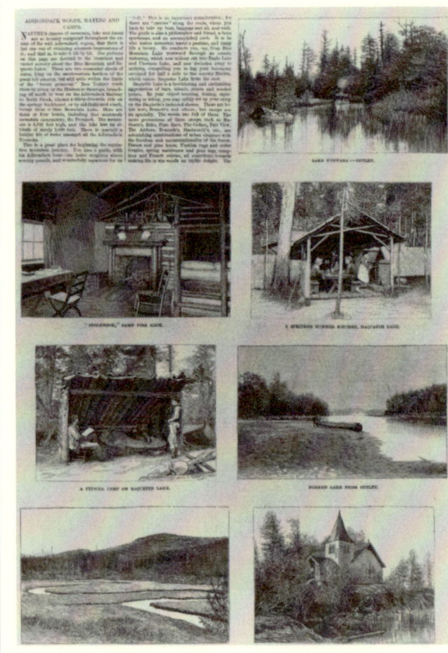

Seneca Ray Stoddard (1843-1917)

❦ 518. "New York. Summer Life in the Adirondacks—Scenes in the Raquette Lake Region." Seven vignettes: "Lake Utowana—Outlet"; "'Inglenook,' Camp Pine Knot"; "A Specimen Summer Kitchen, Raquette Lake"; "A Typical Camp on Raquette Lake"; "Forked Lake from Outlet"; "Ray Brook—Letter 'S'"; "Island Church on Raquette Lake." $13\frac{13}{16}$ x $9\frac{3}{8}$. Published in *Frank Leslie's Illustrated Newspaper* (New York: Mrs. Frank Leslie, Aug. 13, 1887). 79.33.1.

Arthur Fitzwilliam Tait (1819-1905)

519. "No. 182. An Old 'Bar' Narrating his Adventures to an intensely-interested Hunter." $2\frac{1}{4}$ x $2\frac{3}{4}$. Published in *Harper's Weekly* 2 (New York: Harper & Brothers, May 15, 1858). 85.47.1.

520. "'Surprised.' From the Painting by A. F. Tait." $6\frac{1}{2}$ x $9\frac{1}{4}$. The painting was exhibited at the National Academy of Design in 1879. This reproduction published in an unidentified periodical. 73.8.1.

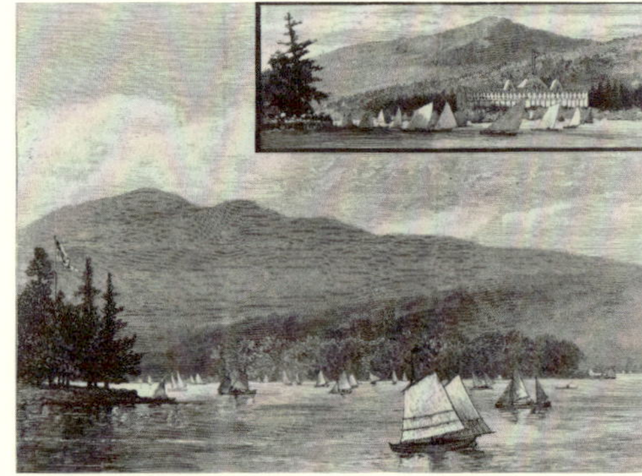

F. H. Taylor

❦ 521. "The Canoe Regatta on Lake George." $6\frac{7}{8}$ x 9. Published in *Harper's Weekly* 26 (New York: Harper & Brothers, Aug. 26, 1882). 81.25.1.

H. D. Turner

522. "Deer on Lake St. Regis, at Night." Crane, engraver. $6\frac{3}{8}$ x $9\frac{3}{8}$. 78.69.7.

523. "Upper Ausable Lake." Crane, engraver. $9\frac{3}{8}$ x $6\frac{3}{8}$. 92.41.7; 94.27.7.

Numbers 522 and 523 published in John David Williams, *America Illustrated* (New York: The Arundel Print, 1874).

Fred T. Vance (ca. 1840-92)

524. "Avalanche Lake." J. Sutton & Co., engraver. $6\frac{5}{8}$ x $8\frac{7}{8}$. 66.45.29; 72.77.1.

525. "Calamity Pond Brook." J. R. Ceraly, engraver. $8\frac{3}{4}$ x $5\frac{7}{8}$. 66.45.32; 72.77.2.

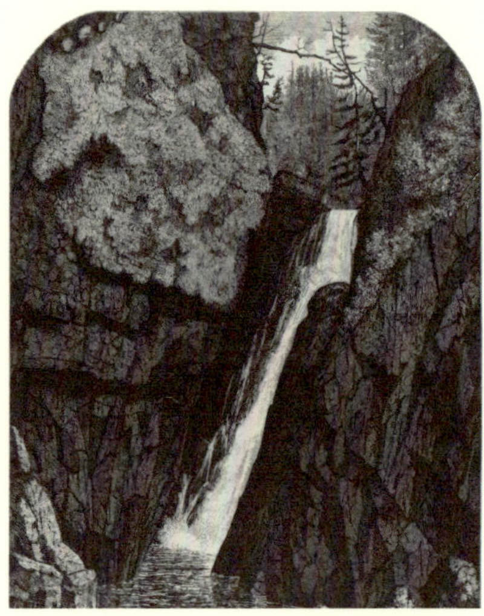

❦ 526. "Flume Falls of the Opalescence [*sic*]." J. Sutton & Co., engraver. $10\frac{7}{8}$ x $8\frac{3}{8}$. 66.45.8; 72.77.5.

Numbers 524-526 published in *The Aldine* 6 (New York: James Sutton & Co., Aug. 1873).

527. "The Glen." C. Welcht, engraver. $9\frac{3}{16}$ x 7. Published in *The Aldine* 5 (New York: James Sutton & Co., Oct. 1872). 66.45.25; 66.45.26.

528. "Lake Colden." $8\frac{15}{16}$ x $12\frac{7}{8}$. Published in *The Aldine* 6 (New York: James Sutton & Co., Aug. 1873. 72.77.3.

529. "Lake Henderson." John Tinkey, engraver. $6\frac{5}{8}$ x $8\frac{7}{8}$. 66.45.19.

530. "Preston Pond, From Bishop's Knoll." C. Welcht, engraver. 9 x 12. 66.45.18; 68.67.2.

Numbers 529 and 530 published in *The Aldine* 5 (New York: James Sutton & Co., Oct. 1872).

JACOB C. WARD (1809-91)
531. "Outlet of Lake George." Samuel Wallin, engraver. $4\frac{1}{2}$ x $6\frac{1}{8}$. Attributed to Ward on the basis of 67.64.5 (checklist 80). 61.53.2.

THOMAS WORTH (1834-1917)
532. "Summer Sports and Pasttimes [*sic*]." $9\frac{15}{16}$ x 9. Published in *The New Yorker* 19 (New York: J. B. Collin & Co., Aug. 22, 1877). 66.45.5.

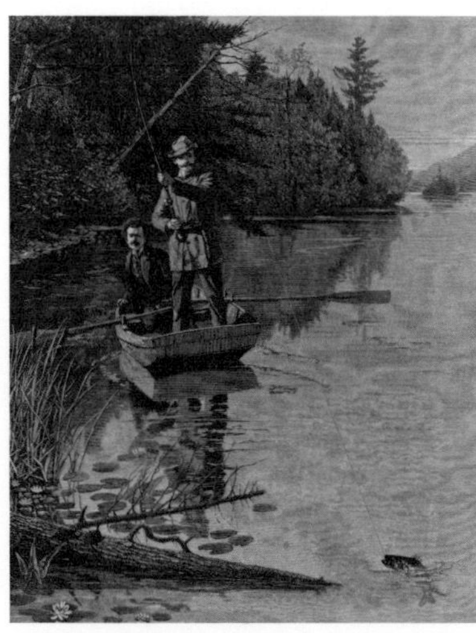

RUFUS FAIRCHILD ZOGBAUM (1849-1925)
533. "Black-Bass Fishing in the Adirondacks." $11\frac{5}{16}$ x $8\frac{11}{16}$. Published in *Harper's Weekly* 28 (New York: Harper & Brothers, Aug. 30, 1884). 66.52.1; 77.196.6.

WOOD ENGRAVINGS BASED ON PHOTOGRAPHS

GEORGE W. BALDWIN (fl. 1870-1903)
534. "New York. The Autumn 'Outing' of Mrs. Cleveland—Saranac Inn, on Upper Saranac Lake, the Favorite Resort of the President—Bringing in a Deer." $4\frac{3}{16}$ x $8\frac{3}{4}$. Baldwin had studios in Plattsburgh and Keeseville, N. Y. Published in *Frank Leslie's Illustrated Newspaper* (New York: Mrs. Frank Leslie, Oct. 6, 1888). 84.3.3.

GEORGE W. BALDWIN (fl. 1870-1903) and SENECA RAY STODDARD (1843-1917)
535. "Summer in the Adirondacks. Glimpses of Lake and Mountain Scenery." Four vignettes: "Owl's Head, Long Lake"; "Going In—Their first trip by Buckboard"; "Chateaugay Lake"; "St. Regis Mountain, from Spitfire Pond." $13\frac{3}{4}$ x $9\frac{3}{8}$. Baldwin had studios in Plattsburgh and Keeseville; Stoddard's studio was in Glens Falls, N. Y. Published in *Frank Leslie's Illustrated Newspaper* (New York: Mrs. Frank Leslie, July 28, 1888). 68.215.2; 94.27.9 (published in German language edition of same newspaper).

CHRISTY R. FAY (1838-1916) and FARMER
536. "The Adirondack Mountains." Nine vignettes: "Old Bridge at Meacham Outlet"; "The Falls from Bartlett's Bridge"; "Looking up the Lake" [St. Regis]; "Corey's Hotel at Indian Carry"; "Indian Carry on the Upper Saranac"; "Big Clear Pond"; "Harrietstown, New York"; "John Brown's Grave"; "John Brown's House." $13\frac{3}{4}$ x $9\frac{1}{4}$. The Fay and Farmer studio was in Malone, N. Y. Published in *Harper's Weekly* 11 (New York: Harper & Brothers, Aug. 31, 1867). Vignettes based on Fay and Farmer photographs in the Adirondack Museum collection: P42816 (Old Bridge—Meacham Outlet); P42823 (Corey's Indian Carry); P42824 (Harrietstown); P42825 (John Brown's House); P42826 (John Brown's Grave); P24836 (Big Clear Pond). 76.168.2; 82.144.1.

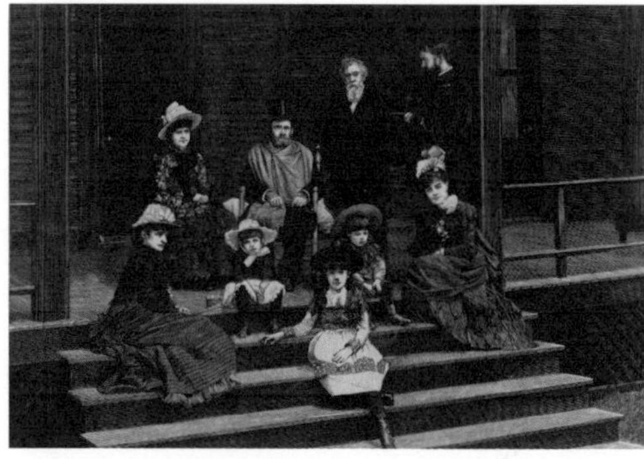

RECORD AND EPLER
537. "General Grant at Mount McGregor." $6\frac{1}{2}$ x $9\frac{1}{4}$. The Record and Epler studio was in Saratoga Springs, N. Y. Probably published in *Harper's Weekly*, 1885. 92.41.8.

SENECA RAY STODDARD (1843-1917)
538. "Adirondack Mountains. 'The Nation's Pleasure-Ground and Sanitarium.'" $14\frac{1}{8}$ x $9\frac{1}{2}$. Stoddard's studio was in Glens Falls, N. Y. Published by the New York Central and Hudson Railroad after 1892. 78.69.5; 94.28.12.
539. "New York.—View of Prospect House, Upper Saranac Lake, with the President's cottage on the left." $2\frac{3}{8}$ x $8\frac{15}{16}$. Published ca. 1880. 84.3.1.

Anonymous Artists, Known Engravers

540. [Advertisement for Winchester Repeating Fire Arms, New Haven, Conn.] Asher-Adams, engraver. Sheet size $24\frac{1}{2}$ x 18. 76.205.1.
541. [Advertisement for the Schenectady Stove Company, Schenectady, N. Y.]. Ferguson [Albany], J. L. Rowe, N. S. Vedder [Troy], J. V. Vrooman & Co., engravers. Sheet size $24\frac{1}{2}$ x 18. 76.205.2.
542. [Advertisement for E. Remington & Sons, Ilion, N. Y.] Ashton [Utica] and Ferguson [Albany], engravers. Sheet size $24\frac{1}{2}$ x 18. 76.205.3.
543. [Advertisement for Joseph Dixon Crucible Company's Works.] Asher-Adams and J. S. Patterson, engravers. Sheet size $22\frac{1}{4}$ x $15\frac{3}{4}$. 82.107.1.

Numbers 540-543 are removed from unidentified volumes, possibly atlases, published in the 1870s.

544. "Lake Colden." Butterworth & Heath, engravers. $3\frac{3}{8}$ x $3\frac{5}{8}$. Published in Benson John Lossing, *The Hudson. From Wilderness to the Sea* (New York: Virtue and Yorston, 1866). 94.27.6A.
545. "Life in the Woods. A Summer Encampment in the Adirondacks." Ed. Lagarde, engraver. $9\frac{1}{4}$ x $14\frac{1}{8}$. Published in *Frank Leslie's Illustrated Newspaper* (New York: Mrs. Frank Leslie, July 15, 1882). 78.69.1.

Anonymous Artists, Unknown Engravers

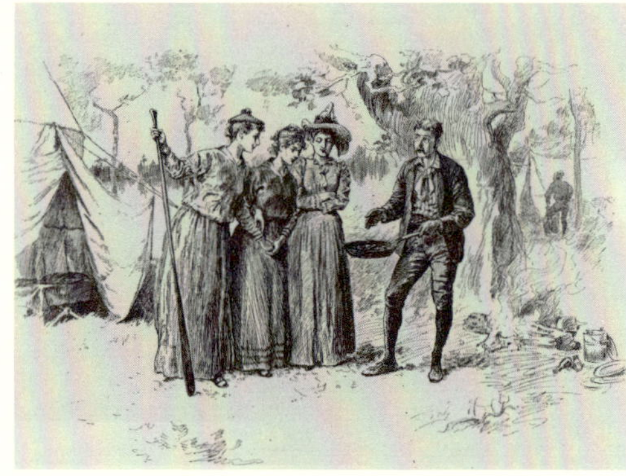

546. "An Amateur Cook." $6\frac{1}{4}$ x $8\frac{1}{4}$. Published in *Harper's Weekly* 35 (New York: Harper & Brothers, Aug. 29, 1891). 81.25.3.
547. [Bear trap]. $2\frac{1}{4}$ x $3\frac{7}{8}$. Impression on paper of stamp for binding Jeptha R. Simm's *Trappers of New York* (1935). 78.16.1; 78.16.2.
548. "Death in the Adirondacks. A Sportsman Mistakes a Kerchief on a Lady's Head for a Gull, and Fires." $6\frac{15}{16}$ x $9\frac{3}{8}$. Published in the *Day's Doings* 9, (New York: Day's Doings Company, Aug. 3, 1872). 91.61.2.
549. "Equipped for Winter Travel in the Adirondacks. A Winter 'Home Camp' in the Adirondacks." $7\frac{1}{2}$ x $4\frac{3}{4}$. Published in *Harper's Weekly* 31 (New York: Harper & Brothers, March 26, 1887). 69.177.1; 78.17.1A-B.
550. [Grasse River Clubhouse]. $1\frac{7}{8}$ x $2\frac{5}{8}$. 76.103.1.

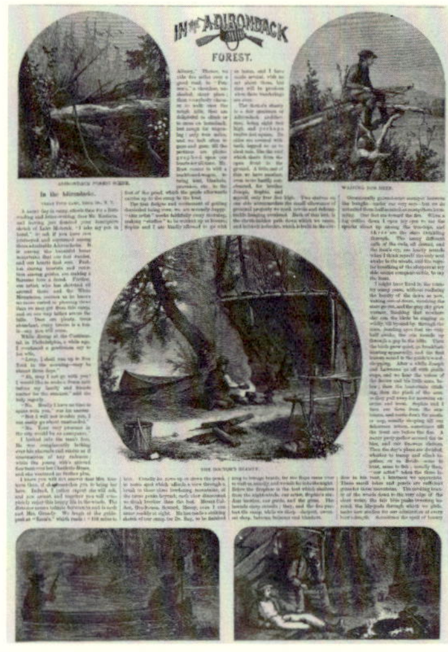
IN THE ADIRONDACK FOREST.

551. "In the Adirondack Forest." Five vignettes: "Adirondack Forest Scene"; "Waiting for Deer"; "The Doctor's Shanty"; "Night-Hunting for Deer"; "The Camp-Fire." 14 x $9\frac{3}{8}$. Published in *Illustrated Christian Weekly* 2 (New York: American Tract Society, Aug. 17, 1872). 91.61.1.
552. "Jay Gould." $4\frac{7}{8}$ x $3\frac{13}{16}$. Published in *Harper's New Monthly Magazine* 71 (New York: Harper & Brothers, 1885). 70.123.189.
553. "A Lodge in the Wilderness." $3\frac{3}{4}$ x $5\frac{11}{16}$. Published in E. R. Wallace, *Descriptive Guide to the Adirondacks* (Syracuse, New York: Watson Gill, and Bible Publishing Co., 1887). 94.28.1.
554. "My First Deer Hunt. The infuriated creature met him half way, and with one sweep of his antlers threw him a dozen feet." $3\frac{3}{8}$ x $6\frac{3}{8}$. Published in *Frank Leslie's Popular Monthly* 4 (New York: Frank Leslie, Sept. 1877). 74.70.4.
555. "New York. The Canoeing Season. Camp on Canoe Islands, Lake George." $6\frac{3}{4}$ x 9. Published in *Frank Leslie's Illustrated Newspaper* (New York: Mrs. Frank Leslie, Aug. 22, 1885). 81.25.4; 94.28.4.

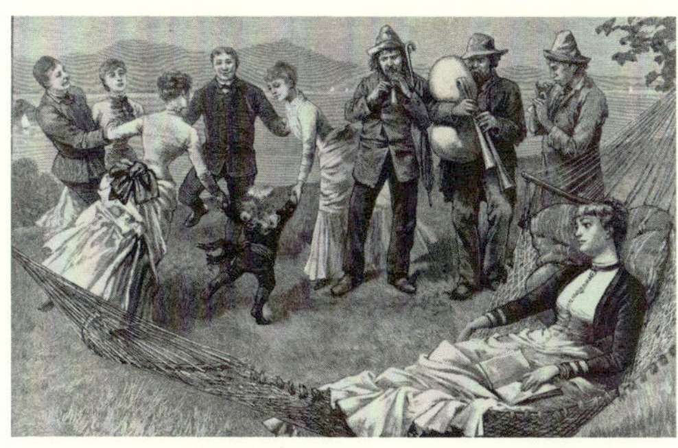

❦ 556. "New York. Cottage Life at Lake George. A Dance to the Music of Strolling Players." $8^{7}/_{8}$ x $13^{13}/_{16}$. Published in *Frank Leslie's Illustrated Newspaper* (New York: Mrs. Frank Leslie, July 10, 1886). 84.3.4.

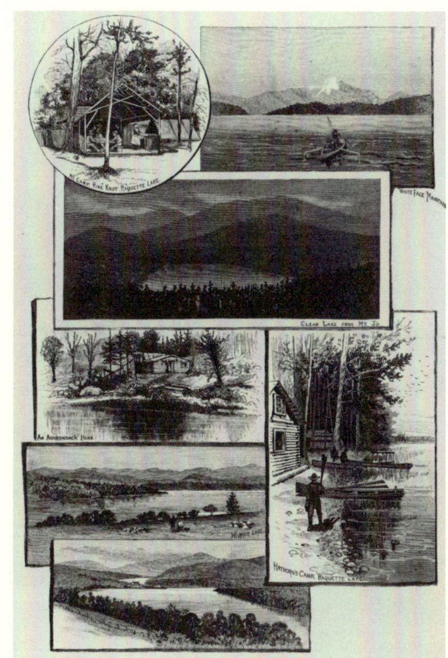

❦ 557. "New York. Lake and Mountain Views in the Adirondack Region." Seven vignettes: "At Camp Pine Knot. Raquette Lake"; "White Face Adirondack Home"; "Mirror Lake"; "Hathorn's Camp. Raquette Lake"; "Lake Placid House, from Grand View House." $13^{11}/_{16}$ x $8^{7}/_{8}$. Published in *Frank Leslie's Illustrated Newspaper* (New York: Mrs. Frank Leslie, July 19, 1884). 84.3.5.

558. "New York. President Cleveland's Visit to the Adirondacks. Deer-hunting on Prospect Lake [Upper Saranac Lake]." $7^{3}/_{4}$ x $8^{7}/_{8}$. Published in *Frank Leslie's Illustrated Newspaper* (New York: Mrs. Frank Leslie, Aug. 28, 1886). 82.32.1A. Same image used in German language edition of Sept. 4, 1886. 94.27.8.

559. "New York. Running the Rapids, Ausable Chasm." $8^{15}/_{16}$ x $6^{13}/_{16}$. 84.3.2.

560. "A Night View of Niagara in Olden Time." $9^{3}/_{16}$ x $6^{3}/_{8}$. Published in John David Williams, *America Illustrated* (New York: The Arundel Print, 1874). 61.55.4.

561. [Old Coeymans Mansion on banks of Hudson River, Albany County, N. Y.]. $3^{1}/_{16}$ x $2^{7}/_{8}$. 66.55.515.

562. "Our Artist in the Adirondacks." $9^{3}/_{16}$ x $6^{3}/_{8}$. Published in *Appleton's Journal of Literature, Science and Art* 8 (New York: D. Appleton & Co., Sept. 21, 1872). 94.28.3.

563. "Our Photographer in the Adirondacks." $4^{3}/_{8}$ x $2^{3}/_{4}$. Published in *Harper's Weekly* 31 (New York: Harper & Brothers, March 26, 1887. 78.17.1C.

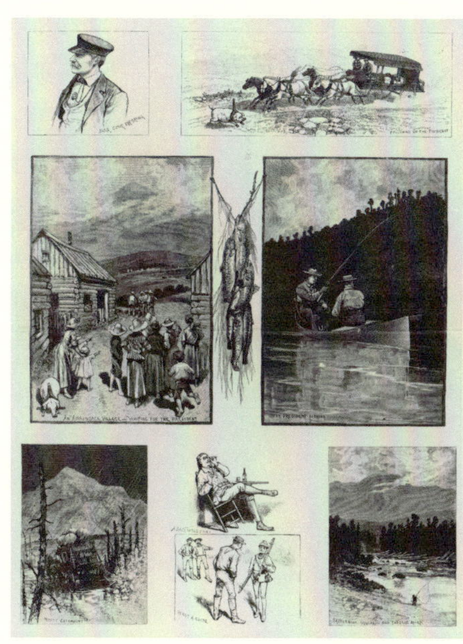

❦ 564. "President Cleveland in the Adirondacks. Scenes and Incidents of his Vacation." Eight vignettes: "Jake Cone, the Driver"; "Following up the President"; "An Adirondack Village—Waiting for the President"; "The President Fishing"; "Mount Catamount"; "A Backwoodsman"; "Want a Guide?"; "Saddleback Mountain and Saranac River." $19^{5}/_{8}$ x $14^{1}/_{2}$. Published in *Frank Leslie's Illustrated Newspaper* (New York: Mrs. Frank Leslie, Aug. 29, 1885). 74.329.2.

565. "President Cleveland in the North Woods." $9^{7}/_{8}$ x $8^{7}/_{8}$. Published in *Frank Leslie's Illustrated Newspaper* (New York: Mrs. Frank Leslie, Aug. 22, 1885). 74.329.1.

566. "Recluse Island, Lake George." $3^{1}/_{4}$ x $5^{7}/_{16}$. Published in *Frank Leslie's Popular Monthly* 3 (New York: Frank Leslie, June 1877). 74.70.3.

567. "Ruse pour prendre toutes bestes sauvages." $5^{3}/_{8}$ x $6^{3}/_{8}$. Published in A. Thevet, *Cosmographie Universelle* (Paris, 1575). 78.149.1.

568. "Sketches of the National Camp-Meeting at Round Lake, New York, July 6-15, 1869." Thirteen vignettes: "Round Lake Station"; "Watering Horses"; "View of Round Lake"; "An Outside Meeting"; "Drinking Fountain"; "Book Store"; "Family Tent"; "Camp-Ground Register"; "The Central Circle"; "Boating on Round Lake"; "The Big Tent"; "The Camp-ground Market"; "Wesley Avenue." Published in *Harper's Weekly* 13 (New York: Harper & Brothers, July 31, 1869. 62.16.23; 92.41.10.

569. "Unfitchen aux Dolgeville, Nordamerica." 12 1/2 x 8 13/16. 82.11.6.

570. "View on the North West Corner of 4th Avenue and 42nd Street." 4 15/16 x 8 3/8. Published ca. 1880. 66.124.29.

571. "Views in the Adirondacks." Scene of open camp surrounded by nine vignettes: "Head Gates and Overflow of Upper Canal"; "Camp on Raquette Lake"; "Hudson River at Luzerne"; "Carry at Buttermilk Falls"; "View near Saranac Inn"; "Ampersand Mountain"; "From Bartlett [Carry]"; "Mount Morris from Outlet of Tupper Lake"; "On Blue Mountain Lake [view of Prospect House]." 9 x 14 1/8. Published in *Harper's Weekly* 32 (New York: Harper & Brothers, Aug. 11, 1888). 61.37.1.

Selected Bibliography

Research for this publication was facilitated by the existence of the many books and articles cited in the endnotes. The curatorial files at the Adirondack Museum and the extensive research files of Peggy O'Brien in the Library of the Adirondack Museum were also extremely useful. I am particularly indebted to the late Patricia C. F. Mandel, the author of *Fair Wilderness: American Paintings in the Collection of The Adirondack Museum* (Blue Mtn. Lake, N.Y.: The Adirondack Museum, 1990). For the major exhibition of the Museum's paintings in 1990 and the accompanying catalogue, Dr. Mandel assembled all that was known about the activities of the nearly one hundred and fifty artists represented in the collection. I relied on this publication a great deal and it facilitated and enhanced my own work.

Other recent books that were particularly useful for the documentation of the landscape artists whose works were reproduced as engravings or wood engravings include *American Paradise: The World of the Hudson River School* (New York: Metropolitan Museum of Art, 1988), *Views and Visions: American Landscape before 1830* (Washington, D.C.: The Corcoran Gallery of Art, 1986), and *Thomas Cole: Landscape into History* (New Haven and London: Yale University Press, and Washington, D.C.: National Museum of American Art, 1994).

In the past twenty years, several exhibitions with a regional focus resulted in publications that have been very useful. *Vermont Landscape Images,* 1776-1976 (Burlington, Vt.: Robert Hull Fleming Museum, 1976), *The White Mountains: Place and Perceptions* (Hanover, N.H.: University Press of New England, 1980), Kenneth Myers' *The Catskills: Painters, Writers, and Tourists in the Mountains, 1820-1895* (Hanover, N.H.: University Press of New England, 1987), and *Impressions of Niagara: The Charles Rand Penney Collection of Prints of Niagara Falls* (Philadelphia: The Philadelphia Print Shop, 1993) relate closely to the present effort on prints of the Adirondacks.

Some of the artists represented in this exhibition are among the best known of their generation. Others are more obscure; a few seem to have vanished without leaving a trace except for their work. Finding information on engravers of the nineteenth century can also be difficult. Many of the best wood engravers were immigrants whose names do not even appear in city directories; we know them only by the signatures on the prints. *The New-York Historical Society's Dictionary of Artists in America, 1564-1860* by George C. Groce and David H. Wallace (New Haven and London: Yale University Press, 1957) is always the first place to check on an artist or engraver. *American Landscape and Genre Paintings in the New-York Historical Society; A Catalogue of the Collections, Including Historical, Narrative, and Marine Art* (New York: New-York Historical Society and Boston: G. K. Hall & Co., 1982) includes many of the artists represented in this project.

Robert Taft's classic *Artists and Illustrators of the Old West, 1850-1900* (New York: Charles Scribner's Sons, 1953) and Catherine H. Campbell's *New Hampshire Scenery* (Canaan, N.H.: Phoenix Publishing for the New Hampshire Historical Society, 1985) contain useful biographical sketches of landscape artists. *The American Personality. The Artist-Illustrator of Life in the United States, 1860-1930* (Los Angeles: The Grunwald Center for the Graphic Arts, 1976), William J. Linton's *American Wood Engraving* (Boston: Estes and Lauriat, 1882; reprint, Watkins Glen, N.Y.: American Life Foundation & Study Institute, 1976), and Frank Weitenkampf's *American Graphic Art* (New York: The Macmillan Company, 1924) are useful in tracing illustrators and wood engravers of the second half of the nineteenth century. Basil Hunnisett's *Steel-engraved book illustration in England* (Boston: David R. Godine, 1980) provides the context for William Henry Bartlett's engravings.

Fortunately many of the standard Adirondack histories have been reprinted in recent years and are therefore very accessible. Alfred L. Donaldson's two volume *A History of the Adirondacks* (New York: Century, 1921; reprint, Fleischmanns, N.Y.: Purple Mountain Press, 1992) contains not only a detailed index but an excellent bibliography that provides references to much of the early literature on the region. Warder H. Cadbury wrote an excellent introduction to the edition of William H. H. Murray's *Adventures in the Wilderness* (Boston: Fields, Osgood, & Co., 1869) reprinted by The Adirondack Museum and Syracuse University Press in 1989. The two institutions also collaborated to reprint Charles Dudley Warner's *In the Wilderness* (Boston: Houghton, Osgood & Company, 1878) in 1990 with an introduction by Alice Wolf Gilborn. Alfred B. Street's *The Indian Pass* (New York: Hurd and Houghton, 1869) was reprinted by the Purple Mountain Press in 1993. These entertaining and informative books have been an excellent introduction to the region.

Index

Patch for Inside back cover page

Back Cover: *Lake George.* Richard William Hubbard (1816-88), artist. Chromolithograph, 15 x 26, 1865. Checklist no. 323.